The
I Hate
Republicans
R·E·A·D·E·R

The I Hate Republicans READER

WHY THE GOP IS TOTALLY WRONG ABOUT EVERYTHING

EDITED BY CLINT WILLIS

THUNDER'S MOUTH PRESS
NEW YORK

The I Hate Republicans Reader:
Why the GOP Is Totally Wrong About Everything

Compilation copyright © 2003 by Clint Willis
Introductions copyright © 2003 by Clint Willis

Published by
Thunder's Mouth Press
An Imprint of Avalon Publishing Group Incorporated
245 West 17th St., 11th floor
New York, NY 10011

Library of Congress Cataloging-in-Publication Data is available.

ISBN 1-56025-508-0

Interior design by Paul Paddock

Printed in the United States of America

Distributed by Publishers Group West

Disclaimers

Ruben Bolling wishes to emphatically state that he does not hate Republicans (nor does he hate Democrats). As many Republicans themselves say: He hates the sin, but loves the sinners.

You can find Ruben Bolling's cartoons on pages 23, 38, 163, 309 and 332.

You can find Ruben Bolling's cartoons on pages 23, 38, 163, 309 and 332.

Official Notice of Non-Partisanship.

Look, as a journalist, I don't like saying, "I hate Republicans." In fact, I don't mind if people are Republicans in the privacy of their own bedrooms. It's just the ones that flaunt it in public, the raging, flaming ones, that give me the creeps.

My problem with saying, "I hate Republicans" is that someone might think I have a thing for Democrats. Yes, I'll admit I've looked at the magazines and maybe perused their websites—just out of curiosity, mind you—but I always come away disappointed. Ultimately, there's just something a bit pathetic in watching invertebrates trying to take a stand. (Nor do I have a taste for inedible Greens.)

The honorable Congresswoman Katherine Harris has written, "Greg Palast is twisted and maniacally partisan." That's not nice. That's not fair. Katie, if the Democrats ever stumble back to office, then I'll turn my spy-glass their way. Until then, as to Democrats, let's let sleeping dogs lie and lying dogs sleep.

In the meantime, lie back, think of England, and enjoy my non-partisan exposé of the Republican Party's putsch in the Sunshine State (*see page 57*).

Greg Palast
New York & London

Greg Palast is author of the New York Times *bestseller* The Best Democracy Money Can Buy. *Subscribe to his writings for Britain's* Observer *and* Guardian *newspapers, and view his investigative reports for BBC Television's* Newsnight, *at www.GregPalast.com.*

For my misguided republican friends,
with love

CONTENTS

INTRODUCTION

First, a word about the title: You don't have to hate republicans to hate Republicans.

The first group—republicans with a small "r"—may include some of your neighbors and colleagues and perhaps even your elderly grandmother. True, such republicans are often boring, sometimes obnoxious and occasionally even hateful—for example, when they tell racist jokes or prattle on about welfare mothers or bully women in the workplace. But many of these republicans are more or less well-meaning Americans, unwitting victims of the corporate-funded lies, manipulations and distortions that are the stock-in-trade of the Republican elite. Many republicans are intelligent, and some are even nice.

The second group—Republicans with a capital "R"—includes the economic and political elite who fund and perpetuate such lies, manipulations and distortions and benefit hugely from them. We're talking about the small-minded, selfish, arrogant, power-mad, murderous little twits and nerds who have stolen our government from us: people like George W. Bush and Dick Cheney, Richard Perle and Pat Buchanan, Gale Norton and Newt Gingrich.

The I Hate Republicans Reader is by and for Americans who are appalled by the policies of Bush and the rest of these insufferable stinkers. We are frustrated when we discover that Republicans have once again cut essential aid to the poor to free up cash for corporate subsidies. We are angry when Republicans eliminate regulations that protect the quality of our air and the sanctity of our shrinking wilderness—while claiming to support the environment. We get mad when a Republican leader slashes education spending—while calling himself "the education president." We are disgusted when Republicans cut taxes for the rich—and call it "tax reform." We are enraged when Republicans steal a presidential election—while wrapping themselves in the flag that represents our precious democracy. We are outraged when Republicans secretly deprive innocent citizens of their civil liberties—while publicly asking God to bless America. We are horrified when Republicans launch a devastating war on the basis of frightening lies about hypothetical nuclear weapons.

Pondering the latest outrage—they come thick and fast these days—we realize just how much we really hate what Republicans are doing to our country. We want to tell the world about it. We want our republican, democrat and independent friends and neighbors and grandmothers to know that they're not getting the real news from the Fox Network—or from any other network, for that matter. We want them to know that the Republicans are wrong about just about everything; that Republicans are destroying our democracy and creating a more dangerous world for all of us.

What's more, we want to prove it to them, and that's where *The I Hate Republicans Reader* comes in. Carry it with you on the subway or bus, in your briefcase, to class, to work, to concerts. Keep a spare copy at your office and one in your car. The next time someone at a party or at your job or school tries to tell you that Republicans are protecting your freedom and making the world a safer place, grab this book and turn to page 327 or 380. When your brother-in-law says that Republicans are against big government, flip to page 189 for a devastating rebuttal. When the moron on your flight to Spokane insists that George W. Bush won the 2000 presidential election, turn to page 57 and shut him the hell up.

We've listened to George Bush and Rush Limbaugh and their ilk for long enough.

We need to start talking back.

—Clint Willis

SECRETS AND LIES

with quotes from Ronald Reagan, Larry Speakes;
cartoons by Ruben Bolling;
and a quiz from Paul Slansky

Republicans from Ronald Reagan to Ari Fleis-cher lie often and outrageously to defend other-wise indefensible policies and positions. It's no wonder that so many of them lose the ability to distinguish truth from falsehood.

This is from Michael Moore's best-selling Stupid White Men.

Dear George

from *Stupid White Men* (2001)

Michael Moore

AN OPEN LETTER TO "PRESIDENT" GEORGE W. BUSH

Dear Governor Bush:

You and I—we're like family. Our personal connection goes back many years. Neither of us has cared to publicize it, for all the obvious reasons—mostly because no one would believe it. But because of something personal, something the Bush family did, my life was profoundly affected.

Let's come clean and admit it: it was your cousin Kevin who shot *Roger & Me.*

At the time I made the movie, I didn't know that your mother and Kevin's mother were sisters. I just thought Kevin, whom I'd met when he was shooting his own film at a cross burning in Michigan, was one of those bohemian artist types who lived in Greenwich Village. Kevin had made a great film, *Atomic Café,* and on a lark I asked him if he would come to Flint, Michigan, and teach me how to make a movie. To my astonishment he said yes, and so for one week in February of 1987 Kevin Rafferty and Anne Bohlen traipsed around Flint with me, showing me how to work the equipment, giving me invaluable tips on how to make a documentary. Without your cousin's generosity, I don't know if *Roger & Me* would have ever been made.

I remember the day your dad was inaugurated as President. I was editing the film in a ratty old editing room in D.C. and decided to go down to watch him be sworn in on the

Capitol steps. How weird it was to see your cousin Kevin, my mentor, sitting next to you up on the dais! I remember also walking down The Mall and seeing the Beach Boys playing "Wouldn't It Be Nice" at a free inaugural concert in honor of your father. Back in the editing room, my friend Ben was on the screen, all choked up about going crazy on the assembly line and singing the same Beach Boys song over scenes of Flint in shreds.

Months later, when the film was released, your dad, the President, ordered a print of *Roger & Me* sent to Camp David one weekend for the family to watch. Oh, to have been a fly on the wall as you all viewed the havoc and despair that had been visited upon my hometown—thanks, in large part, to the actions of Mr. Reagan and your father. Here's something I've always wanted to know: At the end of the film, as the deputy sheriff was tossing the homeless kids' presents and Christmas tree out on the curb because they were $150 behind in their rent, were there any tears in the room? Did anyone feel responsible? Or did you all just think, "Nice camerawork, Kev!"?

Well, that was the late eighties. You'd just given up your hard drinking; after being sober for a few years, you were trying to "find yourself" with Dad's help—an oil venture here, a baseball team there. It's been clear to me for some time that you never had any intention of being President yourself. We all stumble into jobs we don't want at one time or another—who hasn't done that?

For you, though, it must be different. After all, it's not just that you don't want to be there: now that you're there, you're surrounded by the same gang of geezers who used to run the world with Pops. All those men roaming around the White House—Dick, Rummy, Colin—not a single one is a pal of *yours!* It's all the old farts Poppy used to have over to the house for a good cigar and vodka as they dreamed up plans to carpet bomb the civilians of Panama.

But you're one of us—a Boomer, a C student, a partier! What the hell are you doing with that crowd? They're eating you alive and spitting you out like a bad pork rind.

They probably didn't tell you that the tax cut they drew up for you to sign was a swindle to take money from the middle class and give it to the super-rich. I know you don't need the extra money; you're already set for life, thanks to Grandpappy Prescott Bush and his smart trading with the Nazis before and during World War II.[*]

But all those dudes who gave you a record-breaking $190 million to run your campaign (two-thirds of which came from just over seven hundred individuals!), they want it all back—and more. They're going to hound you like dogs in heat, making sure you do exactly as they say. Your predecessor may have been renting out the Lincoln bedroom to Barbra Streisand, but that ain't nothin': before you know it, your pal, Acting President Cheney, will be turning over the keys of the West Wing to the chairmen of AT&T, Enron, and ExxonMobil.

Your critics berate you for taking naps in the middle of the day and ending your workday around 4:30 p.m. You should just tell them you're starting a new American tradition—lunchtime naps for all, and everybody

[*]During the late 1930s and through the 1940s, Prescott Bush, George I's father and W's grandfather, was one of seven directors in the Union Banking Corporation, owned by Nazi industrialists. After filtering their money through a Dutch bank, they hid an estimated $3 million in Bush's bank. As a principal player, it's unlikely that Bush would have been unaware of the Nazi connection. The government eventually seized the assets and the bank dissolved in 1951, after which Prescott Bush—and *his* father, Sam Bush—received $1.5 million.

home by five! Do that, and trust me, you'll be remembered as our greatest President.

How dare they suggest you're not getting anything done in office? Not true! I have never seen a new President busier than you. It's almost as if you think your days as The Man are numbered. With the Senate already gone to the Democrats and the House on its way in 2002—well, hey, look at the bright side, you'll still have two more years before all those sore winners who voted for Gore give you the boot.

Your list of accomplishments—in just your first few months in office—is brutally impressive.

You have:

- Cut $39 million from federal spending on libraries

- Cut $35 million in funding for advanced pediatric training for doctors

- Cut funding for research into renewable energy sources by 50 percent

- Delayed rules that would reduce "acceptable" levels of arsenic in drinking water

- Cut funding for research into cleaner, more efficient cars and trucks by 28 percent

- Revoked rules strengthening the power of the government to deny contracts to companies that violate federal laws, environmental laws, and workplace safety standards

• Allowed Secretary of the Interior Gale Norton to request suggestions for opening up national monuments for foresting, coal mining, and oil and gas drilling

• Broken your campaign promise to invest $100 million per year in rain forest conservation

• Reduced by *86 percent* the Community Access Program, which coordinated care for people without health insurance among public hospitals, clinics, and other health care providers

• Nullified a proposal to increase public access to information about the potential ramifications of chemical plant accidents

• Cut funding for the Girls and Boys Clubs of America programs in public housing by $60 million

• Pulled out of the 1997 Kyoto Protocol agreement on global warming, ultimately signed by 178 other countries

• Rejected an international accord to enforce the 1972 treaty banning germ warfare

• Cut $200 million from workforce training programs for dislocated workers

• Cut $200 million from the Childcare and Development grant, a program that provides child care to low-income families as they are forced from welfare to work

• Eliminated prescription contraceptive coverage to federal employees (though Viagra is still covered)

• Cut $700 million in funds for public housing repairs

• Cut half a *billion* dollars from the Environmental Protection Agency's budget

• Overturned workplace ergonomic rules designed to protect workers' health and safety

• Abandoned your campaign pledge to regulate carbon dioxide emissions, a major contributor to global warming

• Prohibited any federal aid from going to international family planning organizations that provide abortion counseling, referrals, or services with their own funds

• Nominated former mining company executive Dan Lauriski as Assistant Secretary of Labor for Mine Safety and Health

• Appointed Lynn Scarlett, a global warming skeptic and an opponent of stricter standards on air pollution, as Undersecretary of the Interior

• Approved Interior Secretary Gale Norton's controversial plan to auction off areas close to Florida's eastern shore for oil and gas development

• Announced your plans to allow oil drilling in Montana's Lewis and Clark National Forest

• Threatened to shut down the White House AIDS office

• Decided no longer to seek guidance from the American Bar Association on federal judicial appointments

• Denied college financial aid to students convicted of misdemeanor drug charges (though convicted murderers are still eligible for financial aid)

• Allocated only 3 percent of the amount requested by Justice Department lawyers in the government's continued litigation against tobacco companies

• Pushed through your tax cut, 43 percent of which goes to the wealthiest 1 percent of Americans

• Signed a bill making it harder for poor and middle-class Americans to file for bankruptcy, even when facing overwhelming medical bills

• Appointed affirmative action opponent Kay Cole James to direct the Office of Personnel Management

• Cut $15.7 million from programs dealing with child abuse and neglect

• Proposed elimination of the "Reading Is

Fundamental" program, which gives free books to poor children

• Pushed for development of "mini-nukes," designed to attack deeply buried targets—a violation of the Comprehensive Test Ban Treaty

• Tried to reverse regulation protecting sixty million acres of national forest from logging and road building

• Appointed John Bolton, an opponent of nonproliferation treaties and the United Nations, as Undersecretary of State for Arms Control and International Security

• Made Monsanto executive Linda Fisher deputy administrator of the Environmental Protection Agency

• Nominated Michael McConnell, a leading critic of the separation of church and state, to a federal judgeship

• Nominated civil rights opponent Terrence Boyle to a federal judgeship

• Canceled the 2004 deadline for auto makers to develop prototype high-mileage cars

• Named John Walters, an ardent opponent of prison drug *treatment* programs, as drug czar

• Appointed oil and coal lobbyist J. Steven Giles as Deputy Secretary of the Interior

- Named Bennett Raley, who has called for the repeal of the Endangered Species Act, as Assistant Secretary of the Interior for Water and Science

- Sought the dismissal of a class-action lawsuit filed in the United States against Japan by Asian women forced to work as sex slaves in World War II

- Appointed as solicitor general Ted Olson, your chief lawyer in the Florida voting debacle

- Proposed to ease the permit process for constructing refineries and nuclear and hydroelectric dams, including lowering environmental standards

- Proposed the selling of oil and gas tracts in the Alaska Wildlife Preserve

Whew! I'm tired just typing this list! Where do you get the energy? (It is the naps, isn't it?)

Of course, a lot of the above is supported by many Democrats.

But right now, I'm concerned about you. Think back—what was your first act as "President"? You remember: before you would get in the car to ride down Pennsylvania Avenue in your inaugural parade, you insisted someone get a screwdriver and take the D.C. license plates off the limo because they contained the words "Support D.C. Statehood." Here it is, the biggest day of your life, and you're pissed at the license plates? You have GOT to relax!

I guess, though, I started worrying about you long before that day. A number of disturbing revelations regarding your behavior surfaced during the campaign.

Eventually they went away, but I continue to have concerns about your ability to function on the job. Please don't take this as prying or moralizing—we'll leave that to Cheney! It is simply an honest attempt at intervention from a close friend of the family.

Let me be blunt: I'm afraid you may be a threat to our national security.

That may seem a bit strong, but I don't make this statement lightly. It has nothing to do with our minor disagreements regarding executing innocent people on death row, or how much of Alaska to carve up with oil rigs. And I'm not questioning your patriotism—I'm sure you'd love any country that's been this good to you.

Rather, it has to do with a number of behaviors many of us who care for you have witnessed over the years. Some of these habits are a little surprising; some you can't control; and others are, unfortunately, all too common among us Americans.

Because you have your finger on The Button (you know, the one that could blow up the world), and because decisions you make have vast and far-reaching consequences for the stability of said world, I would like to ask you three pointed questions—and I would like you to give me, and the American people, three honest answers:

1. GEORGE, ARE YOU ABLE TO READ AND WRITE ON AN ADULT LEVEL?
It appears to me and many others that, sadly, you may be a functional illiterate. This is nothing to be ashamed of. You have lots of company (just count the typoes in this book. In fact, isn't *that* a typo?). Millions of Americans cannot read and write above a fourth-grade level. No wonder you said "leave no child behind"—you knew what it felt like.

But let me ask this: if you have trouble comprehending the complex position papers you are handed as the Leader of the Mostly-Free World, how can we entrust something like our nuclear secrets to you?

All the signs of this illiteracy are there—and apparently no one has challenged you about them. The first clue was what you named as your favorite childhood book. *"The Very Hungry Caterpillar,"* you said.

Unfortunately, that book wasn't even published until a year after you graduated from college.

Then there's the question of your college transcripts, if those really are your transcripts. How *did* you get into Yale when other applicants in 1964 had higher SATs and much better grades? During the campaign, when asked to name the books you were currently reading, you answered gamely—but when quizzed about the books' contents, you didn't know what to say. No wonder your aides stopped letting you hold press conferences with two months left in the campaign. Your handlers were scared to death of what you might get asked—and how you might answer.

One thing is clear to everyone—you can't speak the English language in sentences we can comprehend. At first, the way you mangled words and sentences seemed cute, almost charming. But after a while it became worrisome. Then in an interview you broke America's decades-long policy toward Taiwan, saying we were willing to do "whatever it took" to defend Taiwan, even suggesting we might deploy troops there. Jeez, George, the whole world flipped out; before you knew it, everyone was at Defcon 3.

If you're going to be Commander-in-Chief, you *have* to be able to communicate your orders. What if these little slipups keep happening? Do you know how easy it would be to turn a little faux pas into a national-security nightmare? No wonder you want to increase the Pentagon budget. We'll need all the firepower we can get after you accidentally order the Russians "wiped out," when what you meant to say was, "I need to wipe the Russian dressing off my tie."

Your aides have said that you don't (can't?) read the briefing papers they give you, and that you ask them to read them for you or to you. Your mother was passionately committed to reading programs as First Lady. Should we assume she knew firsthand the difficulty of raising a child who couldn't read?

Please don't take any of this personally. Perhaps it's a learning disability. Some sixty million Americans have learning disabilities. There's no shame in this. And yes, I believe a dyslexic can be President of the United States. Albert Einstein was dyslexic; so is Jay Leno. (Hey, I finally found a way to work Leno and Einstein into the same sentence! See, language can be fun.)

But if you refuse to seek help with this problem, I'm afraid you may be too great a risk for the country. You need help. You need Hooked on Phonics, not just another Oval Office briefing.

Tell us the truth, and I'll come read to you every night at bedtime.

2. ARE YOU AN ALCOHOLIC, AND IF SO, HOW IS THIS AFFECTING YOUR PERFORMANCE AS COMMANDER-IN-CHIEF?
Again, there is no finger being pointed here, no shame or disrespect intended. Alcoholism is a huge problem; it affects millions of American citizens, people we all know and love. Many are able to recover and live normal lives.

Alcoholics can be, and have been, President of the United States. I greatly admire anyone who can deal with this addiction. You have told us that you cannot handle drinking, and that you haven't touched a drop of alcohol since you were forty. Congratulations.

You have also told us that you used to "drink too much" and that you eventually "realized that alcohol was beginning to crowd out my energies and could crowd, eventually, my affections for other people." That is the definition of an alcoholic. This does not disqualify you from being President, but it does require that you answer some questions, especially after you spent years covering up the fact that in 1976 you were arrested for drunk driving.

Why won't you use the word *alcoholic*? That is, after all, the First Step to recovery. What support system have you set up to make sure you don't fall off the wagon? Being President is perhaps the most stressful job in the world. What have you done to ensure you can handle the pressure and the anxiety associated with being the most powerful man on earth?

How do we know you won't turn to the bottle when faced with a serious crisis? You've never had a job like this. For twenty years, from what I can tell, you had no job at all. When you stopped "drifting," your dad set you up in the oil business with some ventures that failed, and then he helped you get a major league baseball team, which required you to sit in a box seat and watch a lot of long, slow baseball games.

As governor of Texas, you couldn't have had much stress; there just isn't enough to do. Being governor of Texas is a relatively ceremonial job. How will you deal with some unexpected new threat to world security? Do you have a sponsor you can call? Is there a meeting you can attend? You don't have to tell me the answers to these questions; you just have to promise me you've thought them out for yourself.

I know this is very personal, but the public has a right to know. For those who say, "Well, c'mon, it's his personal life—that was twenty-four years ago," I have this to say: I was hit by a drunk driver twenty-eight years ago, and to this day I cannot completely extend my right arm. I'm sorry, George, but when you go out on a public highway drunk, it's no longer just your PERSONAL life we're talking about. It's *my* life, and the lives of my family.

Your campaign people—the enablers—tried to cover for you, lying to the press about the nature of your arrest for driving under the influence. They said the cop pulled you over because you were "driving too slowly." But the arresting officer said it was because you had swerved off on the shoulder of the road. You yourself joined in the denial when asked about the evening you spent in jail.

"I didn't spend time in jail," you insisted. The officer told the local reporter that in fact you were handcuffed, taken to the station, and held in custody for at least an hour and a half. Could it be that you truly don't remember?

This is not just some simple traffic ticket. I can't believe your enablers actually implied your drunk driving conviction wasn't as offensive as Clinton's transgressions. Lying about consensual sex you had with another adult while you are married is wrong, but it is NOT the same as getting behind the wheel of a car when you are drunk and endangering the lives of others (including, George, *the life of your own sister*, who was with you in the car that night).

It is also NOT the same, despite what your defenders said

before the election, as Al Gore volunteering that he smoked pot in his youth. Unless he was driving while stoned, his actions endangered no life but his own—and *he* wasn't trying to cover it up.

You've tried to dismiss the incident by saying "it was back in my youth." But you were NOT a "youth"; you were in your *thirties.*

The night your conviction was finally revealed to the nation, just days before the election, it was painful to watch you swagger as you tried to chalk up your "irresponsible" action as the mere "youthful indiscretion" of having a few beers with the boys (smirk, smirk). I really felt for the families of the *half a million* people who have been killed by drunks like yourself in the twenty-four years since your "little adventure." Thank God you kept drinking for *only another several years* after you "learned your lesson." I think, too, of what you must have put your wife, Laura, through. She knew all too well how dangerous it is when any of us get behind the wheel. At seventeen she killed a high school friend of hers when she ran through a stop sign and collided with his car. I'm hopeful that you can look to her for guidance if ever you feel the pressures of the job getting to you. (Whatever you do, don't turn to Dick Cheney for help: he's had two drunk driving arrests on *his* record for more than twenty-five years!)

Finally, I have to tell you how distressed I was when, back in that crazy week before the election, you hid behind your daughters as your excuse for covering up this conviction. You said you were worried that your history of drunkenness would set a bad example for them. A lot of good that secrecy has done, as proven by the twins' various arrests this year for alcohol possession. In some ways, I admire their rebellion. They asked you, they begged you, they told you: "Please, Dad, *don't* run for President and ruin our lives!" You did. It did. Now, like all good teenagers, it's payback time.

Perhaps the news anchor on *Saturday Night Live* put it best: "George Bush said he didn't reveal the drunk driving charge because of what his daughters might think of him. He had preferred that they think of him as a man with numerous failed business ventures who now executes people."

Here's what I suggest: Get help. Join AA. Take your daughters to Al-Anon. You will all be welcomed with open arms.

3. ARE YOU A FELON?

When you were asked in 1999 about your alleged cocaine use, you replied that you had committed "no felonies in the last twenty-five years." With all we've learned about tricky answers in the last eight years, that kind of response could only lead a reasonable observer to believe that the years before that were a different story.

What felonies did you commit before 1974, George?

Believe me, I'm not asking this in order to seek punishment for anything you did. I am concerned that if there is some deep, dark secret you are hiding, you may in effect be providing ammunition for anyone who uncovers that secret—be it a foreign power (your current favorite, the Chinese) or domestic (like—oh, pick one—say, R.J. Reynolds). If they discover your history of a felony or felonies, they'll have something to hold over you, putting them in a position to blackmail you. That makes you, George, a national security threat.

Trust me, *someone* will find out what you are hiding—and when they do, we'll all be at risk. You have a duty to disclose the nature of whatever felony you imply that you may have committed. Only by revealing it can you neutralize its potential use as a weapon against you—or us.

Also, you recently made it a requirement for any young person seeking financial aid for college to answer a question on the application form that reads: "Have you ever been convicted for any drug offense?" If they have, they are denied student aid—which means that many of them will not be going to college. (Or, to put it another way, according to your new orders Sirhan Sirhan can still receive student aid, but a kid with a joint can't.)

Doesn't this move on your part strike you as a little hypocritical? You would deny a college education to thousands of kids who only did *exactly* what you have implied you did as a young person? Man, that takes some chutzpah! As you'll be receiving $400,000 a year from us until 2004—from the same federal kitty that pays out the college aid—it seems only fair to make you answer the same question: "Have you ever been convicted of selling or possessing drugs (not including alcohol or tobacco)?"

We do know, George, that you have been arrested *three* times. Other than some peace-activist friends of mine, I don't personally know anyone who has been arrested *three* times in their life.

In addition to the drunk driving, you were arrested with some fraternity brothers for stealing a Christmas wreath as a prank. What was *that* all about?

Your third arrest was for disorderly conduct at a football game. Now this I *really* don't get. *Everyone* conducts themselves in a disorderly manner at a football game! I've been to many football games and have had many a beer spilled on my head, but to this day I've never seen anyone arrested. You've gotta work pretty hard to get noticed in a crowd of drunken football fans.

George, I have a theory about why and how all this has happened to you.

Instead of having to earn it, you have been handed the presidency, the same way you've come by everything else in your life. Money and name alone have opened every door for you. Without effort or hard work or intelligence or ingenuity, you have been bequeathed a life of privilege.

You learned at an early age that, in America, all someone like you has to do is show up. You found yourself admitted to an exclusive New England boarding school simply because your name was Bush. You did not have to EARN your place there. It was bought for you.

When they let you into Yale, you learned you could bypass more deserving students who had worked hard for twelve years to qualify for admission to college. You got in because your name was Bush.

You got into Harvard Business School the same way. After screwing off during your four years at Yale, you took the seat that rightfully belonged to someone else.

You then pretended to serve a full stint in the Texas Air National Guard. But one day, according to the *Boston Globe*, you just skipped out and failed to report back to your unit—*for a year and a half!* You didn't have to fulfill your military obligation, because your name was Bush.

Following a number of "lost years" that don't appear in your official biography, you were given job after job by your daddy and other family members. No matter how many of your business ventures failed, there was always another one waiting to be handed to you.

Finally, you got to be a partner in a major league baseball team—another gift—even though you put up only one one-hundredth of the money for the team. And then you conned the taxpayers of Arlington, Texas, into giving you another perk—a brand-new multimillion-dollar stadium that *you* didn't have to pay for.

So it's no wonder you think you deserved to be named President. You didn't earn it or win it—therefore it must be yours!

And you see nothing wrong with this. Why should you? It is the only life you have ever known.

On election night, as the vote swayed back and forth across the nation, you told the press that your brother had assured you Florida was yours. If a Bush said it was so, it was so.

But it ain't so. And when it dawned on you that the presidency had to be earned and won by a vote of the people—yes, the people!—you went berserk. You sent in hatchet man James Baker ("Fuck the Jews, they don't vote for us anyway" was his advice to Poppy in '92) to tell lies to the American people and stoke the nation's fears. When that didn't seem to work, you went to federal court and sued to stop the votes from being counted—because you knew how the vote would turn out. If you were truly sure you had the vote of the people, you wouldn't have minded all those votes being counted.

What startles me is how you turned to the big bad federal government for help. Your mantra during every campaign stop was the following: "My opponent trusts the federal government. *I trust you, the people!*"

Well, we soon learned the truth. You didn't trust the

people at all. You went straight to the *federal* court to get your handout (trust the voting machines, not the people!). At first the judges in Florida didn't buy it—and for perhaps the first time in your life, someone told you no.

But as we've already seen, Daddy's friends on the U.S. Supreme Court were there to take care of everything.

In short, you've been a drunk, a thief, a possible felon, an unconvicted deserter, and a crybaby. You may call that statement cruel. I call it "tough love."

For the sake of all that is decent and sacred, good God, man, take leave immediately and bring some honor to your all-important family name! Make those of us who know there's a thread of decency in your family proud once again to claim that a Bush in the hand is better than a handout to a Bush.

Yours,
Michael Moore

Defense Secretary: The Peculiar Duplicity of Ari Fleischer

from *The New Republic* (6/10/02)

Jonathan Chait

A ri Fleischer, the White House press secretary, is famous. But I knew him back when he was merely infamous, as chief Republican spokesman on the House Ways and Means Committee. He spoke with a cool, quick certainty, unhindered by any sense of conscience. A profile in GQ—not many Hill staffers receive such attention— dubbed him the "flack out of hell."

The typical press secretary shovels out fairly blunt propaganda, the kind reporters can spot a mile away and sidestep easily. But Fleischer has a way of blindsiding you, leaving you disoriented and awestruck. Once, about six years ago, I called to ask him something about tax reform. Knowing Fleischer, I tried to anticipate his possible replies and map out countermeasures to cut off his escape routes. I began the conversation by bringing up what seemed a simple premise: His boss, Bill Archer, favored replacing the income tax with a national sales tax. Fleischer immediately interrupted to insist that Archer did not support any such thing. I was dumbfounded. Forgetting my line of questioning, I frantically tried to recall how it was I knew that Archer had advocated a sales tax. But in the face of this confident assertion, my mind went blank. "Wha . . . uh, really?" I stammered. He assured me it was true. Completely flustered, I thanked him and hung up. I rummaged through my files, trying to piece together my reality. Didn't everybody who followed these things know that Archer favored a sales tax? Yes—here was one newspaper story, and another, and finally a crinkled position paper, authored by Bill Archer, explaining why we needed a national sales tax. Of course he favored it. Fleischer had made the whole thing up.

Most press secretaries "spin." Spin is a clever, lawyerly art, often performed with a knowing wink, which involves casting your boss's actions in the most favorable light. Practitioners of spin don't deny generally accepted facts or contest a reporter's right to ask questions. Rather, they emphasize alternative facts as a way of establishing the difference between what their boss is perceived to have done and what he or she actually did. During the Clinton administration, spin came to symbolize everything reporters loathed about what they saw as a too-clever-by-half presidency. The *Washington Post*'s Howard Kurtz, in his book *Spin Cycle*, describes Bill Clinton's spinsters as trying "to defend the indefensible," by, for instance, insisting that White House coffees with donors were not "fund-raisers" because the money was raised beforehand.

But what Fleischer does, for the most part, is not really spin. It's a system of disinformation—blunter, more aggressive, and, in its own way, more impressive than spin. Much of the time Fleischer does not engage with the logic of a question at all. He simply denies its premises—or refuses to answer it on the grounds that it conflicts with a Byzantine set of rules governing what questions he deems appropriate. Fleischer has broken new ground in the dark art of flackdom: Rather than respond tendentiously to questions, he negates them altogether.

SECRETS AND LIES

I. THE AUDACIOUS FIB

Like any skilled craftsman, Fleischer has a variety of techniques at his disposal. The first is the one he used to such
great effect at Ways and Means: He cuts off the question
with a blunt, factual assertion. Sometimes the assertion is
an outright lie; sometimes it's on the edge. But in either
case the intent is to deceive—to define a legitimate question as based on false premises and, therefore, illegitimate.
Fleischer does this so well, in part because of his breath-
taking audacity: Rather than tell a little fib—i.e., attacking
the facts most open to interpretation in a reporter's
query—he often tells a big one, challenging the question
in a way the reporter could not possibly anticipate. Then
there's his delivery: Fleischer radiates boundless certainty,
recounting even his wildest fibs in the matter-of-fact,
slightly patronizing tone you would use to explain, say,
the changing of the seasons to a child. He neither under-
emotes (which would appear robotic) nor overemotes
(which would appear defensive) but seems at all times so
natural that one wonders if somehow he has convinced
himself of his own untruths.

One month ago, for example, a reporter cited the administration's recent plan to build an education, health, and
welfare infrastructure in Afghanistan and asked Fleischer
when George W. Bush—who during the campaign repeatedly bad-mouthed nation-building—had come around to
the idea. A lesser flack would have given the obvious, spun
response: The Bush administration's policies in
Afghanistan don't constitute nation-building for reasons X,
Y, and Z. The reporter might have expected that reply and
prepared a follow-up accordingly. But Fleischer went the
other way, bluntly asserting that Bush had never derided

nation-building to begin with. "The president has always been for those," Fleischer said. The questioner, likely caught off guard, repeated, "He's always been for . . ." when Fleischer interjected, "Do you have any evidence to the contrary?" In fact, Bush had denounced nation-building just as unambiguously as Archer had endorsed the national sales tax. "I don't think our troops ought to be used for what's called nation-building," said candidate Bush in the second presidential debate, to take one of many examples. The offending reporter, of course, didn't have any of these quotes handy at the press conference, and so Fleischer managed to extinguish the nation-building queries.

To take another example, after the coup in Venezuela last month, Fleischer announced that "it happened in a very quick fashion as a result of the message of the Venezuelan people." But once the coup was reversed, the administration's seeming support proved embarrassing. So at the next press conference, a reporter asked Fleischer, "Last Friday, you said that it—the seizure of power illegitimately in Venezuela—'happened in a very quick fashion as a result of the message of the Venezuelan people'; that the seizure of power, extraconstitutionally, that is, dissolution of the congress and the supreme court happened as a result of the message of the Venezuelan people."

Fleischer could have acknowledged the underlying fact—that the Bush administration initially endorsed the coup—but then expressed regret at its anti-democratic turn, a turn that the United States presumably opposed and perhaps even tried to prevent. Instead, he replied, "No, that's not what I said." And indeed, it wasn't exactly what he said—after quoting Fleischer verbatim reacting to the coup, the reporter went on to describe some of the things that happened after the coup. And that gave Fleischer his opening: "The dissolution that you just referred to did not take place until later Friday afternoon," he noted. "It could not possibly be addressed in my briefing because it hadn't taken place yet." By focusing on the latter, subordinate part of the reporter's question, Fleischer negated the verbatim quote of his earlier remarks—and thus neatly cut off discussion of the administration's early reaction to news of the coup.

The problem with this tactic is that it's always possible to get caught in an outright lie. Speaking to reporters on the morning of February 28, for instance, Fleischer said of Middle East peace negotiations under Clinton: "As a result of an attempt to push the parties beyond where they were willing to go, that led to expectations that were raised to such a high level that it turned to violence." The story went out that the administration blamed Middle East violence on its predecessor's peacemaking. That afternoon, Fleischer insisted he had said no such thing. "That's a mischaracterization of what I said," he protested. But Fleischer's earlier statement was too fresh in the press corps's mind to simply deny, and the press continued to hound him. Later in the day he was forced to issue a statement of regret.

What this episode illustrates is that stating unambiguous falsehoods carries certain risks—and no press secretary can afford to have his factual accuracy repeatedly challenged by the press. So while Fleischer may employ this tactic more frequently than most press secretaries, it is still relatively rare—the p.r. equivalent of a trick play in football: While spectacular to behold and often successful, more frequent usage would dilute its effectiveness and risk disaster.

DEFENSE SECRETARY: THE PECULIAR DUPLICITY OF ARI FLEISCHER

The greater feat is to put yourself in a position where you don't have to lie. This can be accomplished in lots of ways—spinning is the preferred approach for most flacks, but that isn't Fleischer's style; candor, obviously, is out of the question. Fleischer's method of choice is question-avoidance. After all, you can't be accused of answering a question untruthfully if you haven't answered it at all.

II. THE PROCESS NON SEQUITUR

Fleischer has two ways of not answering a question. The first is the non sequitur, a banal statement that, though related to the general topic, sheds no light upon the question at hand. Here, again, Fleischer is an innovator: Whereas most spinners abhor questions about legislative process and try to turn them into questions about their boss's beliefs, Fleischer excels at turning specific questions about Bush's beliefs and intentions into remedial-level civics-class descriptions of process. For example, asked last month if Bush would sign an energy bill that didn't include new drilling in Alaska, here was Fleischer's response in full: "Again, the process, as you know, is the House passes a bill, the Senate passes a bill. And we'll go to conference and try to improve the bill from what the Senate passed. The purpose of energy legislation is to make America more energy-independent. And that's the goal of the conference, in the president's opinion." Will Bush sign a campaign finance bill that doesn't restrict union dues? Fleischer's reply in full: "The president is looking forward to working together to bring people together so he can sign a bill."

At his best, Fleischer can fasten together clumps of non sequiturs into an elaborate web of obfuscation. Last year

Bush persuaded GOP Representative Charlie Norwood to back off his own patients' bill of rights just before the other co-sponsors held a press conference, effectively splitting up a bipartisan coalition. Yet patients' rights was popular, and Bush wanted to present himself as supporting the bill he had just scuttled. The task of disseminating this message fell to Fleischer, and the result was inspired. The transcript of that afternoon's press conference reads like dialogue from a David Mamet film:

FLEISCHER: [W]e're going to be prepared to work with a number of people to get it done.

Q: You would work with the people, including the ones who put the bill forward today? Why won't you work with them?

FLEISCHER: Absolutely. Absolutely we will.

Q: So why are you asking lawmakers not to go with them, to stay with us?

FLEISCHER: Again, I think the president is just in a position now where we want to begin the process, begin this year working directly with some of the more influential people who have been part of the patients' bill of rights in the past, and we'll continue to do that.

A few minutes later Fleischer stated, "We view what's happening today on the Hill"—that is, the press conference Bush had pressured Norwood to abandon—"as very helpful to the process." But, a reporter asked, "If it's helpful . . . why was Norwood asked not to attend today's event?" Fleischer explained, "I think congressmen decide every day whether they want to co-sponsor bills or not co-sponsor bills." His purpose in this exercise was not to make the press corps see Bush's side of the argument, or even to make any argument at all, but simply to befuddle them with non sequitur nonsense until they ran out of questions.

III. The Rules

After the non sequitur, the other kind of non-answer is more straightforward: the open refusal to reply. This is tricky business. A press secretary, after all, is supposed to provide information to the press, not deny it. The straight rebuff, then, must be couched in terms of some broader principle. And it is here that Fleischer's particular genius is on clearest display. As press secretary, Fleischer has developed a complex, arbitrary, and constantly shifting set of rules governing what questions he can answer. If a reporter's question can be answered simply by reciting talking points about process, Fleischer will comply. If he can't, he will find a way to rule it out of order.

Fleischer declines to answer any question he deems "hypothetical." This, too, is a common press-secretary tactic, but Fleischer has a talent for finding hypotheticals buried in what would seem to be extremely concrete questions. Earlier this year, for example, the administration praised an Arab League resolution supporting the Saudi peace plan, but dismissed as irrelevant a resolution condemning a possible U.S. attack on Iraq. A reporter asked why one Arab League resolution mattered but the other didn't. "I'm not going to speculate about plans that the president has said that he has made no decisions on and have not crossed his desk," Fleischer replied. "That wasn't my question," the reporter retorted. Fleischer insisted: "You're asking about an attack on Iraq, and the president has said repeatedly that he has no plans and nothing has crossed his desk. So that enters into the area of hypothetical." Fleischer redefined a question about something that had happened—the Arab League resolution—into a question about something that hadn't—a U.S. attack on Iraq—and then dismissed the latter as hypothetical.

Perhaps the easiest way for Fleischer to dismiss questions is to suggest that he is not the appropriate person to answer them—something he does with remarkable promiscuity. Do the administration and Pakistan agree on extraditing the killers of Daniel Pearl? "You'd have to ask Pakistan," Fleischer replied on February 25. Did Israel's offensive in the West Bank enhance its security? "That's a judgment for Israel to make," he said on April 16. In short, if a question can be said to pertain to another country, that discharges the White House from having to state an opinion.

Fleischer uses the same technique for discussions of domestic policy. Does the administration want Congress to move ahead with campaign finance reform? "The president does not determine the Senate schedule," Fleischer explained on March 19. "The Senate leadership determines the Senate schedule." (That hasn't stopped the White House from demanding the Senate take up other legislation on numerous occasions.) Does an anti-administration court ruling strengthen the U.S. General Accounting Office's case for demanding energy documents? "That's for the courts to judge, not for me,"

Fleischer demurred on February 28. What about the recent decision by Stanley Works to relocate to Bermuda, which several members of Congress condemned? "I can't comment on any one individual corporate action." Indeed, Fleischer will even palm off questions involving other branches of the Bush administration. Asked this spring whether Army Secretary Thomas White has lived up to the standards Bush set out after Enron, Fleischer answered, "Anything particular to Enron, I would refer you to the Department of Justice." What sort of access did GOP donors get to White House officials at a recent fund-raiser? Ask the Republican National Committee, replied Fleischer. Has Colin Powell met with Ariel Sharon? Ask the State Department. Did the administration intervene to allow more pollutants in Alabama? Ask the Environmental Protection Agency. And so on.

When questions cannot be fobbed off on other departments, Fleischer often rephrases them to make them seem so complex and esoteric that he couldn't possibly be expected to answer them. Asked two weeks ago to comment on a blockbuster quote by Bush counterterrorism official Richard Clarke prominently featured in a front-page *Washington Post* story, he replied, "I do not receive a daily briefing on his verbatim quotes." One year ago Fleischer listed six members of Congress who would appear at an event with Bush. Asked how many were Democrats— this was two months into Bush's tenure, when he was making a big deal of meeting with members of the other party—Fleischer said, "I don't have any breakdown here." (The breakdown was six Republicans, no Democrats.) Last year Fleischer ticked off for the press Bush's legislative priorities. "Where does campaign finance rank in those priorities?" asked one. "I don't do linear rankings," Fleischer replied, as if to suggest that answering the question would require a sophisticated mathematical analysis.

To emphasize his inability to answer these complicated questions, Fleischer occasionally pleads lack of expertise. Last year he touted a drop in oil prices since Bush took office and plugged the president's energy plan. Would the energy plan, which would take effect over the long run, impact short-term prices? "I'm not an economist," he demurred. What does the administration think about an unfavorable court ruling? "I'm not a lawyer." Has Yasir Arafat been elected democratically? "I personally am just not expert enough to be able to answer that question. . . . That was before I came to this White House."

For any administration, the most damaging information often comes in the form of anonymous quotes from White House staffers. Leaks rarely happen in this administration; but when they do, they are often more damaging for their infrequency. So in order to avoid answering questions arising from such leaks, Fleischer simply denies their veracity. Asked, in the wake of the Venezuelan coup, about a quote in *The New York Times* attributed to a "Defense Department official," Fleischer went on the attack:

FLEISCHER: And what's the name of the official?

Q: The official is unnamed. But it is . . .

FLEISCHER: Then how do you know he's "top"?

Q: It says, according to *The New York Times*. So is this official mistaken?

FLEISCHER: You don't know the person's name?

Q: No, I don't know the . . .

FLEISCHER: The person obviously doesn't have enough confidence in what he said to say it on the record. . . . So I think if you can establish the name of this person who now without a name you're calling "top," we can further that. But I think you're—you need to dig into that.

(Fleischer himself, of course, makes a regular practice of speaking to reporters off the record.)

In the even rarer case that an administration official cuts against the party line on the record, Fleischer still manages to come up with a set of rules that enables him not to acknowledge it. A few weeks ago a reporter asked him if Bush agreed with Treasury Secretary Paul O'Neill, who had said he "can't find too many Americans who believe that they are overtaxed." Fleischer enthusiastically replied in the affirmative. The reporter, realizing Fleischer must have misunderstood the quote, helpfully repeated it. "Oh, I'm sorry. I thought your question was—I hadn't heard that Secretary O'Neill said that," Fleischer backtracked, proceeding to declare, "I have a long-standing habit in this briefing room, when a reporter describes to me the statements that are made by government officials, I always like to see those statements myself with my own eyes before I comment." Needless to say, that "longstanding habit" had not prevented Fleischer from commenting when he thought the statement concurred with Bush's own view.

Fleischer likewise reserves the right to close off topics because of timing. This applies first to events that have already taken place. Upon taking office, Fleischer wouldn't comment on allegations (fed by White House leaks) of massive vandalism by departing Clintonites because "the president is looking forward and not backwards." He wouldn't discuss the firing of Army Corps of Engineers head Mike Parker because it was "over and dealt with."

But Fleischer also refuses to address events that have yet to take place. When campaign finance reform moved through the Senate last year, he declined to explain Bush's position: "It's too early, yet, to say." After it passed, and went to the House, Fleischer continued to demur because "[i]t hasn't even made its way through the House yet." After it passed the House, he still wouldn't express a view, because "you just don't know what the Senate is going to do. . . . There's a lot of talk about will the Senate try to amend it, will they be unsuccessful in amending it? Will the Senate basically take the House bill and put it in a photocopier, and, therefore, send it directly to the president?" Well, a reporter asked, what if they do photocopy it? Fleischer retorted—you guessed it—"I don't answer hypotheticals."

The reporter tried, valiantly, to get an answer one more time, with a query that was clear, nonhypothetical, White House-related, and present tense: "Of the two bills that have been passed, is there any reason to veto either one?" Fleischer's answer? "We're going to go around in circles on this." You can't argue with that.

Quiz
Paul Slansky

True or False:

Five weeks after White house spokesman Ari Fleischer implied that Bill Clinton was to blame for the current violence in the Middle East, and was quickly forced to retract the implication, George W. Bush implied that Bill Clinton was to blame for the current violence in the Middle East, and was forced to retract the implication.

Answer: True

Standard Operating Procedure

from the *New York Times* (6/3/03)

PAUL KRUGMAN

The mystery of Iraq's missing weapons of mass destruction has become a lot less mysterious. Recent reports in major British newspapers and three major American news magazines, based on leaks from angry intelligence officials, back up the sources who told my colleague Nicholas Kristof that the Bush administration "grossly manipulated intelligence" about W.M.D.'s.

And anyone who talks about an "intelligence failure" is missing the point. The problem lay not with intelligence professionals, but with the Bush and Blair administrations. They wanted a war, so they demanded reports supporting their case, while dismissing contrary evidence.

In Britain, the news media have not been shy about drawing the obvious implications, and the outrage has not been limited to war opponents. *The Times of London* was ardently pro-war; nonetheless, it ran an analysis under the headline "Lie Another Day." The paper drew parallels between the selling of the war and other misleading claims: "The government is seen as having 'spun' the threat from Saddam's weapons just as it spins everything else."

Yet few have made the same argument in this country, even though "spin" is far too mild a word for what the Bush administration does, all the time. Suggestions that the public was manipulated into supporting an Iraq war gain credibility from the fact that misrepresentation and deception are standard operating procedure for this administration, which—to an extent never before seen in U.S. history—systematically and brazenly distorts the facts.

Am I exaggerating? Even as George Bush stunned reporters by declaring that we have "found the weapons of mass destruction," the Republican National Committee declared that the latest tax cut benefits "everyone who pays taxes." That is simply a lie. You've heard about those eight million children denied any tax break by a last-minute switcheroo. In total, 50 million American households— including a majority of those with members over 65—get nothing; another 20 million receive less than $100 each. And a great majority of those left behind do pay taxes.

And the bald-faced misrepresentation of an elitist tax cut offering little or nothing to most Americans is only the latest in a long string of blatant misstatements. Misleading the public has been a consistent strategy for the Bush team on issues ranging from tax policy and Social Security reform to energy and the environment. So why should we give the administration the benefit of the doubt on foreign policy?

It's long past time for this administration to be held accountable. Over the last two years we've become accustomed to the pattern. Each time the administration comes up with another whopper, partisan supporters—a group that includes a large segment of the news media— obediently insist that black is white and up is down. Meanwhile the "liberal" media report only that some people say that black is black and up is up. And some Democratic politicians offer the administration invaluable cover by making excuses and playing down the extent of the lies.

If this same lack of accountability extends to matters of war and peace, we're in very deep trouble. The British seem to understand this: Max Hastings, the veteran war correspondent—who supported Britain's participation in the war—writes that "the prime minister committed British troops and sacrificed British lives on the basis of a deceit, and it stinks."

It's no answer to say that Saddam was a murderous tyrant. I could point out that many of the neoconservatives who fomented this war were nonchalant, or worse, about mass murders by Central American death squads in the 1980's. But the important point is that this isn't about Saddam: it's about us. The public was told that Saddam posed an imminent threat. If that claim was fraudulent, the selling of the war is arguably the worst scandal in American political history—worse than Watergate, worse than Iran-contra. Indeed, the idea that we were deceived into war makes many commentators so uncomfortable that they refuse to admit the possibility.

But here's the thought that should make those commentators really uncomfortable. Suppose that this administration did con us into war. And suppose that it is not held accountable for its deceptions, so Mr. Bush can fight what Mr. Hastings calls a "khaki election" next year. In that case, our political system has become utterly, and perhaps irrevocably, corrupted.

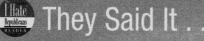

They Said It . . .

"I'm no linguist, but I have been told that in the Russian language there isn't even a word for freedom."

—Ronald Reagan, 1985

Note: The Russian word for freedom is *svoboda*.

"If you tell the same story five times, it's true."

—Reagan White House spokesman Larry Speakes, 1983

Apocryphal Anecdotes

from *Rush Limbaugh Is a Big Fat Idiot* (1996)

Al Franken

Republicans have a very annoying habit of proving political points by telling horror stories that aren't even true to begin with. You know, things like "we should abolish seat belts because I know someone who got strangled by one once."

The master of the apocryphal story was Ronald Reagan, the most successful Republican politician of the last thirty years. Remember Reagan's welfare queen in Chicago? She had bilked the government for $150,000 by applying for benefits using eighty different names, thirty addresses, a dozen social security cards, and four fictional dead husbands.

Attempts to confirm the story yielded only one woman who received $8,000 by using two false names.

Now you might say, "Well, it's a good story, though. It made the point, didn't it?" That's exactly what Reagan's press secretary said after he learned that another one of Reagan's stories was untrue. This one about England, where "if a criminal carried a gun, even if he didn't use it, he was tried for first-degree murder and hung if he was found guilty." Not true. But wouldn't it be cool if it was!?

Reagan told so many whoppers that the press basically held him to a lower standard. And that's a shame. Because the man felt so strongly about the importance of telling the truth. I know this because he used to tell a great anecdote about telling the truth.

I first ran across the anecdote in an article written by award-winning Reagan biographer Lou Cannon. The story was from his days on his high school varsity football team in Dixon, Illinois. It was during his senior year, and, as Reagan tells it, his team was behind in the last few seconds of the fourth quarter. Just as the final gun went off, Reagan caught a pass in the end zone for the winning touchdown. Only trouble was, Reagan had been offside. So he did the only thing he could. He went to the ref and told him about the infraction. "I told the truth, the penalty was ruled, and Dixon lost the game." The punch line of the story was that none of Reagan's teammates was upset. After all, he told the truth.

Cannon went back to Dixon, and no one could recall the incident. In fact, in the only varsity game in which Reagan played, Dixon lost 24-0. Well, it's a good story though. It made the point.

Reagan, of course, was a B-movie actor. So nobody really expected him to be authoritative on complicated facts and such. But Newt Gingrich, you'll recall, has a Ph.D. in history. That's why it's particularly puzzling when the Speaker of the House turns into the fellow I like to call Bizarro Newt.

See, in Superman's Bizarro World, everything is the opposite of things on Planet Earth. So if you like a hot dog in Bizarro World and would like another one, you would say, "Me hate hot dog. Me want more, me hate them so much." It's a little confusing, but believe me, so is Bizarro Newt.

BIZARRO NEWT: "Most people don't know that it's illegal to pray. When they learn that a ten-year-old boy in St. Louis was put in detention for saying grace privately over his lunch, they think that's bizarre. . . ."

PLANET EARTH: According to the school's superintendent, the boy in St. Louis was *not* disciplined for praying. Prayer is not illegal in school. *Organized* prayer is prohibited.

BIZARRO NEWT: Gingrich complained in December 1994 that a heart pump that was "invented in Denmark increases by 54 percent the number of people given CPR who get to the hospital with a chance to recover. The Food and Drug Administration makes illegal [a product] that minimizes brain damage, increases the speed of recovery, and saves money."

PLANET EARTH: The pump was invented in the United States. The Danish company which licensed the pump had yet to apply to the FDA for approval. Initial field tests conducted by the University of California, San Francisco, have "unfortunately showed the pump to be of absolutely no value."

BIZARRO NEWT: Gingrich claimed, also in December 1994, that 800 babies a year were being left in Dumpsters in Washington, D.C.

PLANET EARTH: In this case Bizarro Newt was off by 796 babies. The four babies found in Dumpsters in 1994 were rescued and cared for by government bureaucrats.

BIZARRO NEWT: In February 1995, Bizarro Newt told members of the National Restaurant Association that a federal shelter in Denver had 120 beds and cost $8.8 million a year to operate, while a similar-sized but private shelter in the same area costs only $320,000 a year and saves more lives in the process. Members of the audience gasped, "Oh my God!" and "Wow!"

PLANET EARTH: The "federal" shelter doesn't exist. What Bizarro Newt was apparently referring to is a rehab clinic run by Arapahoe House, Colorado's largest drug and alcohol treatment program, which operates its multiple clinics and 16 school-based counseling programs at a total cost of $11 million, of which $4.3 million is federal money. The "private shelter" is a homeless shelter which offers some drug counseling but no formal treatment or detoxification program.

Bizarro Newt told the restaurateurs that he wanted to discuss Denver's shelter to show "how totally different our vision of the world is from the welfare state. . . . Twenty-five times as much money to ruin lives. This is why we don't believe the big-spending theory of what liberal compassion is."

In fact, all reliable studies on Planet Earth show that for every dollar spent, good drug rehabs like Arapahoe House save society approximately seven dollars in medical expenses, crime, and lost productivity. They don't "ruin" lives, they save them.

If Newt's apocryphal anecdotes and Reagan's share a certain carefree indifference to the truth, Newt's usually lack the warm personal touch that Reagan could bring to his. That's why my favorite new Republican Apocryphal Horror Story is House majority leader Dick Armey's warm yet tragic tale of Charlie, the semi-retarded janitor.

Armey tells the story often. Charlie, it seems, swept the floors of Wooten Hall, the building where Armey worked as a professor at North Texas State University. Armey took a liking to Charlie and they talked a lot. (That's the warm part.) Well, one day Armey noticed that Charlie was gone. A few months went by before Armey ran into a degraded Charlie on the checkout line, buying his groceries with *food stamps*. "What happened, Charlie?" Charlie told him. The federal government had raised the minimum wage, and the university could no longer afford to pay his salary. (That's the tragic part.) From that moment on, Armey tells his audiences, he swore his undying hostility to the federal minimum wage.

(Here comes the truth part.)

Washington Post reporter David Maraniss spoke to four different professors who also worked at Wooten Hall during that period. None could remember a janitor named Charlie. The current chancellor of the university told Maraniss that, as state employees, university janitors are paid well over the minimum wage, and so Armey's story doesn't make sense. When pressed, Armey changed the tragic, moving story. He said that the head of the university's physical plant ("his name was Dale something") told him Charlie was fired because they could no longer afford him.

Still, there's nothing like a really dumb apocryphal horror story. Republican congressman David McIntosh of Indiana claimed on the House floor and in hearings before the Senate Judiciary Committee that the Consumer Product Safety Commission had issued a guideline requiring that all five-gallon and larger buckets used on worksites be built *with a hole in them* to "avoid the danger of somebody falling face down in the bucket and drowning."

You have to admit. Requiring a hole in a bucket would be really stupid. It would defeat the entire purpose of the bucket! I mean, why have a bucket if you're going to have a hole in it?! And, let's get real. What hardhat is going to fall face down in a bucket and drown?! Man, the federal government is stupid!

Do I even have to finish this one? Okay. Here goes: The CPSC never issued such a guideline. It did study the issue of small children—not adults, as McIntosh implies—drowning in such buckets (228 died in this manner between 1984 and 1994), but closed the investigation after the bucket industry agreed to put warning labels on the buckets and spend money for an information campaign regarding the problem.

Are there badly written, unnecessary, stupid government regulations? Yes. Are there enough of them that the Republicans don't have to make them up to give interesting examples? Evidently not.

Here's a good one. House Republican whip Tom Delay tells of a dentist who refused to give a child's baby teeth to his parents because the teeth were classified as toxic waste.

I didn't bother to check that one.

Instead I thought I'd spend my time trying to make up my own Democratic apocryphal story. Something really touching and horrible. Here goes.

There's this kid named Jason on my son's Little League team for which I'm the assistant coach. Hell. Let's make me the coach. Jason has Attention Deficit Disorder. No, wait. He's semi-retarded. And we play on a beautiful field that was once a Superfund site. Some corporate polluter had put carcinogens in the groundwater and the EPA forced them to pay for the cleanup, which was a huge success.

Anyway. Jason is semi-retarded. As coach, I've kind of taken him under my wing, and taught him the intricacies of the game. So, one day we're playing a game against a team of bullies. They're a better team, but we're only down by one run in the bottom of the sixth with two outs and the bases loaded. Jason is up and the entire game is on the line. It's the league championship! And the count is three and two. So Jason gets hit in the head with a pitch. He's fine, because he's wearing a helmet, which is a government regulation. And our team is cheering because that forces in the tying run. Only Jason stops everyone and says his head was in the strike zone, and he should be called out. So the umpire calls him out, but everyone on our team is happy because Jason told the truth. He didn't really; his head wasn't in the strike zone. He just thought it was because he's semi-retarded. But everyone's happy anyway.

So we all go out for hamburgers. I buy because that's the kind of guy I am. Jason's burger is undercooked. It's got the *E. coli* bacteria, because the Republicans deregulated meat inspection, and Jason dies.

I forgot. When he got hit in the head, he was okay, except the shock knocked out two of his baby teeth. And on his deathbed he gave them to his parents and told them to put them under his little sister's pillow so the tooth fairy would give her a quarter.

Unfortunately, she also died from eating an *E. coli* hamburger. As did every kid on the team. And a pregnant woman. And three tourists from Kansas. It was real tragic.

The Poetry of D. H. Rumsfeld

from Slate.com (4/02/03)

Hart Seely

Secretary of Defense Donald Rumsfeld is an accomplished man. Not only is he guiding the war in Iraq, he has been a pilot, a congressman, an ambassador, a businessman, and a civil servant. But few Americans know that he is also a poet.

Until now, the secretary's poetry has found only a small and skeptical audience: the Pentagon press corps. Every day, Rumsfeld regales reporters with his jazzy, impromptu riffs. Few of them seem to appreciate it.

But we should all be listening. Rumsfeld's poetry is paradoxical: It uses playful language to address the most somber subjects: war, terrorism, mortality. Much of it is about indirection and evasion: He never faces his subjects head on but weaves away, letting inversions and repetitions confuse and beguile. His work, with its dedication to the fractured rhythms of the plainspoken vernacular, is reminiscent of William Carlos Williams'. Some readers may find that Rumsfeld's gift for offhand, quotidian pronouncements is as entrancing as Frank O'Hara's.

And so *Slate* has compiled a collection of Rumsfeld's poems, bringing them to a wider public for the first time. The poems that follow are the exact words of the defense secretary, as taken from the official transcripts on the Defense Department web site.

The Unknown
As we know,
There are known knowns.
There are things we know we know.
We also know
There are known unknowns.
That is to say
We know there are some things
We do not know.
But there are also unknown unknowns,

The ones we don't know
We don't know.

—Feb. 12, 2002,
Department of Defense news briefing

Glass Box
You know, it's the old glass box at the—
At the gas station,
Where you're using those little things
Trying to pick up the prize,
And you can't find it.
It's—

And it's all these arms are going down in there,
And so you keep dropping it
And picking it up again and moving it,
But—

Some of you are probably too young to remember those—
Those glass boxes,
But—
But they used to have them
At all the gas stations
When I was a kid.

—Dec. 6, 2001,
Department of Defense news briefing

A Confession
Once in a while,
I'm standing here, doing something.

And I think,
"What in the world am I doing here?"
It's a big surprise.

> —*May 16, 2001, interview with the*
> New York Times

Happenings
You're going to be told lots of things.
You get told things every day that don't happen.

It doesn't seem to bother people, they don't—
It's printed in the press.
The world thinks all these things happen.
They never happened.

Everyone's so eager to get the story
Before in fact the story's there
That the world is constantly being fed
Things that haven't happened.

All I can tell you is,
It hasn't happened.
It's going to happen.

> —*Feb. 28, 2003,*
> *Department of Defense briefing*

The Digital Revolution
Oh my goodness gracious,
What you can buy off the Internet
In terms of overhead photography!

A trained ape can know an awful lot
Of what is going on in this world,
Just by punching on his mouse
For a relatively modest cost!
                    —June 9, 2001, following European trip

The Situation
Things will not be necessarily continuous.
The fact that they are something other than
    perfectly continuous
Ought not to be characterized as a pause.
There will be some things that people will see.
There will be some things that people won't see.
And life goes on.

                              —Oct. 12, 2001,
                    Department of Defense news briefing

Clarity
I think what you'll find,
I think what you'll find is,
Whatever it is we do substantively,
There will be near-perfect clarity
As to what it is.
And it will be known,
And it will be known to the Congress,
And it will be known to you,
Probably before we decide it,
But it will be known.

                              —Feb. 28, 2003,
                    Department of Defense briefing

DIRTY TRICKS

with a quote from Richard Nixon;
quizzes from Paul Slansky;
and anagrams

Republicans have a huge fund-raising advantage come election time (thank you, NRA, Enron, et al.). But their policies are so destructive and heartless that they must resort to still other forms of cheating to pursue and maintain power, turning the country upside down and spending millions to investigate trumped up scandals; smearing innocent citizens' reputations; stealing votes; and abusing the power of our most sacred institutions, from Congress to the Supreme Court.

Greg Palast is an American journalist in exile in the U.K., where he published most of his ground-breaking and utterly convincing reporting on the 2000 presidential election. His work was largely ignored by the U.S. media—which is one reason so many people still don't understand that the Republicans stole the election.

from Jim Crow in Cyberspace

from *The Best Democracy Money Can Buy* (2003)

Greg Palast

In the days following the presidential election, there were so many stories of African Americans erased from voter rolls you might think they were targeted by some kind of racial computer program. They were.

I have a copy of it: two silvery CD-ROM disks right out of the office computers of Florida Secretary of State Katherine Harris. Once decoded and flowed into a database, they make for interesting, if chilling, reading. They tell us how our president was elected—and it wasn't by the voters.

Here's how it worked: Mostly, the disks contain data on Florida citizens—57,700 of them. In the months leading up to the November 2000 balloting, Florida Secretary of State Harris, in coordination with Governor Jeb Bush, ordered local elections supervisors to purge these 57,700 from voter registries. In Harris's computers, they are named as felons who have no right to vote in Florida.

Thomas Cooper is on the list: criminal scum, bad guy, felon, *attempted* voter. The Harris hit list says Cooper was convicted of a felony on January 30, 2007.

2007?

You may suspect *something's wrong* with the list. You'd be right. At least 90.2 percent of those on this "scrub" list, targeted to lose their civil rights, are innocent. Notably, over half—about 54 percent—are Black and Hispanic voters. Overwhelmingly, it is a list of Democrats.

Secretary of State Harris declared George W. Bush winner of Florida, and thereby president, by a plurality of 537 votes over Al Gore. Now do the arithmetic. Over 50,000 voters wrongly targeted by the purge, mostly Blacks. My BBC researchers reported that Gore lost at least 22,000 votes as a result of this smart little black-box operation.

The first reports of this extraordinary discovery ran, as you'd expect, on page one of the country's leading paper. Unfortunately, it was in the wrong country: Britain. In the USA, it ran on page *zero*—the story was simply not covered in American newspapers. The theft of the presidential race in Florida also grabbed big television coverage. But again, it was the wrong continent: on BBC Television, broadcasting from London worldwide—everywhere, that is, but the USA.

Was this some off-the-wall story that the British press misreported? Hardly. The chief lawyer for the U.S. Civil Rights Commission called it the first hard evidence of a systematic attempt to disenfranchise Florida's Black voters. So why was this story investigated, reported and broadcast only in *Europe*, for God's sake? I'd like to know the answer. That way I could understand why a Southern California ho'daddy like me has to commute to England with his wife and kiddies to tell this and other stories about my country.

In this chapter, I take you along the path of the investigation, step by step, report by report, from false starts to unpretty conclusions. When I first broke the story, I had it wrong. Within weeks of the election, I said the Harris crew had tried to purge 8,000 voters. While that was enough to change the outcome of the election (and change history), I was way off. Now, after two years of peeling the Florida elections onion, we put the number of voters wrongly barred from voting at over 90,000, mostly Blacks and Hispanics, and by a wide majority, Democrats.[*]

That will take us to the Big Question: Was it *deliberate*, this purge so fortunate for the Republicans? Or just an honest clerical error? Go back to the case of Thomas Cooper, Criminal of the Future. I counted 325 of these time-traveling bandits on one of Harris's scrub lists. Clerical error? I dug back into the computers, the e-mail traffic in the Florida Department of Elections, part of the secretary of state's office. And sure enough, the office clerks were screaming: They'd found a boatload like Mr. Cooper on the purge list, convicted in the future, in the next century, in the *next millennium*.

---

[*]Two years into the investigation, we are still uncovering evidence. The stories of Thomas Cooper and the thousands of other "felons" convicted in the future are new to this edition.

"We" are a team. There's no way on earth I could have conducted this investigation without scores of researchers, some the top names in their technical fields, some inspired amateurs, and many unpaid volunteers. Cyber-wizard Fredda Weinberg of Delray Beach, Florida, deserves special praise for cracking the disks and for indefatigable fact-mining; as do my colleagues at the *Guardian*, BBC, *The Nation*, and Salon.com; database expert Mark Swedlund and so many others. I regret I cannot list them all.

The jittery clerks wanted to know what to do. I thought I knew the answer. As a product of the Los Angeles school system, where I Pledged my Allegiance to the Flag every morning, I assumed that if someone was wrongly accused, the state would give them back their right to vote. But the Republican operatives had a better idea. They told the clerks to *blank out* the wacky conviction dates. That way, the county elections supervisors, already wary of the list, would be none the wiser.[*] The Florida purge lists have over 4,000 blank conviction dates.

You've seen barely a hair of any of this in the U.S. media. Why? How did 100,000 U.S. journalists sent to cover the election *fail* to get the vote theft story (and preferably *before* the election)?

PART I: Silence of the Lambs: AMERICAN JOURNALISM HEARS NO EVIL, SEES NO EVIL, REPORTS NO EVIL

Investigative reports share three things: They are risky, they upset the wisdom of the established order and they are *very expensive* to produce. Do profit-conscious enterprises, whether media companies or widget firms, *seek* extra costs, extra risk and the opportunity to be attacked? Not in any business text I've ever read. I can't help but note that Britain's *Guardian* and *Observer* newspapers, the only papers to report this scandal when it broke just weeks after the 2000 election, are the world's only major newspapers owned by a not-for-profit corporation.

---

[*] E-mail from Janet Mudrow (Florida Department of Elections), "Subject: Future Conviction Dates," to Marlene Thorogood (Database Technologies), cc: Bucky Mitchell (Florida Department of Law Enforcement); dated June 15.

But if profit lust is the ultimate problem blocking significant investigative reportage, the more immediate cause of comatose coverage of the election and other issues is what is laughably called America's "journalistic culture." If the Rupert Murdochs of the globe are shepherds of the New World Order, they owe their success to breeding a flock of docile sheep—snoozy editors and reporters content to munch on, digest, then reprint a diet of press releases and canned stories provided by government and corporate public-relations operations.

Take this story of the list of Florida's faux felons that cost Al Gore the presidential election. Shortly after the U.K. story hit the World Wide Web, I was contacted by a CBS TV network news producer eager to run a version of the story. The CBS hotshot was happy to pump me for information: names, phone numbers, all the items one needs for your typical quickie TV news report.

I freely offered up to CBS this information: The office of the governor of Florida, Jeb Bush, brother of the Republican presidential candidate, had illegally ordered the removal of the names of felons from voter rolls—real felons who had served time but obtained clemency, with the right to vote under Florida law. As a result, *another 40,000 legal voters* (in addition to the 57,700 on the purge list), almost all of them Democrats, could not vote.

The only problem with this new hot info is that I was still in the midst of investigating it. Therefore, CBS *would have to do some actual work*—reviewing documents and law, obtaining statements.

The next day I received a call from the producer, who

said, "I'm sorry, but your story didn't hold up." And how do you think the multibillion-dollar CBS network determined this? Answer: "We called Jeb Bush's office." Oh.

I wasn't surprised by this type of "investigation." It is, in fact, standard operating procedure for the little lambs of American journalism. One good, slick explanation from a politician or corporate chieftain and it's *case closed*, investigation over. The story ran on television, but once again, in the wrong country: I reported it on the BBC's *Newsnight*. Notably, the BBC is a publicly owned network—I mean a *real* public network, with no "funds generously provided by Archer Mobil Bigbucks."

Let's understand the pressures on the CBS TV producer that led her to kill the story simply because the target of the allegation said it ain't so. The story demanded massive and quick review of documents, dozens of phone calls and interviews—hardly a winner in the slam-bam-thank-you-ma'am school of U.S. journalism. Most difficult, the revelations in the story required a reporter to stand up and say that the big-name politicians, their lawyers and their PR people were *freaking liars*.

It would be much easier, a heck of a lot cheaper and no risk at all to wait for the U.S. Civil Rights Commission to do the work, then cover the commission's report and press conference. No one ever lost their job writing canned statements from a press release. Wait! You've watched *Murphy Brown* so you think reporters hanker to uncover the big scandal. Bullshit. Remember, *All the President's Men* was so unusual they had to make a movie out of it.

The Election Fix Story Steals Into the States

In London the *Guardian* and *Observer* received about two thousand bless-you-Britain-for-telling-us-the-truth-about-our-elections letters from U.S. Internet readers circulating the *samizdat* presidential elections coverage. I also received a few like this:

> *You pansey brits seem to think that the average American is as undereducated and stupid as the average british subject. Well comrad* [sic], *I'm here to tell you . . .*

. . . which ended with some physically unfeasible suggestions of what to do with the Queen.

My *Observer* report went to print within three weeks of the election. The vote count in Florida was still on. Watching the vote-count clock ticking, Joe Conason, the most determined of American investigative reporters, insisted to his editors at Salon.com, the Internet magazine, that they bring my story back to America. Salon posted "Florida's Ethnic Cleansing of the Voter Rolls" to the Net on December 4, 2000. It wasn't exactly "print," but at least it was American. Still not one U.S. news editor called, not even from my "sister" paper, the *Washington Post*, with whom the *Guardian* shares material and prints an international weekly.

From a news perspective, not to mention the flood of site hits, this was Salon's biggest politics story ever—and they named Part I their political story of the year. But where was Part II? On their Web site and on radio programs the magazine was announcing Part II would appear in two days . . . and in two days . . . and in two days . . . and *nothing appeared*. Part II was the story blown off by the CBS *Evening News* about an additional 40,000-plus voters whom Jeb Bush barred from voting. The fact that 90 percent of these 40,000 voters were Democrats should have made it news . . . because this maneuver alone more than accounted for Bush's victory.

I was going crazy: Gore had not yet conceded . . . the timing of Part II was crucial. Where the hell was it? Finally, an editor told me, "The story doesn't check out. You see, we checked with Jeb Bush's office and they said . . ."

Argh! It was déjà vu all over again.

Another staffer added, as a kind of explanation, "The *Washington Post* would never run this story."

Well, he had me there. They hadn't, they didn't. Not yet. At least Salon helped me sneak the first report past the border patrols. So God bless America.

While waiting for the United States to awaken, I took my BBC film crew to Florida, having unearthed a smoking-gun document: I had a page marked "confidential" from the contract between the State of Florida and the private company that had purged the voter lists. The document contained cold evidence that Florida knew they were taking the vote away from thousands of innocent voters, most of them Black.

It was February. I took my camera crew into an agreed interview with Jeb Bush's director of the Florida Department of Elections. When I pulled out the confidential sheet, Bush's man ripped off the microphone and did a fifty-yard dash, locking himself in his office, all in front of our cameras. It was killer television and wowed the British viewers. We even ran a confession from the company that was hired to carry out the purge operation. Newsworthy? Apparently not for the United States.

My program, BBC *Newsnight,* has a film-trading agreement with the ABC television network. A record twenty thousand Net-heads in the United States saw the BBC Webcast; and several banged on the door of ABC TV's *Nightline* to run our footage, or at least report what we found. Instead, *Nightline* sent its own crew down to Florida for a couple of days. They broadcast a story that ballots are complex and Blacks are not well educated about voting procedures. The gravamen of the story was, *Blacks are too frigging dumb to figure out how to vote.* No mention that in white Leon County, machines automatically kicked back faulty ballots for voter correction; whereas in Gadsden County, very Black, the same machines were programmed to *eat* mismarked ballots. That was in our story, too.

Why didn't ABC run the voter purge story? Don't look for some big Republican conspiracy. Remember the three elements of investigative reporting: risk, time, money. Our BBC/*Guardian* stories required all of those, in short supply in U.S. news operations.

Finally, in February, my Part II—the report that was too scary and difficult for Dan Rather's show—found asylum in the *Nation* magazine, that distant journalistic planet not always visible to the naked eye.

And then, mirabile dictu, the *Washington Post* ran the story of the voter purge on page one, including the part that "couldn't stand up" for CBS and Salon . . . and even gave me space for a by-lined comment. Applause for the *Post*'s courage! Would I be ungrateful if I suggested otherwise? The *Post* ran the story in *June*, though they had it at hand seven months earlier when the ballots were still being counted. They waited until they knew the findings of the U.S. Civil Rights Commission Report, which verified BBC's discoveries, so they could fire from behind that big safe rock of Official Imprimatur. In other words, the *Post* had the courage to charge out and shoot the wounded.

PART II: THE REPORTS

These are the stories you weren't supposed to see: from reports that ran in Britain's *Observer* and *Guardian*, bits of script from the BBC Television investigation and, to help set out the facts, the U.S. stories from Salon, the *Nation* and the *Washington Post*—followed by new material, never before printed or broadcast on either continent. Documents keep bubbling up from the cesspool of the Florida state offices. I've saved them for you here, having run out of the patience needed to knock heads with "respectable" U.S. papers and networks.

How did British newspapers smell the Florida story all the way across the Atlantic? At the time, I was digging into George Bush Sr.'s gold-mining business, when one of my researchers spotted a note on the *Mother Jones* Internet bulletin board flagging a story in the *Palm Beach Post* printed months before the election. The Post's back pages mentioned that 8,000 voters had been removed from the voter rolls by mistake. That's one heck of a mistake. Given the Sturm und Drang in Florida, you'd think that an American journalist would pick up the story. Don't hold your breath. There were a couple of curious reporters, but they were easily waylaid by Florida's assurances that the "mistake" had been *corrected*, which the *Post* ran as truth.

But what if the Florida press puppies had been wrong? What if they had stood on their hind legs and swallowed a biscuit of bullshit from state officials—and the "mistakes" had *not* been corrected?

It was worth a call.

From London, I contacted a statistician at the office of the county elections supervisor in Tampa. Such an expert technician would have no reason to lie to me. The question at the top of my list: *"How many of the voters on the scrub list are BLACK?"*

And the statistician said, "You know, I've been waiting for someone to ask me that." From his leads, I wrote:

"Black-Out in Florida"
The Observer, London, November 26, 2000
Vice-President Al Gore would have strolled to victory in Florida if the state hadn't kicked up to 66,000 citizens off the voter registers five months ago as former felons. In fact, not all were ex-cons. Most were simply guilty of being African-American. A top-placed election official told me that the government had conducted a quiet review and found—surprise!—that the listing included far more African-Americans than would statistically have been expected, even accounting for the grievous gap between the conviction rates of Blacks and Whites in the U.S.

One list of 8,000 supposed felons was supplied by Texas. But these criminals from the Lone Star State had committed nothing more serious than misdemeanors such as drunk driving (like their governor, George W. Bush).

The source of this poisonous blacklist: Database Technologies, acting under the direction of Governor Jeb Bush's frothingly partisan secretary of state, Katherine Harris. DBT, a division of Choice-Point, is under fire for misuse of personal data in state computers in Pennsylvania. ChoicePoint's board is loaded with Republican sugar daddies, including Ken Langone, finance chief for Rudy Giuliani's aborted Senate run against Hillary Clinton.

Voting with the Alligators

When the *Observer* report hit the streets (of London), Gore was still in the race.

Reporter Conason pushed Salon.com to pick up my story and take it further. But that would not be easy. The Texas list error—8,000 names—was corrected, said the state. That left the tougher question: What about the 57,700 *other* people named on that list? The remaining names on the list were, in the majority, Black—not unusual in a nation where half of all felony convictions are against African Americans. But as half the names were Black, and if this included even a tiny fraction of innocents, well, there was the election for Bush.

The question was, then, whether the "corrected" list had in fact been corrected. Finding the answer would not be cheap for Salon. It meant big bucks; redirecting their entire political staff to the story and making hotshot reporters knuckle down to the drudgery of calling and visiting county elections offices all over Florida. But they agreed, and

Salon's Alicia Montgomery, Daryl Lindsey and Anthony York[*] came back with a mother lode of evidence proving that, by the most conservative analysis, Florida had purged enough innocent Black voters—several thousand—to snatch the presidency from Al Gore.

At that time the presidential race was wide open. Word was, Gore's camp was split, with warriors fighting the gray-heads of the Establishment who were pushing him to lie down and play dead, advice he'd ultimately follow. Just before we hit the electronic streets with it, someone called a key player in the White House and Gore's inner circle about the story Salon would soon break. The Big Insider said, "That's fantastic! Who's the reporter?" The tipster said, "This American, he's a reporter in Britain, Greg Palast."

Mr. White House Insider replied, "Shit! We *hate* that guy." But that's another story.

On December 4, 2000, I sent this to Salon:

"Florida's Ethnic Cleansing of the Voter Rolls"
from *Salon.com*

If Vice President Al Gore is wondering where his Florida votes went, rather than sift through a pile of chads, he might want to look at a "scrub list" of 57,700 names targeted to be knocked off the Florida voter registry by a division of the office of Florida Secretary of State Katherine Harris. A close examination suggests thousands of voters may have

[*]Thank you all.

lost their right to vote based on a flaw-ridden list of purported "felons" provided by a private firm with tight Republican ties.

Early in the year, the company ChoicePoint gave Florida officials the names of 8,000 ex-felons to "scrub" from their list of voters.

But it turns out none on the list was guilty of felonies, only misdemeanors.

The company acknowledged the error, and blamed it on the original source of the list—the state of Texas.

Florida officials moved to put those falsely accused by Texas back on voter rolls before the election. Nevertheless, the large number of errors uncovered in individual counties suggests that thousands of other eligible voters have been turned away at the polls.

Florida is the only state that pays a private company that promises to provide lists for "cleansing" voter rolls. The state signed in 1998 a $4 million contract with DBT Online, since merged into ChoicePoint, of Atlanta. The creation of the scrub list, called the central voter file, was mandated by a 1998 state voter fraud law, which followed a tumultuous year that saw Miami's mayor removed after voter fraud in the election, with dead people discovered to have cast ballots. The voter fraud law required all 67 counties to purge voter registries of duplicate registrations, deceased voters and felons, many of whom, but not all, are barred from voting in Florida. In the process, however, the list invariably targets a minority population in Florida, where 31 percent of all Black men cannot vote because of a ban on felons.

If this unfairly singled out minorities, it unfairly handicapped Gore: in Florida, 93 percent of African-Americans voted for the vice president.

In the ten counties contacted by Salon, use of the central voter file seemed to vary wildly. Some found the list too unreliable and didn't use it at all. But most counties appear to have used the file as a resource to purge names from their voter rolls, with some counties making little—or no—effort at all to alert the "purged" voters. Counties that did their best to vet the file discovered a high level of errors, with as many as 15 percent of names incorrectly identified as felons.

News coverage has focused on some maverick Florida counties that rejected the scrub lists, including Palm Beach and Duval. The *Miami Herald* blasted the counties for not using the lists; but local officials tell us they had good reason to reject the scrub sheets from Harris's office. Madison County's elections supervisor, Linda Howell, had a peculiarly personal reason for distrusting the central voter file. She had received a letter saying that since she had committed a felony, she would not be allowed to vote.

Howell, who said she has never committed a felony, said the letter she received in March 2000 shook her faith in the process. "It really is a mess," she said.

"I was very upset," Howell said. "I know I'm not a felon." Though the one mistake did get corrected and law enforcement officials were quite apologetic, Howell decided not to use the state list because its "information is so flawed."

She's unsure of the number of warning letters that were sent out to county residents when she first received the list in 1999, but she recalls that there were many problems. "One day we would send a letter to have someone taken off the rolls, and the next day, we would send one to put them back on again," Howell said. "It makes you look like you must be a dummy."

Dixie and Washington counties also refused to use the scrub list. Starlet Cannon, Dixie's deputy assistant supervisor of elections, said, "I'm scared to work with it because [a] lot of the information they have on there is not accurate."

Carol Griffin, supervisor of elections for Washington, said, "It hasn't been accurate in the past, so we had no reason to suspect it was accurate this year."

But if some counties refused to use the list altogether, others seemed to embrace it all too enthusiastically. Etta Rosado, spokeswoman for the Volusia County Department of Elections, said the county essentially accepted the file at face value, did nothing to confirm the accuracy of it and doesn't inform citizens ahead of time that they have been dropped from the voter rolls.

"When we get the con felon list, we automatically start going through our rolls on the computer. If there's a name that says John Smith was convicted of a felony, then we enter a notation on our computer that says convicted felon—we mark an 'f' for felon—and the date that we received it," Rosado said.

"They're still on our computer, but they're on purge status," meaning they have been marked ineligible to vote.

"I don't think that it's up to us to tell them they're a convicted felon," Rosado said. "If he's on our rolls, we make a notation on there. If they show up at a polling place, we'll say, 'Wait a minute, you're a convicted felon, you can't vote.' Nine out of ten times when we repeat that to the person, they say 'Thank you' and walk away. They don't put up arguments." Rosado doesn't know how many people in Volusia were dropped from the list as a result of being identified as felons.

Hillsborough County's elections supervisor, Pam Iorio, tried to make sure that the bugs in the system didn't keep anyone from voting. All 3,258 county residents who were identified as possible felons on the central voter file sent by the state were sent a certified letter informing them that their voting rights were in jeopardy. Of that number, 551 appealed their status, and 245 of those appeals were successful. (By the rules established by Harris's office, a voter is assumed guilty and convicted of a crime and conviction unless and until they provide documentation certifying their innocence.) Some had been convicted of a misdemeanor and not a felony, others were felons who had had their rights restored and others were simply cases of mistaken identity.

An additional 279 were not close matches with names on the county's own voter rolls and were not notified. Of the 3,258 names on the original list, therefore, the county concluded that more than 15 percent were in error. If that ratio held statewide, *no fewer than 7,000* voters were incorrectly targeted for removal from voting rosters.

Iorio says local officials did not get adequate preparation for purging felons from their rolls. "We're not used to dealing with issues of criminal justice or ascertaining who has a felony conviction," she said. Though the central voter file was supposed to facilitate the process, it was often more troublesome than the monthly circuit court lists that she had previously used to clear her rolls of duplicate registrations, the deceased and convicted felons. "The database from the state level is not always accurate," Iorio said. As a consequence, her county did its best to notify citizens who were on the list about their felony status.

"We sent those individuals a certified letter, we put an ad in a local newspaper and we held a public hearing. For those who didn't respond to that, we sent out another letter by regular mail," Iorio said. "That process lasted several months."

"We did run some number stats and the number of Blacks [on the list] was higher than expected for our population," says Chuck Smith, a statistician for the county. Iorio acknowledged that African-Americans made up 54 percent of the people on the original felons list, though they constitute only 11.6 percent of Hillsborough's voting population.

Smith added that the DBT computer program automatically transformed various forms of a single name. In one case, a voter named "Christine" was identified as a felon based on the conviction of a "Christopher" with the same last name. Smith says ChoicePoint would not respond to queries about its proprietary methods. Nor would the company provide additional verification data to back its fingering certain individuals in the registry purge. One supposed felon on the ChoicePoint list is a local judge.

While there was much about the lists that bothered Iorio, she felt she didn't have a choice but to use them. And she's right. Section 98.0975 of the Florida Constitution states: "Upon receiving the list from the division, the supervisor must attempt to verify the information provided. If the supervisor does not determine that the information provided by the division is incorrect, the supervisor must remove from the registration books by the next subsequent election the name of any person who is deceased, convicted of a felony or adjudicated mentally incapacitated with respect to voting."

But the counties have interpreted that law in different ways. Leon County used the central voter file sent in January 2000 to clean up its voter rolls, but set aside the one it received in July. According to Thomas James, the information systems officer in the county election office, the list came too late for the information to be processed.

According to Leon election supervisor Ion Sancho, "there have been some problems" with the file. Using the information received in January,

Sancho sent 200 letters to county voters, by regular mail, telling them they had been identified by the state as having committed a felony and would not be allowed to vote. They were given 30 days to respond if there was an error. "They had the burden of proof," he says.

He says 20 people proved that they did not belong on the list, and a handful of angry phone calls followed on election day. "Some people threatened to sue us," he said, "but we haven't had any lawyers calling yet." In Orange County, officials also sent letters to those identified as felons by the state, but they appear to have taken little care in their handling of the list.

"I have no idea," said June Condrun, Orange's deputy supervisor of elections, when asked how many letters were sent out to voters. After a bit more thought, Condrun responded that "several hundred" of the letters were sent, but said she doesn't know how many people complained. Those who did call, she said, were given the phone number of the Florida Department of Law Enforcement so that they could appeal directly to it.

Many Orange County voters never got the chance to appeal in any form.

Condrun noted that about one-third of the letters, which the county sent out by regular mail, were returned to the office marked undeliverable. She attributed the high rate of incorrect addresses to the age of the information sent by DBT, some of which was close to 20 years old, she said.

Miami-Dade County officials may have had

similar trouble. Milton Collins, assistant supervisor of elections, said he isn't comfortable estimating how many accused felons were identified by the central voter file in his county. He said he knows that about 6,000 were notified, by regular mail, about an early list in 1999. Exactly how many were purged from the list? "I honestly couldn't tell you," he said. According to Collins, the most recent list he received from the state was one sent in January 2000, and the county applied a "two-pass system." If the information on the state list seemed accurate enough when comparing names with those on county voter lists, people were classified as felons and were then sent warning letters. Those who seemed to have only a partial match with the state data were granted "temporary inactive status."

Both groups of people were given 90 days to respond or have their names struck from the rolls.

But Collins said the county has no figures for how many voters were able to successfully appeal their designation as felons.

ChoicePoint spokesman Martin Fagan concedes his company's error in passing on the bogus list from Texas. ("I guess that's a little bit embarrassing in light of the election," he says.) He defends the company's overall performance, however, dismissing the errors in 8,000 names as "a minor glitch—less than one-tenth of 1 percent of the electorate" (though the total equals 15 times Governor George W. Bush's claimed lead over Gore). But he added that ChoicePoint is responsible only for turning over its raw list, which is then up to Florida officials to test and correct.

Last year, DBT Online, with which ChoicePoint would soon merge, received the unprecedented contract from the state of Florida to "cleanse" registration lists of ineligible voters—using information gathering and matching criteria it has refused to disclose, even to local election officials in Florida.

Atlanta's ChoicePoint, a highflying dot-com specializing in sales of personal information gleaned from its database of four billion public and not-so-public records, has come under fire for misuse of private data from government computers.

In January 2000, the state of Pennsylvania terminated a contract with ChoicePoint after discovering the firm had sold citizens' personal profiles to unauthorized individuals.

Fagan says many errors could have been eliminated by matching the Social Security numbers of ex-felons on DBT lists to the Social Security numbers on voter registries. However, Florida's counties have Social Security numbers on only a fraction of their voter records. So with those two problems—Social Security numbers missing in both the DBT's records and the counties' records—that fail-safe check simply did not exist.

Florida is the only state in the nation to contract the first stage of removal of voting rights to a private company. And ChoicePoint has big plans. "Given the outcome of our work in Florida," says Fagan, "and with a new president in place, we think our services will expand across the country."

Especially if that president is named "Bush." ChoicePoint's board, executive suite and consultant rosters are packed with Republican stars, including former New York Police Commissioner Howard Safir and former ultra-Right congressman Vin Weber, ChoicePoint's Washington lobbyist.

More Votes Fished Out of the Swamps

Following the Salon investigation I was confident that at least 7,000 innocent voters had been removed from voter rolls, half of them Black, and that swung the election. But my investigation was far from over—and I found yet another 2,834 eligible voters targeted for the purge, almost all Democrats.

It was December 10, 2000—Gore was still hanging in there—when I wrote this for British readers:

"A Blacklist Burning for Bush"
The Observer, London, December 10, 2000

Hey, Al, take a look at this. Every time I cut open another alligator, I find the bones of more Gore voters. This week, I was hacking my way through the Florida swampland known as the Office of Secretary of State Katherine Harris and found a couple thousand more names of voters electronically "disappeared" from the vote rolls. About half of those named are African-Americans.

They had the right to vote, but they never made it to the balloting booths.

On November 26, we reported that the Florida Secretary of State's office had, before the election, ordered the elimination of 8,000 Florida voters on the grounds that they had committed felonies in Texas. None had.

For Florida Governor Jeb Bush and his brother, the Texas blacklist was a mistake made in Heaven. Most of those targeted to have their names "scrubbed" from the voter roles were African-Americans, Hispanics and poor white folk, likely voters for Vice-President Gore. We don't know how many voters lost their citizenship rights before the error was discovered by a few skeptical county officials before ChoicePoint, which has gamely 'fessed-up to the Texas-sized error, produced a new list of 57,700 felons. In May, Harris sent on the new, improved scrub sheets to the county election boards.

Maybe it's my bad attitude, but I thought it worthwhile to check out the new list. Sleuthing around county offices with a team of researchers from Internet newspaper Salon, we discovered that the "correct" list wasn't so correct.

Our ten-county review suggests a minimum 15 percent misidentification rate. That makes another 7,000 innocent people accused of crimes and stripped of their citizenship rights in the run-up to the presidential race, a majority of them Black.

Now our team, diving deeper into the swamps, has discovered yet a third group whose voting rights were stripped. The state's private contractor, Choice-Point, generated a list of about two thousand names of people who, earlier in their lives, were convicted of felonies in Illinois and Ohio. Like most American states, these two restore citizenship rights to people who have served their time in prison and then remained on the good side of the law.

Florida strips those convicted in its own courts of voting rights for life. But Harris's office concedes, and county officials concur, that the state of Florida has no right to impose this penalty on people who have moved in from these other states. (Only 13 states, most in the Old Confederacy, bar reformed criminals from voting.)

Going deeper into the Harris lists, we find hundreds more convicts from the 37 other states that restored their rights at the end of sentences served. If they have the right to vote, why were these citizens barred from the polls? Harris didn't return my calls. But Alan Dershowitz did. The Harvard law professor, a renowned authority on legal process, said: "What's emerging is a pattern of reducing the total number of voters in Florida, which they know will reduce the Democratic vote."

How could Florida's Republican rulers know how these people would vote?

I put the question to David Bositis, America's top expert on voting demographics.

Once he stopped laughing, he said the way Florida used the lists from a private firm was "a patently obvious technique to discriminate against Black voters." In a darker mood, Bositis, of Washington's Center for Political and Economic Studies, said the sad truth of American justice is that 46 percent of those convicted of felony are African-American. In Florida, a record number of Black folk, over 80 percent of those registered to vote, packed the polling booths on November 7. Behind the curtains, nine out of ten Black people voted for Gore.

Mark Mauer of the Sentencing Project, Washington, pointed out that the "White" half of the purge list would be peopled overwhelmingly by the poor, also solid Democratic voters.

Add it up. The dead-wrong Texas list, the uncorrected "corrected" list, plus the out-of-state ex-con list. By golly, it's enough to swing a presidential election. I bet the busy Harris, simultaneously in charge of both Florida's voter rolls and George Bush's presidential campaign, never thought of that.

Thursday, December 7, 2 A.M. On the other end of the line, heavy breathing, then a torrent of words too fast for me to catch it all. "Vile . . . lying . . . inaccurate . . . pack of nonsense . . . riddled with errors . . . " click! This was not a ChoicePoint whistleblower telling me about the company's notorious list. It was ChoicePoint's own media communications representative, Marty Fagan, communicating with me about my "sleazy disgusting journalism" in reporting on it.

Truth is, Fagan was returning my calls. I was curious about this company that chose the president for America's voters.

They have quite a pedigree for this solemn task.

The company's Florida subsidiary, Database Technologies (now DBT Online), was founded by one Hank Asher. When US law enforcement agencies alleged that he might have been associated with Bahamian drug dealers—although no charges were brought—the company lost its data management contract with the FBI. Hank and his friends left and so, in Florida's eyes, the past is forgiven.

Thursday, 3 A.M. A new, gentler voice gave me ChoicePoint's upbeat spin. "You say we got over 15 percent wrong—we like to look at that as up to 85 percent right!" That's 7,000 votes-plus—the bulk Democrats, not to mention the thousands on the faulty Texas list. (Gore lost the White House by 537 votes.)

I contacted San Francisco–based expert Mark Swedlund. "It's just fundamental industry practice that you don't roll out the list statewide until you have tested it and tested it again," he said. "Dershowitz is right: they had to know that this jeopardized thousands of people's registrations. And they would also know the [racial] profile of those voters."

"They" is Florida State, not ChoicePoint. Let's not get confused about where the blame lies. Harris's crew lit this database fuse, then acted surprised when it blew up. Swedlund says ChoicePoint had a professional responsibility to tell the state to test the list; ChoicePoint says the state should not have used its "raw" data.

Until Florida privatized its Big Brother powers, laws kept the process out in the open. This year,

when one county asked to see ChoicePoint's for-
mulas and back-up for blacklisting voters, they
refused—these were commercial secrets.

So we'll never know how America's president
was chosen.

ANAGRAM

Republican National Committee:
Inept ballot count: America mine!

Correction
from *The Economist* (11/17/01)

I n the issues of December 16th 2000 to November 10th
2001, we may have given the impression that George W.
Bush had been legally and duly elected president of the
United States. We now understand that this may have been
incorrect, and that the election result is still too close to call.
The Economist apologizes for any inconvenience.

Alan Dershowitz investigates the motives of the five Supreme Court justices who voted to stop the vote count while Bush was ahead.

The Inconsistency of the Majority Justices

from *Supreme Injustice* (2001)

Alan M. Dershowitz

JUSTICE O'CONNOR

The patriotic-partisan motive alone might well have caused Sandra Day O'Connor to decide the case in favor of Bush, even if she had not also had a unique personal motive to help guarantee a Bush victory. A closer look at the O'Connor situation may help us to understand both the difficulty and the importance of trying to assess motive in this kind of a situation. It may also help us understand why we need prophylactic rules of judicial disqualification in close cases involving the possible combination of proper and improper motives.

It has been widely reported that O'Connor was hoping for a Bush victory so that she could retire from the Supreme Court with the assurance that her replacement would be named by a Republican president. According to reports, O'Connor—who is seventy years old and a breast cancer survivor—was anxious to join her ailing husband in Arizona but planned to delay her retirement in the event of a Gore victory. A story in *Newsweek* reported that while watching the media coverage on election night with friends, she responded to news projections that Gore had won Florida by exclaiming, "This is terrible!" The *Newsweek* report continued:

> She explained to another partygoer that Gore's reported victory in Florida meant that the election was "over," since Gore had already carried two other swing states, Michigan and Illinois.
>
> Moments later, with an air of obvious disgust, she rose to get a plate of food, leaving it to her husband to explain her somewhat uncharacteristic outburst. John O'Connor said his wife was upset because they wanted to retire to Arizona, and a Gore win meant they'd have to wait another four years. O'Connor, the former Republican majority leader of the Arizona State Senate and a 1981 Ronald Reagan appointee, did not want a Democrat to name her successor. Two witnesses described this extraordinary scene to *Newsweek*. Responding through a spokesman at the high court, O'Connor had no comment.

Personal retirement plans constitute self-interest under the codes of judicial conduct, and so if these reports are true, then O'Connor probably should not have participated in any of the presidential election cases. Whether or not she was actually influenced by this personal motivation, the possibility that she might have been—or that reasonable observers could honestly believe she was—is enough to raise a serious question about the appearance of justice. One former Supreme Court law clerk, noting O'Connor's "newly petulant attitude during oral arguments" in this case, commented that the high court's 5–4 vote "has raised the specter that some of the conservative justices, yearning for retirement, suffered from a serious conflict of interest when deciding the case." The only other justice to whom he could have been referring is Chief Justice Rehnquist, who suffers from severe back problems; it has been widely reported that he wishes to retire from the high court, but only if his replacement will be named by a Republican president. Unlike O'Connor, he apparently did not talk as openly about his retirement plans or about how "terrible" a Gore victory would have been. But the Bush administration is aware of Rehnquist's wish to retire, and it is already gearing up to find a suitable replacement.

Some of the lawyers with whom I have discussed the matter have suggested that in O'Connor's case, her *personal* motive may not have been the deciding factor, since she already had a strong *political* inclination toward favoring a Bush victory, and what she meant by "terrible" was terrible for the country, not terrible for her and her retirement plans, despite her husband's statement to the contrary. She is, after all, a lifelong Republican who has served in various leadership roles in that party. She was "extremely active in the Arizona Republican Party and in Barry Goldwater's 1964 presidential campaign" and was co-chair of Richard Nixon's Arizona reelection campaign; she served as the Republican leader of the state senate and was considered as a Republican candidate for governor. "She was a very political animal," said one observer at the time of her nomination. "She started out as a moderate Republican and then . . . moved toward the right." After paying her dues to the Republican Party, she was brought to the attention of President Ronald Reagan by her law school classmate William Rehnquist and by Senator Barry Gold-water, though she had served as an Arizona intermediate appellate court judge for less than two years at the time." She was interviewed by then–Justice Department lawyer Kenneth Starr, who reported back that she was a law-and-order judge who was likely to defer to other branches of government. She was quickly nominated and confirmed as the first woman to serve on the Supreme Court.

She was not, of course, the first politically active elected official to serve on the high court, but traditionally politicians have left their partisanship behind when joining the Court. Not so with O'Connor. While serving as a justice, she has been criticized by judicial ethics experts on at least two occasions for using her position as a justice to support partisan Republican causes. Such criticism is rare in the Court's history.

The first incident that raised ethical questions occurred in 1987, when O'Connor agreed to conduct a "private briefing" on the workings of the Supreme Court for Republicans who had contributed at least $10,000 to a political action group called GoPac, which was seeking to gain Republican control of Congress. She bowed out of this partisan fund-raising event only after ethics experts publicly criticized her actions as violating the American Bar Association's Code of Judicial Conduct—but not until after her name had been used successfully in the fund-raising solicitation. Two years later O'Connor responded to a request from an Arizona Republican asking her to write a letter in support of a proposed Republican Party resolution declaring the United States to be "a Christian Nation . . . based on the absolute law of the Bible, not a democracy." She did so, and her reply—written on Court stationery—was circulated as part of the campaign to help the Arizona Republican Party. When her letter was publicly disclosed, Justice O'Connor issued a statement regretting that the "letter she had written to an acquaintance . . . was used in a political debate." The Court press office said that she had "had no idea" the letter would be used politically. The available evidence points to the opposite conclusion. The request itself made it unmistakably clear that she was being asked to write her letter specifically for use in the campaign by conservative Republicans to take votes away from Democrats in Arizona:

> Republicans are making some interesting advances in this heavily controlled Democratic area. Some of us are proposing a resolution which acknowledges that the Supreme Court ruled in 1892 that this is a Christian Nation. It would be beneficial and interesting to have a letter from you.

Justice O'Connor has thus twice publicly endorsed partisan Republican causes. Her regrets—which were incomplete and misleading—came only after public criticism. Nothing in her background suggests that she would have risked criticism for comparable Democratic causes. In light of the close association she has maintained with Republican causes and officials, it came as no surprise when, in 1988, an aide to George H. Bush, then a presidential candidate, characterized O'Connor as a Bush "dream pick" for vice president if he received the Republican presidential nomination.

Although O'Connor has not repeated her openly partisan mistakes in recent years, her obvious dismay at

Gore's apparent victory on election night shows that her allegiance to her old party is still strong. The conservative Republican columnist Robert Novak, in a recent article praising Justice O'Connor's role as a "flexible politician" on the high court, quoted a "well-connected conservative lawyer" as saying that after nearly twenty years on the Court, she is "what she always has been and always will be: the Republican floor leader of the Arizona Senate." If we accept this picture of O'Connor as a still-loyal Republican politician who has already acknowledged that she wants her replacement to be picked by a Republican president, we can certainly speculate that she might have voted for the Republican candidate for these reasons alone. According to this scenario, her vote was motivated not by personal, material considerations—namely, her wish to retire—but instead by party loyalty. Or, to put the best partisan face on it, she was motivated by a desire to see the best man elected as president.

She was also reportedly "furious" at the Florida Supreme Court for what she believed was its partisan intervention in favor of Gore. It is impossible to know whether this fury was institutional or personal: Would she have been as angry had a state court similarly intervened in favor of Bush?

There is, of course, no way to separate completely the personal from the partisan in this situation, because it is O'Connor's *choice* not to retire unless her replacement would be named by a Republican president. Were it not for this partisan choice, she could have satisfied her personal desire to retire at any time, regardless of who won the election.

Of course, even if the personal could be separated from

the partisan, the suggestion that the deciding factor in her decision was her partisan support for the Republican candidate rather than her personal desire to retire does not put O'Connor in a much better light. Her judicial vote was improper if it was influenced by *either* personal or partisan political considerations. Her vote would be proper only if she would have voted exactly the same way if stopping the recount would have ensured a "terrible" Gore victory, rather than a personally and politically beneficial Bush victory. In order to prove this highly unlikely—and incomplete— defense, one would have to demonstrate a pattern of judicial voting, in other relevant cases not involving personal or partisan outcomes, consistent with her vote in this case. Such a pattern is, to say the least, not evident.

If Election 2000 had been decided by a legislature of which O'Connor was a member, she certainly would have been questioned about her apparent conflict of interest. But because she is a justice of the Supreme Court—an institution deemed above partisanship—there is a tendency to resolve doubts in favor of her integrity. In this case, however, there do not appear to be real doubts to resolve. The available evidence, in my view, strongly suggests that Justice O'Connor, at the very least, had the appearance of a conflict of interest following her revealing statement on the night of the election. How much of a role, if any, her retirement motive played in causing her to fail the shoe-on-the-other-foot test is impossible to calibrate. That she did fail this test seems clear from the totality of evidence.

While O'Connor was in the process of being confirmed to the high court, she told the senators that she would like to be remembered with the following epitaph: "Here lies a good judge who upheld the Constitution." She has recently acknowledged to a mutual friend that her vote in the election case may have hurt her reputation and endangered her place in history. She is right.

The crowning irony is that O'Connor may not now be able to retire from the Court without confirming the worst suspicions about her motives. A recent story in the *New York Times* has reported that "associates of Justice O'Connor have signaled that she wants it known that she will not retire after this term" (which ends in July, 2001). I have also been told that O'Connor wants more time to rebuild her tarnished legacy and does not wish to be remembered by her vote in *Bush v. Gore.*

JUSTICE KENNEDY

Mixed motives may also have been at play with regard to Anthony Kennedy's decision to join the majority. I have been told by a source close to the Court that Anthony Kennedy has a quiet but determined ambition that could be satisfied only if Bush became president: He wants to become the next chief justice of the United States when William Rehnquist steps down, as he is expected to do now that a Republican president is in office.

Kennedy realized that because of his own background in Republican politics—he had ties to Ronald Reagan during Reagan's governorship and to Reagan's executive secretary, Edwin Meese, and had worked as a lobbyist—he would stand little chance of being promoted to chief justice by a Democratic president. He has confided his ambition to trusted friends and former law clerks, who have shared this information with my source. One former clerk has pointed out that in recent years, as the prospect of a vacancy has drawn closer, Kennedy has changed his vote in several cases to enhance his standing as a strong candidate to fill that vacancy.

This speculation has also been reported by Robert Novak, who has excellent sources within the conservative movement: "Kennedy's recent swing to the right led court-watchers to conclude that he was readying himself for a chief justice vacancy in a Republican administration." Novak had previously pinpointed one decision by Kennedy that "raised suspicions in legal circles that he is launching a campaign to be the next chief justice if a Republican is elected president."

It has now been reliably reported—and I have been able to confirm independently—that Justice Kennedy was the primary author of the Court's final per curiam opinion. I have also been told that Justice Kennedy wishes to have his authorship known to the Bush administration. In his campaign for the chief justiceship, he has emphasized that because of his generally moderate views, he is the only inside candidate who is confirmable by the Senate, but—as evidenced by his vote in *Bush v. Gore*—he is also a moderate who can be counted on when push comes to shove.

We can't know for certain whether my source is correct about Kennedy's ambition and, if so, whether it played any role in his vote in the Florida recount case. What we do know is that his vote and the arguments he presented in the opinion to support it were inconsistent with his previously expressed substantive views on equal protection, with his long-held attitudes toward the force of precedent, with his previous votes on stay applications, and with his frequently stated position on the limited role of courts in cases involving large issues of politics and policy. So at the very least, there is evidence of a motive other than the desire to follow his previous decisions and rule fairly.

There is no public information that would have justified Kennedy's recusal in this case, but if he in fact chose personal ambition or party loyalty over principle, then he has, in my view, morally disqualified himself from becoming chief justice or earning a place of honor in the history of the Supreme Court. A justice who once bends the rules to favor a particular litigant can never again be trusted not to break them if the stakes are sufficiently high. A justice who allows himself to become blinded by personal ambition should not be rewarded by having his ambition satisfied.

JUSTICE THOMAS

Clarence Thomas is a reliable member of the Court's right wing and is also, according to people who know him well, consumed by the need to strike back at those Democrats who put him through the "high-tech lynching" of the Anita Hill hearings. Thomas divides the world into friends and enemies. "Good versus evil" is how his wife, Virginia Thomas, described the "spiritual warfare" of his confirmation hearings, which left Thomas with a long enemies list consisting primarily of Democratic senators who voted against his confirmation—among them Al Gore and Joseph Lieberman.

At the time, Gore said his negative vote was based on Thomas's "judicial philosophy" and his testimony—which Gore did not believe—that he had never discussed *Roe v. Wade*, implying that he had no fixed views on the abortion issue. Lieberman, who originally supported

Thomas's nomination, changed his mind after hearing Anita Hill's testimony, which, he concluded, was "believable." Gore also found Hill to be "believable and credible," which carried the implicit assertion that Thomas was lying. On the other hand, George W. Bush's father nominated Thomas to the Supreme Court, declaring him to be "the best man for the job," and stood behind him in the face of Democratic attacks. During the campaign, George W. Bush characterized Thomas, along with Antonin Scalia, as his two favorite justices. Gore criticized Bush for singling out these two justices, saying that "when the names of Scalia and Thomas are used as benchmarks for who would be appointed, those are code words." One can only imagine how Thomas must have reacted to being characterized as a code word.

Following his close confirmation, Thomas began to withdraw, both publicly and privately. He almost never spoke during Supreme Court arguments, though he had been an active questioner during his days on the Court of Appeals. According to one observer, Thomas "not only remained unvaryingly silent but looked uninterested, often not even bothering to remove the rubber band from his stack of briefs." He stopped watching the news on television or reading mainstream newspapers or magazines. He limited his information sources to "reliably conservative publications" and to Rush Limbaugh—"[f]or entertainment, he says he likes to listen to tapes of Rush Limbaugh poking fun at feminists, environmentalists and all manner of liberal crusaders." The groups he publicly says he likes to hear fun made of are, of course, often litigants in cases before him. He almost always rules against them.

Thomas speaks primarily to right-wing groups, and he,

too, was criticized for agreeing to give a dinner speech to the Claremont Institute, a group that was actively seeking President Clinton's impeachment, that was scheduled for just three days before the impeachment vote. According to the *Los Angeles Times*, Thomas, "alone among the justices, . . . has spoken regularly before groups that espouse strongly conservative views," despite the Judicial Code of Conduct, which prohibits a judge from "being a speaker or guest of honor at an organization's fundraising events" or "making speeches for a political organization." Thomas has spoken to and been honored by several partisan organizations that supported his nomination. At one such event, he expressed his "sense of gratitude and sense of loyalty." Thomas not only provided an "exclusive and challenging message deep from his heart" to the Concerned Women for America, but sat on cases in which they had filed briefs—and voted in favor of their positions. His loyalty to those who supported him is as powerful—and as influential on his decisions—as his hatred for those who opposed him.

At the time of the Supreme Court's decision in the Florida recount case, Virginia Thomas was working for the Heritage Foundation, a conservative group with close ties to the Bush campaign, gathering resumes for the Bush transition team. Many observers, including a federal judge, believe that Justice Thomas should have recused himself from the case because of his wife's connections to the Republican Party and her substantial interest in a Bush victory.

An even more compelling argument for his recusal would have been his abiding hatred for Gore and Lieberman (coupled with his deep sense of loyalty to the

Bush family). According to Court watchers, even Thomas's "jurisprudence on the Court seemed guided to an unusual degree by raw anger." Jeffrey Toobin quoted a longtime friend of the Thomases about the effect of the confirmation hearings on his role as a justice: "The real tragedy of this event is that his behavior on the court has been affected. He's still damaged. He's still reeling. He was hurt more deeply than anyone could comprehend." His anger continues to "churn within" him. According to a close friend, "[h]e never wants the world to forget the price he paid to get" on the Court. He refuses to "let bygones be bygones" lest that be seen as "capitulation" to his enemies. His rage on the subject of his confirmation "is evergreen." Thomas has acknowledged that he was a very angry man even before the hearings. After that transforming event, he became consumed with anger, hatred, and revenge. "His votes on the Supreme Court— and his public life as a justice—have reflected, with great precision, the grievance that simmers inside him." His chambers "exuded a sense of score settling," and his wife has said that he "doesn't owe any of the groups who opposed him anything"—suggesting that he does owe something to those who supported him. As Jeffrey Toobin has put it: "The heart of Thomas's strategy for striking back at his liberal critics is, of course, to utilize the Supreme Court itself." Both sides regarded him as a sure vote for Bush, despite the fact that his previous decisions seemed to have favored the Gore positions on their merits.

JUSTICE SCALIA

Antonin Scalia is certainly the most ideological and opinionated justice on the Court today. Although some critics sought his recusal because two of his sons worked for law firms that represented the Bush side, I find it difficult to believe he was actually motivated by such personal factors. According to people who know him, Scalia's primary motive is to pack the high court, as well as the lower courts, with judges who share his ideology. He has a loyal and dedicated following among former clerks, members of the conservative Federalist Society, and other like-minded right-wing Republicans. As his former colleague at the University of Chicago, Judge Richard Posner, recently put it:

> The real conflict of interest is that justices are not indifferent to their colleagues and successors, and the president appoints them. That's an inherent serious conflict, because even if the justices play it straight and each says to himself or herself, I'm not going to think about the effect of this decision on my legacy as a Supreme Court justice, you can't exclude the possibility of an unconscious influence. If these justices had not been so interested in this case for themselves, they might not have picked up on some of the mistakes by the Florida Supreme Court. What a judge notices as "something bad enough to require action" is likely to be influenced by unconscious factors. You are just alert to things the way a drug-sniffing police dog is alert to cocaine.

Scalia himself does not fit neatly into any familiar political or ideological category. He is not a classic conservative, as that term has traditionally been defined in this country. American conservatism has always had more of a libertarian streak than Scalia seems to embrace. His conservatisms, according to a professor who is an expert in these matters, are "of the Old World European sort, rooted in the authority of the Church and the military. It is more reminiscent of French, Italian and Spanish clerical conservatism than of American conservatism with its libertarian bent." According to a *Washington Post* story, Antonin Scalia was sent to "an elite church-run military prep school in Manhattan," where one of his classmates remembered him at age seventeen as "an archconservative Catholic [who] could have been a member of the curia." When he was nominated to the Supreme Court in 1986, the American Civil Liberties Union presciently summarized his views in the following terms:

> In virtually every opinion that he has written addressing civil liberties issues, Judge Scalia has decided against the individual. He has restricted the protection of the First Amendment, made it more difficult for plaintiffs in discrimination cases to proceed and succeed, always upheld the state's position against that of the accused, almost always restricted the public's access to government information and has insulated executive action from judicial review.

One of Scalia's staunchest supporters was far less prescient—at least about the justice's vote in the Florida election case. Norman Podhoretz, editor of *Commentary*, wrote in 1986 that "Scalia has decided against judicial intrusion into the business of the political branches." If he had been truly prescient, he would have added: ". . . except when necessary to get his candidate elected."

Scalia's vote in *Bush v. Gore* has shown that the most accurate guide to predicting his judicial decisions is to follow his political and personal preferences rather than his lofty rhetoric about judicial restraint, originalism, and other abstract aspects of his so-called constraining judicial philosophy, which turns out to be little more than a cover for his politics and his desire to pack the Court with like-minded justices. Because I like Justice Scalia as a person, I was most disappointed with his precipitous abandonment of principle in the name of partisanship.

CHIEF JUSTICE REHNQUIST

I was neither surprised nor disappointed by the actions of Chief Justice Rehnquist. No one I know seriously consid-ered the possibility that Rehnquist had an open mind in this case—and not only because of his wish to retire and have his successor named by a Republican. He has always been a partisan justice. He was appointed for that reason. The tapes made in the Oval Office during Nixon's admin-istration recorded White House chief of staff H. R. Haldeman telling President Nixon that Rehnquist "wouldn't have a snowball's chance of getting on that court" if the Senate hadn't been exhausted from the battle over the failed nominations of Clement Haynsworth and G. Harrold Carswell. On the tapes, Henry Kissinger asks whether Rehnquist is "pretty far right," and Haldeman replies, "Oh, Christ, he's way to the right of Patrick Buchanan."

Despite Rehnquist's prior decisions limiting equal-protection claims to racial grounds and his strong support for state sovereignty under the Tenth Amendment, he too was considered a sure vote for Bush. His motive may have been mixed and somewhat more difficult to decipher than some of the other justices', but his vote was a sure thing for the Republican candidate. Lawyers on both sides did not bother to speculate about why Rehnquist would vote in favor of Bush, because they were absolutely certain he would do so.

ANAGRAM

George Walker Bush, President of the USA:
Pretender grabs White House—flag use OK?

Scandals and Lies

from Democraticunderground.com (3/29/02)

Bridget Gibson

When is a scandal not a scandal? When a scandal appears to be connected with a member of the Republican Party, it is not reported as a "scandal." Only when a member of the Democratic Party has involvement in anything that broaches the questionable grey area is something "determined" to be a "scandal."

After an eight-year-long investigation of William Jefferson and Hillary Clinton was concluded with "no evidence," it is still reported as a "scandal." That $70 million in taxpayer dollars and untold hours were devoted to finding something, anything, to throw at the Clintons has shown that there was nothing to throw. The media (and I mean the major corporate media) still consider it to be a "scandal." One that just won't go away. One that has to be lied about and drummed constantly into the psyche of the American public until something resonates. What is resonating are the words that have been repeated endlessly until almost everyone can recite them verbatim.

But let me tell you what was not a "scandal."

There was no "scandal" when Republican President George Herbert Walker Bush pardoned Caspar Weinberger with an indictment filed against him, thus avoiding any questions regarding the involvement of that same Republican President in the Iran-Contra Affair. There was no "scandal" when a partisan court appointed the highest elected official in this country.

There was no "scandal" when an intern was found dead of mysterious causes in Florida Republican Congressman Joe Scarborough's office. There was no "scandal" when Republican Mayor Philip Giordano of Waterbury, Connecticut, was caught and charged as a sexual predator of young girls.

There was no "scandal" when the Republican President George Walker Bush nominated Theodore Olson (investigated for obstruction of justice and lying to Congress during the Superfund investigation) to the office of Solicitor General. There was no "scandal" when Florida

Governor Jeb Bush's daughter, Noelle Bush, was charged with felony fraud in obtaining a controlled substance.

There was no "scandal" when Republican President George Walker Bush's daughters, Jenna and Barbara Bush, then 18, were convicted with using illegally obtained and false identification to obtain alcohol. There was no "scandal" when Mark A. Grethen, a Republican activist, nominated for "Republican of the Year" was convicted and is serving a more than 20 year sentence in prison for six counts of sex crimes involving children.

There was no "scandal" when Wendy Gramm, the wife of prominent Republican Senator Phil Gramm, approved illegal partnerships and waived the code of ethics for those partnership formations while on the Board of Directors of Enron. There is no "scandal" when Kenneth "Kenny Boy" Lay (Enron and Lay contributed $2.16 million to Republicans in the 2000 election cycle, the largest contributor to the sitting Republican President, George Walker Bush) currently is being investigated for leading one of the largest American companies, Enron, into bankruptcy following fraudulently filed earnings reports.

There was no "scandal" when Enron was allowed to price-gouge consumers and the sitting Republican President George Walker Bush refused to allow the Federal Energy Regulatory Committee (FERC) to impose price caps to control excess profiteering. There was no "scandal" when the current sitting Republican President George Walker Bush appointed Elliott Abrams (convicted of lying to Congress about the Iran-Contra Affair) to the Human Rights Commission of the United Nations.

There was no "scandal" when John Ashcroft, the current Republican Attorney General, spuriously gave a "reprieve" and discontinued the lawfully entered agreement for damages to The Adams Mark Hotel, owned by Fred S. Kummer Jr, a personal friend and $25,700 senatorial campaign contributor, for charges of serious violations of racial discrimination.

There was no "scandal" when key figures John Negroponte (complicit in the Honduran Death Squads), Richard Armitage (linked to illegal arms transfers and CIA drug-running operations), Otto Reich (propaganda operative), John Poindexter (convicted of conspiracy {obstruction of inquiries and proceedings, false statements, falsification, destruction and removal of documents}; two counts of obstruction of Congress and two counts of false statements) of the Iran-Contra Affair have re-appeared in official governmental positions by appointment by George Walker Bush, the sitting Republican President, the son of the former Republican President, George Herbert Walker Bush, for whom these men worked.

There is no "scandal" when the current Republican Vice President Richard Cheney refuses to release what should be public records of meetings held in the formulation of public policy (The Energy Policy) after being ordered to do so by three Federal Judges (U.S. District Judge Gladys Kessler, U.S. District Judge Emmet Sullivan and U.S. District Judge Paul L. Friedman). There is no "scandal" when the personal fortune of George Walker Bush, the sitting Republican President, is being bolstered by governmental war contracts to The Carlyle Group, partially owned by his father, former Republican President George Herbert Walker Bush.

The only exception to this "scandal" rule that you will be able to easily recall is the Watergate scandal presided over by Republican President Richard Milhouse Nixon, who was forced to resign his office in disgrace.

Don't worry about those "scandals," you know the "liberal" major media corporations (Rupert Murdoch of FOX—$30,033 to RNC . . . AOL/Time Warner/Walter Isaacson of CNN—$6,150 to RNC . . . GE/Jack Welch of NBC—$160,350 to RNC . . . Disney/Michael Eisner/ABC—$208,052 to RNC) are surely going to tell you every "scandal" that they want you to know.

They do not want you to remember Republican "scandals." It makes it easier to demonize Democrats. They do not want you to look around. They do not want you to question their version of the news. There are only Democrat "scandals." You can recite them as easily as you can recite the Pledge of Allegiance: Whitewater. The Blue Dress. Chandra Levy. Chappaquiddick. You know the drill.

As citizens of this once great country, we must demand the truth from our media. We must demand the truth from our politicians. We must demand our country back. Each of us, you and I, has that power and the right to make these demands. Call your local television station. Write your representatives. Our voices must be heard. And we must hear the truth.

The following exchange is from an e-mail correspondence between novelist Richard Bausch and Senator John Warner (R–VA) during the Clinton impeachment trial.

Representative Government: A Correspondence

from the *New York Observer*

Richard Bausch

Date: Sat, 30 Jan 1999

Dear Senator Warner,

The impeachment of President Clinton is going to be remembered as the manner in which the radical right finally brought the Republican Party, the party of Lincoln, down. Nothing Clinton did or didn't do endangers the republic; this trial does.

I urge you to seek an end to this madness, this nearly McCarthyesque vendetta by a group of zealots who seem willing to trample everything in order to accomplish their purpose—what Senator Bumpers called "wanting to win too badly."

Sincerely,

Richard Bausch

Date: Mon, 01 Feb 1999

Dear Fellow Virginian:

It is important that you have provided me with your views concerning the impeachment of President Clinton. I share your deep concern, and I assure you that I am proceeding in a manner that aims to preserve the integrity of the United States Constitution and to provide fairness and due process to all involved parties.

I am listening carefully to the views of the people of Virginia, and I commit to you that I will reach decisions based not on politics but rather on the best interests of the nation.

Sincerely,
John Warner
United States Senator

Date: Mon, 01 Feb 1999
Dear Senator Warner,

Is it to be the contention of the party that ONLY Republicans are following the Constitution, and that the entire Democratic Party is trying to circumvent it? Americans are not the dupes some of your colleagues apparently think they are. The people, quite clearly, see this for what it is: a partisan attack on the presidency.

It is very difficult to suppose that the lines of conflict would fall so sharply along party lines if EVERYBODY were voting his conscience. I believe you are. I very much admired your refusal to support the election of Oliver North a few years back. I believe you have the courage to stand against the kind of animus toward a man that may end up changing this government against the expressed will of the people.

Sincerely,
Richard Bausch

Date: Thu, 04 Feb 1999
Dear Fellow Virginian:

It is important that you have provided me with your

views concerning the impeachment of President Clinton. I share your deep concern, and I assure you that I am proceeding in a manner that aims to preserve the integrity of the United States Constitution and to provide fairness and due process to all involved parties.

I am listening carefully to the views of the people of Virginia, and I commit to you that I will reach decisions based not on politics but rather on the best interests of the nation.

Sincerely,
John Warner
United States Senator

Date: Thu, 04 Feb 1999
Dear Senator Warner,

I see from this answer that your writers have crafted a global response letter to be used in all cases. The letter THIS letter answers was the SECOND letter I sent, and was in response to THIS letter. So it is as though I am addressing one of those Chatty Cathy dolls, where you pull the string, and the same words come out, no matter what ELSE is said. In fact, I'm sure I'll get this same form letter in answer to THIS e-mail. I hope you are true to form.

Richard Bausch
(Fellow Virginian)

Date: Fri, 05 Feb 1999
Dear Fellow Virginian:

It is important that you have provided me with your views concerning the impeachment of President Clinton. I share your deep concern, and I assure you that I am proceeding in a manner that aims to preserve the integrity of the United States Constitution and to provide fairness and due process to all involved parties.

I am listening carefully to the views of the people of Virginia, and I commit to you that I will reach decisions based not on politics but rather on the best interests of the nation.

Sincerely,
John Warner
United States Senator

Date: Fri, 05 Feb 1999
Dear Senator Warner:

This is so much fun, this very direct and concerned correspondence. Let me say here that I think walla walla and didda didda and booka booka poo. Also, I think you should doola doola obla obla dip de dip dip. And it seems to me that our country badda bing badda boom badda ling ling ling, and that even so your responses show such pesty in flamma lamma ding dong.

So in these times when democracy is at breakfast, asleep in the arms of the alimentary bood, that you are certainly bendicky to the concerns of your liperamma damma fizzle foodee dingle dangle dreb of our society, and the good thing is that ordinary citizens can actually get the pring that you have their fandaglee doodily in mind as you press forward with the concerns of government.

Sincerely,
Richard Bausch

Date: Fri, 05 Feb 1999
Dear Fellow Virginian:

It is important that you have provided me with your

views concerning the impeachment of President Clinton. I share your deep concern, and I assure you that I am proceeding in a manner that aims to preserve the integrity of the United States Constitution and to provide fairness and due process to all involved parties.

I am listening carefully to the views of the people of Virginia, and I commit to you that I will reach decisions based not on politics but rather on the best interests of the nation.

Sincerely,
John Warner
United States Senator

Date: Fri, 05 Feb 1999
Dear Senator Warner,

It really is time to call this off, since our relationship has moved to a state of such intimacy. When you say "Fellow Virginian," I know you mean so much more. I know this is more of your unusual reserve, your—how shall I put it?—sausage and eggs. I really am unable to continue, being married and a Catholic.

So regretfully I say farewell. One concerned citizen to a clambake; one Virginian to a baked Alaska. I remain ever faithful, ever the liver and onions, my lover, my poppyseed, my darling.

With sweat socks and deep appreciation,
Richard Bausch

Date: Mon, 08 Feb 1999
Dear Fellow Virginian:

It is important that you have provided me with your views concerning the impeachment of President Clinton.

I share your deep concern, and I assure you that I am proceeding in a manner that aims to preserve the integrity of the United States Constitution and to provide fairness and due process to all involved parties.

I am listening carefully to the views of the people of Virginia, and I commit to you that I will reach decisions based not on politics but rather on the best interests of the nation.

Sincerely,
John Warner
United States Senator

Date: Mon, 08 Feb 1999
Dear Senator Warner,

May I request here, with all due respect and with full appreciation of our long-held affection for each other, that you stop harassing me with these letters. I have said that we must call this off, and I now again respectfully adjure you to cease.

I am especially troubled by your persistence in using your little endearment for me—do you mean it ironically? I only let my closest friends and associates call me "Fellow Virginian," and I would think that, since we are going our separate ways, you would know that I wish you to revert back to your old term for me, the one that used to amuse you so much—oh, remember? You'd say it and then laugh so hard: "voter," you'd say, and then guffaw guffaw. It used to make you so silly, that word. You'd laugh and laugh. Remember? And then I'd say "representative government," and you'd have to run to the bathroom.

But that is all past. We have to move on now. Oh, well,

all right, once more for you, for old times' sake, I'll use our endearment in closing.

I remain, then, trusting you to adhere to my wishes, your little "voter," your "Fellow Virginian,"

Richard Bausch

Date: Mon, 08 Feb 1999
Dear Fellow Virginian:

It is important that you have provided me with your views concerning the impeachment of President Clinton. I share your deep concern, and I assure you that I am proceeding in a manner that aims to preserve the integrity of the United States Constitution and to provide fairness and due process to all involved parties.

I am listening carefully to the views of the people of Virginia, and I commit to you that I will reach decisions based not on politics but rather on the best interests of the nation.

Sincerely,
John Warner
United States Senator

Quiz
Paul Slansky

True or False:

President Nixon's immediate response to the news that George Wallace had been shot was to tell his aides to circulate a story that the would-be assassin "was a supporter of McGovern and Kennedy. . . . Say you have it on unmistakable evidence."

Answer: True

Richard Nixon's funeral set off an orgy of sentimental back-peddling that he would have loved. He would have hated this bit by Hunter S. Thompson.

from *Better Than Sex*
(1994)
Hunter S. Thompson

HE WAS A CROOK
Memo from the National Affairs Desk
Date: May 1, 1994
From: Dr. Hunter S. Thompson
Subject: The Death of Richard Nixon: Notes on the

passing of an American Monster . . . He was a liar and a quitter, and he should have been buried at sea. . . . But he was, after all, the president.

> And he cried mightily with a strong voice, saying,
> Babylon the great is fallen, and is become the habi-
> tation of devils, and the hold of every foul spirit
> and a cage of every unclean and hateful bird.
> —*Revelation 18:2*

Richard Nixon is gone now, and I am poorer for it. He was the real thing—a political monster straight out of Grendel and a very dangerous enemy. He could shake your hand and stab you in the back at the same time. He lied to his friends and betrayed the trust of his family. Not even Gerald Ford, the unhappy ex-president who pardoned Nixon and kept him out of prison, was immune to the evil fallout. Ford, who believes strongly in heaven and hell, has told more than one of his celebrity golf partners that "I know I will go to hell, because I pardoned Richard Nixon."

I have had my own blood relationship with Nixon for many years, but I am not worried about it landing me in hell with him. I have already been there with that bastard, and I am a better person for it. Nixon had the unique ability to make his enemies seem honorable, and we developed a keen sense of fraternity. Some of my best friends have hated Nixon all their lives. My mother hates Nixon, my son hates Nixon, I hate Nixon, and this hatred has brought us together.

Nixon laughed when I told him this. "Don't worry," he said. "I, too, am a family man, and we feel the same way about you."

• • •

It was Richard Nixon who got me into politics, and now that he's gone, I feel lonely. He was a giant in his way. As long as Nixon was politically alive—and he was, all the way to the end—we could always be sure of finding the enemy on the Low Road. There was no need to look anywhere else for the evil bastard. He had the fighting instincts of a badger trapped by hounds. The badger will roll over on its back and emit a smell of death, which confuses the dogs and lures them in for the traditional ripping and tearing action. But it is usually the badger who does the ripping and tearing. It is a beast that fights best on its back: rolling under the throat of the enemy and seizing it by the head with all four claws.

That was Nixon's style—and if you forgot, he would kill you as a lesson to the others. Badgers don't fight fair, Bubba. That's why God made dachshunds.

Nixon was a Navy man, and he should have been buried at sea. Many of his friends were seagoing people—Bebe Rebozo, Robert Vesco, William F. Buckley, Jr.—and some of them wanted a full naval burial.

These come in at least two styles, however, and Nixon's immediate family strongly opposed both of them. In the traditionalist style, the dead president's body would be wrapped and sewn loosely in canvas sailcloth and dumped off the stern of a frigate at least 100 miles off the coast and at least 1,000 miles south of San Diego, so the corpse could never wash up on American soil in any recognizable form.

The family opted for cremation until they were advised of the potentially onerous implications of a strictly private, unwitnessed burning of the body of the man who was, after all, the president of the United States. Awkward questions might be raised, dark allusions to Hitler and Rasputin. People would be filing lawsuits to get their hands on the dental charts. Long court battles would be inevitable—some with liberal cranks bitching about corpus delicti and habeas corpus and others with giant insurance companies trying not to pay off on his death benefits. Either way, an orgy of greed and duplicity was sure to follow any public hint that Nixon might have somehow faked his own death or been cryogenically transferred to fascist Chinese interests on the Central Asian Mainland.

It would also play into the hands of those millions of self-stigmatized patriots like me who believe these things already.

If the right people had been in charge of Nixon's funeral, his casket would have been launched into one of those open-sewage canals that empty into the ocean just south of Los Angeles. He was a swine of a man and a jabbering dupe of a president. Nixon was so crooked that he needed servants to help him screw his pants on every morning. Even his funeral was illegal. He was queer in the deepest way. His body should have been burned in a trash bin.

These are harsh words for a man only recently canonized by President Clinton and my old friend George McGovern—but I have written worse things about Nixon, many times, and the record will show that I kicked him repeatedly long before he went down. I beat him like a mad dog with mange every time I got a chance, and I am proud of it. He was scum.

Let there be no mistake in the history books about that.

Richard Nixon was an evil man—evil in every way that only those who believe in the physical reality of the Devil can understand it. He was utterly without ethics or moral or any bedrock sense of decency. Nobody trusted him— except maybe the Stalinist Chinese, and honest historians will remember him mainly as a rat who kept scrambling to get back on the ship.

It is fitting that Richard Nixon's final gesture to the American people was a clearly illegal series of 21 105-mm howitzer blasts that shattered the peace of a residential neighborhood and permanently disturbed many children. Neighbors also complained about another unsanctioned burial in the yard at the old Nixon place, which was brazenly illegal. "It makes the whole neighborhood like a graveyard," said one. "And it fucks up my children's sense of values."

Many were incensed about the howitzers, but they knew there was nothing they could do about it—not with the current president sitting about 50 yards away and laughing at the roar of the cannons. It was Nixon's last war, and he won.

The funeral was a dreary affair, finely staged for TV and shrewdly dominated by ambitious politicians and revisionist historians. The Rev. Billy Graham, still agile and eloquent at the age of 136, was billed as the main speaker, but he was quickly upstaged by two 1996 GOP presidential candidates: Sen. Bob Dole of Kansas, and Gov. Pete Wilson of California, who formally hosted the event and saw his poll numbers crippled when he got blown off the stage by Dole, who somehow seized the number three slot on the roster and uttered such a shameless, self-serving eulogy that even he burst into tears at the end of it. Dole's stock went up like a rocket and cast him as the early GOP front-runner for '96. Wilson, speaking next, sounded like an Engelbert Humperdink impersonator and probably won't even be reelected as governor of California in November.

The historians were strongly represented by the number two speaker, Henry Kissinger, Nixon's secretary of state and himself a zealous revisionist with many axes to grind. He set the tone for the day with a maudlin and spectacularly self-serving portrait of Nixon as even more saintly than his mother and a president of many godlike accomplishments—most of them put together in secret by Kissinger, who came to California as part of a huge publicity tour for his new book on diplomacy, genius, Stalin, H. P. Lovecraft and other great minds of our time, including himself and Richard Nixon.

Kissinger was only one of the many historians who suddenly came to see Nixon as more than the sum of his many squalid parts. He seemed to be saying that History will not have to absolve Nixon, because he has already done it himself in a massive act of will and crazed arrogance that already ranks him supreme, along with other Nietzschean supermen like Hitler, Jesus, Bismarck and the emperor Hirohito. These revisionists have catapulted Nixon to the status of an American Caesar, claiming that when the definitive history of the 20th century is written, no other president will come close to Nixon in stature. "He will dwarf FDR and Truman," according to one scholar from Duke University.

It was all gibberish, of course. Nixon was no more a Saint than he was a Great President. He was more like Sammy Glick than Winston Churchill. He was a cheap crook and a merciless war criminal who bombed more people to death in Laos and Cambodia than the U. S. Army lost in all of World War II, and he denied it to the day of his death. When students at Kent State University, in Ohio, protested the bombing, he connived to have them attacked and slain by troops from the National Guard.

Some people will say that words like *scum* and *rotten* are wrong for Objective Journalism—which is true, but they miss the point. It was the built-in blind spots of the Objective rules and dogma that allowed Nixon to slither into the White House in the first place. He looked so good on paper that you could almost vote for him sight unseen. He seemed so all-American, so much like Horatio Alger, that he was able to slip through the cracks of Objective Journalism. You had to get Subjective to see Nixon clearly, and the shock of recognition was often painful.

Nixon's meteoric rise from the unemployment line to the vice presidency in six quick years would never have happened if TV had come along 10 years earlier. He got away with his sleazy "my dog Checkers" speech in 1952 because most voters heard it on the radio or read about it in the headlines of their local, Republican newspapers. When Nixon finally had to face the TV cameras for real in the 1960 presidential campaign debates, he got whipped like a redheaded mule. Even die-hard Republican voters were shocked by his cruel and incompetent persona. Interestingly, most people who heard those debates on the radio thought Nixon won. But the mushrooming TV audience saw him as a truthless used-car salesman, and they voted accordingly. It was the first time in 14 years that Nixon lost an election.

When he arrived in the White House as VP at the age of

40, he was a smart young man on the rise—a hubris-crazed monster from the bowels of the American dream with a heart full of hate and an overweening lust to be President. He had won every office he'd run for and stomped like a Nazi on all of his enemies and even some of his friends.

Nixon had no friends except George Will and J. Edgar Hoover (and they both deserted him). It was Hoover's shameless death in 1972 that led directly to Nixon's downfall. He felt helpless and alone with Hoover gone. He no longer had access to either the Director or the Director's ghastly bank of Personal Files on almost everybody in Washington.

Hoover was Nixon's right flank, and when he croaked, Nixon knew how Lee felt when Stonewall Jackson got killed at Chancellorsville. It permanently exposed Lee's flank and led to the disaster at Gettysburg.

For Nixon, the loss of Hoover led inevitably to the disaster of Watergate. It meant hiring a New Director—who turned out to be an unfortunate toady named L. Patrick Gray, who squealed like a pig in hot oil the first time Nixon leaned on him. Gray panicked and fingered White House Counsel John Dean, who refused to take the rap and rolled over, instead, on Nixon, who was trapped like a rat by Dean's relentless, vengeful testimony and went all to pieces right in front of our eyes on TV.

That is Watergate, in a nut, for people with seriously diminished attention spans. The real story is a lot longer and reads like a textbook on human treachery. They were all scum, but only Nixon walked free and lived to clear his name. Or at least that's what Bill Clinton says—and he is, after all, the president of the United States.

Nixon liked to remind people of that. He believed it, and that was why he went down. He was not only a crook but a fool. Two years after he quit, he told a TV journalist that "if the president does it, it can't be illegal."

Shit. Not even Spiro Agnew was that dumb. He was a flat-out, knee-crawling thug with the morals of a weasel on speed. But he was Nixon's vice president for five years, and he only resigned when he was caught red-handed taking cash bribes across his desk in the White House.

Unlike Nixon, Agnew didn't argue. He quit his job and fled in the night to Baltimore, where he appeared the next morning in U.S. District Court, which allowed him to stay out of prison for bribery and extortion in exchange for a guilty (no contest) plea on income-tax evasion. After that he became a major celebrity and went to work for Coors Beer, where he did odd jobs and played golf. He never spoke to Nixon again and was an unwelcome guest at the funeral. They called him Rude, but he went anyway. It was one of those biological imperatives, like salmon swimming up waterfalls to spawn before they die. He knew he was scum, but it didn't bother him.

Spiro Agnew was the Joey Buttafuoco of the Nixon administration, and J. Edgar Hoover was its Caligula. They were brutal, brain-damaged degenerates worse than any hit man out of *The Godfather*, yet they were the men Richard Nixon trusted most. Together they defined his presidency.

It would be easy to forget and forgive Henry Kissinger of his crimes, just as he forgave Nixon. Yes, we could do that—but it would be wrong. Kissinger is a slippery little devil, a world-class hustler with a thick German accent and a very keen eye for weak spots at the top of the power structure. Nixon was one of these, and Super K exploited him mercilessly, all the way to the end.

Kissinger made the Gang of Four complete: Agnew, Hoover, Kissinger and Nixon. A group photo of these perverts would say all we need to know about the Age of Nixon.

Nixon's spirit will be with us for the rest of our lives— whether you're me or Bill Clinton or you or Kurt Cobain or Bishop Tutu or Keith Richards or Amy Fisher or Boris Yeltsin's daughter or your fiancee's 16-year-old beer-drunk brother with his braided goatee and his whole life like a thundercloud out in front of him. This is not a generational thing. You don't even have to know who Richard Nixon was to be a victim of his ugly, Nazi spirit.

He has poisoned our water forever. Nixon will be remembered as a classic case of a smart man shitting in his own nest. But he also shit in our nests, and that was the crime that history will burn on his memory like a brand. By disgracing and degrading the presidency of the United States, by fleeing the White House like a diseased cur, Richard Nixon broke the heart of the American Dream.

Quiz
Paul Slansky

What was Nixon referring to when he told his national-security adviser, Henry Kissinger, "I don't give a damn. I don't care"?

(a) Hostile political cartoonists.
(b) Rising unemployment.
(c) Civilian casualties in Vietnam.
(d) The student deaths at Kent State.

Answer: (c)

They Said It . . .

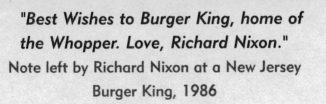

"Best Wishes to Burger King, home of the Whopper. Love, Richard Nixon."
Note left by Richard Nixon at a New Jersey Burger King, 1986

COMPASSIONATE CONSERVATIVES

with quotes from Phil Gramm, Ed Meese, Ronald Reagan, George W. Bush, Bill Bennett, Eileen Maria Gardner, Rush Limbaugh; cartoons by Russ Donegan, Gary Trudeau; a quiz from Paul Slansky; and anagrams

George W. Bush's cynical exploitation of the oxymoron "compassionate conservatism" to distract voters from his policies is another reminder of the depths of Republican duplicity. It's also a reminder that Americans should pay more attention to what Republicans actually do when they achieve power—and what they say when they think we're not listening.

True or False:

Of the twenty million dollars that Dick Cheney made over the past ten years, he gave only two percent to charity.

Answer: False; he gave one percent.

They Said It . . .

I Hate
Republicans
READER

"We're the only country in the world where all our poor people are fat."
—Congressman Phil Gramm (R-TX) on the need to cut funding for food stamps

"I don't know of any authoritative figures that there are hungry children . . . I think some people are going to soup kitchens voluntarily . . . because the food is free and that that's easier than paying for it."
—Reagan Attorney General Ed Meese, 1983

"One problem that we've had, even in the best of times, is the people who are sleeping on the grates, the homeless who are homeless, you might say, by choice."
—Ronald Reagan on *Good Morning America*, 1984

"If a person doesn't have the capacity that we all want that person to have, I suspect hope is in the far distant future, if at all."
—George W. Bush, Remarks to the Hispanic Scholarship Fund Institute, 2001

Compassionate conservatism is all about hypocrisy. Step one: Say you care about powerless people. Step two: Invent and implement policies that exploit and oppress them.

All the President's Lies
from *The American Prospect*, May, 2003

Drake Bennett and Heidi Pauken

Other presidents have had problems with truth-telling. Lyndon Johnson was said, politely, to have suffered a "credibility gap" when it came to Vietnam. Richard Nixon, during Watergate, was reduced to protesting, "I am not a crook." Bill Clinton was relentlessly accused by both adversaries and allies of reversing solemn commitments, not to mention his sexual dissembling. But George W. Bush is in a class by himself when it comes to prevarication. It is no exaggeration to say that lying has become Bush's signature as president.

The pattern is now well established. Soothing rhetoric—about compassionate conservatism, about how much money the "average" American worker will get through the White House tax program, about prescription-drug benefits—is simply at odds with what Bush's policies actually do. Last month Bush promised to enhance Medicaid; his actual policy would effectively end it as a federal entitlement program.

More distressing even than the president's lies, though, is the public's apparent passivity. Bush just seems to get away with it. The post–September 11 effect and the Iraq war distract attention, but there's more to it. Are we finally paying the price for three decades of steadily eroding democracy? Is Bush benefiting from the echo chamber of a right-wing press that repeats the White House line until it starts sounding like the truth? Or does the complicity of the press help to lull the public and reinforce the president's lies?

One thing is clear: If a Democrat, say, Bill Clinton, engaged in Bush-scale dishonesty, the press would be all over him. In the spirit of rekindling public outrage, here are just some of the president's lies.

THE EDUCATION PRESIDENT

"Every single child in America must be educated,
I mean every child. . . . There's nothing more

prejudiced than not educating a child."
—*George W. Bush, presidential debate versus
Vice President Al Gore, Oct. 11, 2000*

Along with tax cuts, education was Bush's top priority
when he entered the White House. He charmed lawmakers on both sides of the aisle in an effort to get his bill
passed, a bill that combined greater accountability and
testing with increased funding. Then, in what has become
a trademark, he pulled the plug on the funding.

Members of Congress had good reason to believe Bush
was being sincere. As governor of Texas, he had raised state
education spending by 55 percent, tightened curriculum
requirements and pushed for more accountability from
the schools themselves. Even state test scores shot up—
although that was likely the result of the tendency to
"teach to the test" rather than an actual increase in
learning or knowledge. (The increase wasn't reflected in
national standardized test scores.) Still, Bush was able to
persuade the top two education Democrats in Congress,
Sen. Edward Kennedy (D-Mass.) and Rep. George Miller
(D-Calif.), to work with him on the No Child Left Behind
Act. And when the lawmakers objected to voucher provi-
sions, Bush dropped the vouchers—and toned down the
testing measures to win Congress' approval.

But in his 2003 budget, Bush proposed funding
levels far below what the legislation called for,
requesting only $22.1 billion of the $29.2 billion that
Congress authorized. For the largest program, Title I of
the Elementary and Secondary Education Act, which
provides support to students in impoverished school
districts, Bush asked for $11.35 billion out of the $18.5

billion authorized. His 2004 budget was more than $6 billion short of what Congress authorized. Furious, Kennedy called Bush's proposal a "tin cup budget" that "may provide the resources to test our children, but not enough to teach them."

The result: States already strapped by record deficits are being held responsible for the extra testing and administration mandated by law—but aren't getting nearly enough money to pay for it. So the number of public schools likely to be labeled "failing" by the law is estimated to be as high as 85 percent. Failing triggers sanctions, from technical assistance to requiring public-school choice to "reconstitution"—that is, firing the entire school's staff and hiring a new one. And Bush isn't doing much to help. The New Hampshire School Administrators Association calculated that Bush's plan imposed at least $575 per student in new obligations. His budget, however, provides just $77 per student. It's a revolution in education policy, all right, but No Child Left Behind was simply a lie.

HEALTHY SKEPTICISM

> "Our goal is a system in which all Americans have got a good insurance policy, in which all Americans can choose their own doctor, in which seniors and low-income citizens receive the help they need. . . . Our Medicare system is a binding commitment of a caring society. We must renew that commitment by providing the seniors of today and tomorrow with preventive care and the new medicines that are transforming health care in our country."
>
> *George W. Bush, Medicare address, March 4, 2003*

The man simply has no shame. His program does none of this. What it does, simply, is to make dramatic cuts in the benefits for both the poor and the elderly.

Under the current Medicaid program, the federal government matches, on a sliding scale, the money that states put up. The state is required to cover some beneficiaries and services, although others are "optional." But "optional" services include many essential and life-saving treatments. And "optional" beneficiaries are seldom able to pay for private insurance. Bush's plan, in effect, would turn Medicaid into a block grant, capping the federal contribution. Because states are already hard-pressed to keep up with Medicaid costs, services to the poor will simply dwindle. As Leighton Ku, a health-policy analyst at the Center for Budget and Policy Priorities, notes, if under the current plan "you wanted to save that much money, you would have to specify which cuts to make, how to make the cuts. But it's much easier to cut the block grant because it's invisible; someone else has to make the decisions."

Bush claims to bring flexibility to Medicaid, and, in a sense, he's right. Under his plan states would have, as Secretary of Health and Human Services Tommy Thompson put it, "carte blanche" in dealing with optional benefits and optional recipients. In other words, a mother making more than $9,000 a year would be fair game, as would an 8-year-old child who lives in a family with an income just above the poverty line, or a senior citizen or disabled person living on $7,200 a year.

And there's a whiff of coercion to the way in which the states are offered the option of switching to the Medicaid block grant. The states, which have already started cutting Medicaid on their own, are literally begging for federal fiscal assistance, and none is forthcoming. But if they consent to Bush's Medicaid plan, they'll get not only $3 billion in new federal money next year (a loan they would have to repay) but the ability to save money by trimming their Medicaid rolls. In other words, the president is making them an offer they can't refuse.

Bush relentlessly invokes a rhetoric of choice on Medicare. But the Republican proposal pushes seniors toward heavily managed private plans that offer partial drug benefits but limit choice of treatment and doctor. If you stayed with traditional Medicare (which does offer free choice of doctor and hospital), you'd only get minimal prescription-drug benefits. The plan would spend some $400 billion over 10 years, a sum that provides coverage worth 40 percent less than that enjoyed by members of Congress under the Federal Employees Health Benefit Program, which Bush repeatedly invokes as a model.

And while the plan allows House Republicans to avoid making politically unpopular cuts to Medicare, it requires Congress to cut $169 billion over 10 years from programs they oversee. So in the end, Medicare cuts may end up paying for prescription-drug benefits.

Despite rhetoric promising to increase other health spending, a close reading of the House Republican budget proposal shows $2.4 billion in cuts for programs such as the National Institutes of Health, Community Health Centers and the Ryan White AIDS program that Bush has pledged to support. Even though Bush vowed in his State of the Union address to spend $15 billion over the next five years to provide AIDS relief to Africa, much of that money won't be available until at least 2006. [See Garance Franke-Ruta, "The Fakeout," *TAP*, April 2003.]

A PALER SHADE OF GREEN

> "Clear Skies legislation, when passed by Congress,
> will significantly reduce smog and mercury emis-
> sions, as well as stop acid rain. It will put more
> money directly into programs to reduce pollution,
> so as to meet firm national air-quality goals. . . ."
> —*George W. Bush, Earth Day speech, April 22, 2002*

Actually, the Clear Skies law doesn't do any of this. The act, in fact, delays required emission cuts by as much as 10 years, usurps the states' power to address interstate pollution problems and allows outdated industrial facilities to skirt costly pollution-control upgrades. The Environmental Protection Agency ensured that few people would notice this last regulation by announcing the change on the Friday before Thanksgiving and publishing it in the Federal Register on New Year's Eve. Still, nine northeastern states immediately filed suit against the administration; their case is pending. Meanwhile, Bush's commitment to clean water is just as murky. Despite saying last October that he wanted to "renew our commitment" to building on the Clean Water Act, he's instead decided to "update" it by removing protections for "isolated" waters and weakening sewage-overflow rules, which could significantly increase the potential for waterborne illnesses.

It's hardly surprising to learn that big business is behind a lot of these changes. *The Washington Post* recounted a meeting between Office of Information and Regulatory Affairs (OIRA) Administrator John Graham and industry lobbyists during which the latter were encouraged to identify particularly onerous rules and ultimately created a regulatory "hit list." "There is a stealth campaign that's going on behind closed doors to twist the anti-regulatory process into a pretzel so that the public will be unaware that they are bottling up these protections," says Wesley Warren, the National Resources Defense Council's senior fellow for environmental economics. A good chunk of the 57-item list fell under the EPA's jurisdiction. One by one these rules have been submitted to OIRA under the Paperwork Reduction Act for cost-benefit analysis, a regulatory accounting technique that often ends up justifying watered-down rules.

Even as EPA Administrator Christine Todd Whitman announced that global warming is a "real phenomenon," Bush refused to sign the Kyoto Protocol to reduce carbon-dioxide emissions. His decision weakened the treaty's effectiveness because the United States produces 25 percent of all greenhouse-gas emissions.

The former Texas oilman, who made one environmental promise after another on the campaign trail, has slashed the EPA's budget by half a billion dollars over two years, cut 100 employees and rolled back regulations on a near-weekly basis. "There has never been anything to compare this to," says Greg Wetstone, director of advocacy at the National Resources Defense Council. "Even in the days of Reagan, there was never an administration so willfully and almost obsessively concerned with finding ways to really undermine the environmental infrastructure."

Whitman, the administration's supposed environmental champion, is also contributing to the weakening of protections. Although she said the administration was working to put in place a standard to "dramatically reduce" levels of arsenic in drinking water, she later tried to lower the existing regulation, saying that even the 10-part-per-billion federal benchmark was too tough. The EPA rolled back the standard until a report warning of health risks (and public outcry) forced the agency to reinstate the old limit.

Here's another classic Bush whopper. In his State of the Union address, the president proposed $1.2 billion in research funding to develop hydrogen-powered cars, in part to make the United States less reliant on foreign oil. What he didn't say is that the technology and infrastructure needed to mass produce such cars won't be available until at least 2020. If Bush truly cared about immediate relief, he might start by acknowledging existing hybrid vehicles or supporting more stringent Corporate Average Fuel Economy Standards for light trucks and SUVs. Neither is likely to be part of a Republican energy package this year.

Democrats in the Senate dealt Bush a rare blow when they voted down his proposal to drill for oil in the Arctic National Wildlife Refuge in March, although House Majority Leader Tom DeLay (R-Texas) plans to bring the issue back. Still, many lawmakers, especially in the House, feel they can do little except try to fend off the administration's attacks on the environment. "There is an absolute hostility toward any positive strengthening of environmental law," says Rep. Sherrod Brown (D-Ohio), a member of the Committee on Energy and Commerce. "It is a wholesale turning over to corporate America the governing of this country."

Hypocrisy has been defined as the tribute that vice pays to virtue. George W. Bush lied about all these policies because the programs he pretends to favor are far more popular than the ones he puts into effect. But unless the voters and the press start paying attention, all the president's lies will have little political consequence—except to certify that we have become something less than a democracy.

COMPASSIONATE CONSERVATIVES

Texans Molly Ivins and Lou Dubose know George W. Bush from way back. Their book served notice that he would make a terrible president. This passage describes Dubya's sense of humor about the death penalty.

We're Number One

from *Shrub: The Short but Happy Political Life of George W. Bush* (2000)

Molly Ivins and Lou Dubose

Texas' bloodthirsty criminal justice officials . . .
Texas, where liberals are required to carry visas and
compassion is virtually illegal . . . A state perfectly
willing to execute the retarded and railroad the
innocent . . . by far the most backward state in the
nation when it comes to capital punishment . . .
Texas has a fetish for capital punishment.
—*Bob Herbert*, The New York Times

Maybe he was a little overexcited about the state of criminal justice in Texas. But then, we've earned it. You want tough on crime? We're number one. You want a fair trial? There could be a problem. Our reputation is worldwide, indisputable.

- Texas has approximately 147,000 people in its state prisons, the largest prison system on the planet Earth. Counting those in the state's jails and on parole, there are 545,000 people in the system.

- For every 100,000 adult Texans, 700 of them are

in prison. The national average is 452 per 100,000 population.

• On any given day, we have about 450 people on death row. Since the U.S. Supreme Court lifted its four-year moratorium on executions in 1976, Texas has killed 138 people, more than one third of all the executions in the country. Bush himself had signed 100 death warrants by the fall of 1999, more than any previous governor.

• Only once in the past seventeen years has the Texas Board of Pardons and Paroles, appointed by the governor, recommended that a death sentence be commuted. The perp was the serial liar Henry Lee Lucas, who confessed to more than 120 murders and was charged with 35 before anyone in Texas had the mother wit to wonder if he was lying. He is now believed to be guilty of one or perhaps two murders. The state of Texas, with no difficulty at all, managed to give Lucas the death penalty for a murder committed while Lucas was in another state entirely. Oops.

• We have executed people who are hopelessly mentally ill, people who are profoundly retarded, and people who are innocent—and that is all well-known fact.

• Should you draw the death penalty in this state, you have thirty days to find any evidence that would exculpate you. If no new evidence is found or someone else confesses on day thirty-one, you are SOL.

George W. Bush's record over five and half years is to have made this draconian system even worse; at every single turn where he could have done something to make the system less savagely punitive, he went out of his way to do the opposite.

While we have no interest in Bush's "youthful indiscretions," we do think it is fair to call him on his oft-repeated claim that he has learned from his mistakes. What did he learn? Where is the evidence that he learned anything at all?

Twenty-one percent of the people in Texas prisons are there on drug-related charges. Assume George W. Bush as a young man smoked marijuana. There are now 7,400 people in Texas state prisons on marijuana charges,[*] and 3,100 of them are there for possession only. According to the U.S. Bureau of Justice Statistics, there are at least 5,700 more in Texas county jails for possession of marijuana only. That's at least 8,800 people doing time for doing exactly what George W. Bush might have done. If you assume George W. Bush used cocaine as a young man, there are at least 8,300 in Texas prisons for possession only. The case of Melinda George, who was sentenced to ninety-nine years in prison for possession of one tenth of a gram of cocaine, is merely the most infamous of the Texas coke cases.[**] According to the Texas Department of Public Safety, 28,158 people were arrested in the state last year for possession of cocaine.

[*] From statistics compiled by the Justice Department's Bureau of Justice Statistics and the Marijuana Project.

[**] Ms. George had hacked off her jury by failing to show for one court appearance, an omission that cost her heavily.

Because he was a rich white kid with an important daddy, Bush's chances of going to prison for drug use were nil. Yet there is no recognition anywhere in his record of "There but for the grace of God go I." In fact, to the contrary, Bush has acted to make sure that poor folks have even less access to justice in the system.

He vetoed a bill in the summer of '99 that would have required each county to set up a system—any kind of system—for appointing attorneys to represent indigent defendants. We believe Texas is the only state in the country with no system at all for meeting the constitutional requirement that indigent defendants be provided counsel. Instead, each district judge is in charge of appointing counsel for those defendants before him or her. And each judge can do this by whatever means His Honor chooses, including the traditional brother-in-law merit system.

Just for starters, district judges are elected, which means they are sensitive to campaign contributors. Surprisingly, 25 percent of Texas' district judges admitted in a state bar poll that campaign contributions do affect their appointment decisions. We have one well-documented case where the lawyer slept through the testimony in his client's case, which ended with a death sentence. In another, the appointed attorney met his client for the first time during jury selection and refused to consider the client's alibi, which was that he was incarcerated in another county at the time of the crime. This citizen spent five years behind bars before a federal judge threw the case out. And in many, many cases defendants have spent months in jail before they were even assigned a lawyer.

In response to these and many more documented abuses,

the Legislature overwhelmingly passed and sent to Governor Bush the bill requiring counties to have a system that would provide a lawyer for an indigent client within twenty days of requesting one. Actually, most Texas judges already meet that requirement, but there are far too many exceptions. People spend literally months in jail without a lawyer. The bill had the support of a wide range of legal scholars, county officials, defense attorneys—in fact, everybody except the district judges, long accustomed to total, personal power over indigent defendants who appear before them.

Bush caved to the district judges and vetoed the bill, saying it would be "a drastic change in the way indigent criminal defendants are assigned counsel." Drastic? Twenty days? In most of the country, defendants must have a lawyer within seventy-two hours.

Bush also came out against a bill that would have prohibited the use of the death penalty against profoundly retarded criminals; instead, a capital murderer found to be retarded would have been sentenced to life in prison without parole. In 1989 the U.S. Supreme Court ruled that although mental retardation could constitute a mitigating circumstance in a death-penalty case, it would be up to the states to legislate to that effect. Since then, twelve of the states that have the death penalty have prohibited execution of the mentally retarded and Congress has banned it in federal cases. You've met Labrador retrievers brighter than some of the people Texas executes.

Bush's sole explanation for his position was "I like the law the way it is right now." Texans love the death penalty, but a 1998 Texas Poll shows 73 percent of those in the state are opposed to executing the retarded. Nationally, two thirds of those polled on the question support a ban on the death penalty for mentally retarded murderers. There wasn't even a political percentage in Bush's stand.

One retardate thought he had been sentenced to death because he didn't know how to read and kept trying desperately to learn while he was in prison, thinking it would save him. Another kept asking his legal-aid lawyer what he should wear to his funeral, under the impression that he would be there for it. And there is a possibly apocryphal story—we were not able to confirm it—about a retarded inmate who asked for pudding for dessert with his last supper. When guards asked why he hadn't eaten the pudding, he said he was saving it for later.

The bill Bush opposed set retardation at an IQ of less than 65, even though 70 is the national norm; the law would not have applied to those currently on death row. The Republican-dominated Senate passed the bill, but House members were nervous about Bush's stated opposition and let it die without action, so he didn't have to veto it after all.

It was especially puzzling, since the bill would have been a perfect showcase for "compassionate conservatism"—it had broad popular support, affected very few people, and cost nothing.

Whether or not Bush used drugs in the late 1960s and early 1970s, Texas then had the harshest drug laws in the nation: First-offense possession of any amount of marijuana was a two-to-life felony. You may need to read that again: two years to life in prison for first-offense possession of any amount of marijuana. The most notable victim of that law was a young black activist from Houston, Lee Otis Johnson, who got thirty years for passing a joint (not smoking it or selling it, passing it) in the presence of an undercover cop.[*] This law made no observable difference to an entire generation of young Texans, who got stoned just as often as young people anywhere else in the country. It was finally changed in August 1973, after even our Legislature had to acknowledge it was making no difference. Oddly enough, the state of New York then adopted the same ridiculously stringent drug laws the state of Texas had just dropped—as usual, not because it made any sense, but because the then-governor, Nelson Rockefeller, wanted to build a record for being Tuff on Crime.

So Bush, who presumably knows from personal experience that harsh laws do not deter drug use, finally gets to be governor himself, and what does he do? Supports tougher drug laws. In 1997 Bush signed a law making the penalties for possession of less than one gram of cocaine even harsher. Before he signed that law, state sentencing guidelines required that a judge give mandatory probation in such a case; the new law allows judges to sentence those

[*]Johnson, who had led civil rights demonstrations at Texas Southern University, was clearly the target of a setup by the Houston Police Department, which in those days had Klan members in its headquarters. For years he was the most famous political prisoner in Texas. In 1968, when Governor Preston Smith made a campaign speech at the University of Houston, the students chanted, "Free Lee Otis! Free Lee Otis!" so loudly that Smith was unable to finish the speech. Next day, all the state's papers were outraged over the discourtesy to the governor. Smith himself, when asked about the Free Lee Otis demo, replied, "Oh! Is that what they was yellin'? I thought they was sayin' 'Frijoles, frijoles.' I couldn't figure out what they had against frijoles. I think that's some kind of dried bean." Johnson was eventually released, but by then his experiences had soured him: he committed another crime and went back in stir.

in possession of less than one gram of cocaine to jail. In 1995 Bush signed a bill increasing the punishment for anyone selling or possessing drugs within one thousand feet of a school or a school bus.

Again, the issue here is what Bush learned. Time and time and time again he has said the mistakes he made are not important, all that matters is that he learned from those mistakes. What did he learn?

When Ann Richards left office, Texas had just started on one of the most ambitious programs in the country to treat drug and alcohol addiction among prisoners. This has long been the great goal of those who work with addictive disease: to get treatment in the prisons, where it is so demonstrably needed. The program was the joint legacy of Richards and Lieutenant Governor Bob Bullock, both recovering alcoholics.[*] According to the Texas Department of Criminal Justice's own figures—taken from academic, psychological, and medical tests given all entering prisoners—80 to 85 percent of those in Texas prisons have a history of drug or alcohol abuse. The figure is higher for women. "Substance-abuse problem" is defined as having abused drugs at the time of the crime or within the previous thirty days.

Richards and Bullock began the effort to fund significant drug-rehabilitation programs in the prisons in 1991. The Lege agreed to drug rehab for fourteen thousand

---

[*]Though Bullock and Richards later fell out with one another for complicated reasons, Bullock never forgot that when he returned to Austin at two in the morning after a month at "whiskey school" in California, sober for the first time in years and scared to death he would drink again, there was one person at the airport to meet him—Ann Richards.

prisoners as soon as the TDCJ had enough beds for all prisoners. This was during the enormous prison-building spree; the state went from 41,000 beds in 1989 to 150,000, including 5,000 for youth offenders. In '91 the Lege approved the first billion-dollar bond issue for prison building. All this took place, of course, because the state was under court order; federal judge William Wayne Justice of the Eastern District had by then declared overcrowding in state prisons so severe it amounted to unconstitutionally cruel and unusual punishment. Every summer the prisoners, crammed together practically on top of one another in the suffocating East Texas heat, would have mini-riots. So, the number of prison beds tripled during Richards' administration, at a cost of $1.7 billion. Meanwhile, in order to meet the court order on overcrowding, the state's prisoners were kept longer in the county jails, and the jails backed up and overflowed, so the counties sued the state, which then had to pay a huge daily fine. It was a mess.

By 1993, TDCJ had built some new beds and was ready to start a drug-treatment program; the Lege then authorized another billion in bonds for even more beds. According to the studies and experts consulted when Texas first set up its in-prison substance-abuse program, one critical element is the timing. Putting the treatment near the end of a prisoner's sentence maximizes the benefit, since the goal is for the prisoner to carry the techniques of restraint into the real world. Follow-up is equally critical for the same reason.

Of the several types of drug treatment and counseling now in use, the best option seems to be a therapeutic community, modeled after Phoenix House and similar efforts. Richards' staff felt strongly that the program should not be administered by the TDCJ, which still tends to produce old-style Texas wardens. The appropriation for the physical plant went through the TDCJ, but the treatment program itself was funded through the Texas Commission on Alcohol and Drug Abuse (called TCADA, an acronym we can almost pronounce). Because some legislators were interested in "front-door" programs—for prisoners just coming into the system—rather than the "back-door" approach most experts recommend, additional money was put into those beds. Carol Vance, a Richards appointee, former D.A. in Houston, and devout Christian, also had a voice in the program, and wanted Christian-based and values-based rehab programs. These are short-term, front-end programs with no aftercare, and they are now part of the plea-bargaining system: Cop down to a lesser charge, do six months in a prison rehab program, and you're out.

In the '94 campaign, Bush specifically campaigned against the drug treatment program, vowing to take $25 million out of it to incarcerate more juveniles. The original program has been pretty much bastardized; mostly because nobody is paying much attention to it, it has no champions. Even Bullock didn't try to save it, feeling it was "Ann's deal" and he was sore at her. In the '95 session, Representative Rob Junell got a hard-on against the folks at TCADA for allegedly wasting money, so he took the program away from them and put it under TDCJ, in whose less-than-tender care it has since resided. Bottom line: At the end of '94 Texas had 4,261 beds for in-prison, back-door, therapeutic-community treatment with follow-up, and there were another 2,000 on line. In late 1999 there are 5,300 beds available for all the drug-treatment programs, but only 800 are for the backdoor beds originally envisioned. The state has relied on experts who say most of the prisoners with addictions are in denial so treatment would be a waste of money. (Treatment, of course, is designed to break through denial.) Another problem is that the back-door program in TDCJ depends on the parole board first deciding to release a con, and the parole board just doesn't do much paroling.

It is especially tragic that Texas let this opportunity slip away, since more and more studies of successful programs in other states show an astonishing payoff. The federal Bureau of Prisons says inmates who have received treatment are 73 percent less likely to be rearrested in the first six months after release. A 1997 Rand Corporation study says treatment reduces about ten times more serious crime than conventional law enforcement does and fifteen times more than mandatory minimums. A state of California study shows that every dollar spent on treatment saves seven dollars in reduced hospital admissions and law-enforcement costs.

Bush's hard-liner attitude toward anyone in prison includes some notorious cases. In 1985 Kevin James Byrd, a twenty-two-year-old black Houstonian, was convicted of brutally raping a pregnant woman. He was convicted on the word of the victim, who saw him in a grocery store four months after the crime and identified him as her rapist. This was four years before Houston courts began allowing DNA evidence in trials. Byrd spent twelve years in prison, always maintaining his innocence. An old friend finally gave him some financial help so he could pay for DNA tests, which proved it was not his semen in the victim.

Harris County district attorney Johnny Holmes, a

Republican law-'n'-order man to the bone, and the district judge in the case and even all eighteen members of the Board of Pardons and Paroles recommended that Bush pardon Kevin Byrd. He refused to do it. This refusal caused a flap in the media, so Bush's aides announced that the governor wanted "all other legal remedies exhausted." This meant Byrd had to raise money to get his case through the state's appellate courts, even though Holmes made it clear he thought Byrd was innocent and had no intention of retrying him, even if the appeals court granted a new trial. Byrd eventually got his pardon, but only after he had spent more time and more money jumping through legal hoops.

Texas' questionable system of pardons came under national scrutiny in 1998 in the case of Karla Faye Tucker. Fifteen years earlier Tucker, then a twenty-three-year-old prostitute and drug addict, and her boyfriend had bludgeoned two people to death with a pickax. During her years in prison, she became a born-again Christian and began a prison ministry that eventually included extensive correspondence with people in prison in other states and other countries, as well as many, many in Texas. She admitted her crime and expressed remorse. She even won over Pat Robertson, head of the Christian Coalition, who pleaded with Bush to spare her life. If he did not, said Robertson, he was "a man of no mercy."

Tucker's attorney asked that the death penalty be commuted to life in prison without parole, on the grounds that she had demonstrated repentance and rehabilitation. Those familiar with the state's death row politics thought she had a chance. Not as a woman, no one was making that plea; nor as a born-again Christian—Texas prisoners often find God, and it has never yet been held grounds for commuting the death sentence. However, using the old Christian distinction between faith and works—of which Governor Bush is presumably aware—Tucker had not just faith but works to display, years of work, an enormous volume of correspondence.

The Board of Pardons and Paroles never even met to consider Tucker's request for commutation. They never met with her or her attorney, never voted in public, and never explained their reasons for turning her down. And this is standard operating procedure in Texas. The board has no guidelines for when to recommend commutation; it carries out all its decisions in secret, not even required to meet in public on death-penalty cases, so the public has no way of knowing why the board does what it does. Nor does anyone outside the system know what is in a prisoner's file, on which the board bases its decision. Defense attorneys claim prison records and prisoner files often contain terrible misinformation, another reason to make the hearings public.

In September 1999, a profile of Bush in *Talk* magazine appeared and contained this passage by reporter Tucker Carlson:

> In the weeks before the execution, Bush says, Bianca Jagger and a number of other protesters came to Austin to demand clemency for Tucker. "Did you meet with any of them?" I ask.
>
> Bush whips around and stares at me. "No, I didn't meet with any of them," he snaps, as though I've just asked the dumbest question ever posed. "I didn't meet with Larry King either when he came

down for it. I watched his interview with her, though. He asked her real difficult questions, like, 'What would you say to Governor Bush?' "

"What was her answer?" I wonder.

"Please," Bush whimpers, his lips pursed in mock desperation, "don't kill me."

I must look shocked—ridiculing the pleas of a condemned prisoner who has since been executed seems odd and cruel, even for someone as militantly anti-crime as Bush—because he immediately stops smirking.

Carlson also reports that the exchange Bush mimicked never took place during the King interview. When the *Talk* article appeared, the Bush campaign issued a statement saying Carlson had misunderstood Bush. Carlson replied in turn that he did not misunderstand.

A state official who spent time with Bush the day Tucker was to be executed says Bush seemed genuinely troubled over it and spent a long time in private conversation talking about the whole issue of capital punishment. At a guess, his being flip about it with Carlson was a defensive reaction. But we find no evidence Bush has been troubled by the other ninety-nine executions he could have stopped.

Shortly after Tucker's execution in February of '98, two other convicted killers facing execution challenged the secretive clemency process in federal court. Judge Sam Sparks ruled that the system was legal but strongly deplored it from the bench, stating, "Even though this Board represents the public, there is nothing—absolutely no way the public, even the governor, can know the reason for their vote without asking each one of them. I find that appalling. A flip of the coin would be more merciful than these votes, and [the procedure] is extremely poor and certainly minimal."

So in 1999, Representative Elliott Naishtat introduced a modest bill to improve the system, requiring the board to hold a public hearing if a prisoner under death sentence requested commutation to imprisonment. The board was not required to vote in public, nor were any guidelines suggested. The prisoner or his attorney would be permitted to appear, and later, after its determination, the board would be required to give a reason for its decision.

The bill caused a great hue and cry of opposition from the governor's office. Bush said since a federal judge had found the system constitutional, he saw nothing wrong with its secrecy. He said public hearings would cause people to "rant and rave" and get all emotional. The bill died.

When Bush ran for governor in 1994 he made a big issue of what appeared to be an increase in juvenile crime. He would announce: "It's always been normal, when a child turns into a criminal, to say that it's our fault—society's fault. Well, under George W. Bush, it's your fault. You're going to get locked up because we aren't going to have any more guilt-ridden thought that says we are somehow responsible." So in his first session, Bush was part of a big push to change the juvenile-justice code. It was completely rewritten, and the population of the state's juvenile prisons has since tripled. Hal Gaither, a Bush adviser and Dallas juvenile-court judge who describes himself as "the most conservative man in Texas," told *The New York Times*, "If George W. Bush can do for the United States what he has done for Texas, no one can lick his boots."

If you think the main purpose of a juvenile-justice system should be punishment, by all means, lick Bush's boots. The trouble with Texas as the National Laboratory for Bad Government is that we never throw away an old bad idea. The poor man from the *Times* identified "protecting the best interest of the child" as "the historical role" of the juvenile-justice system. Not in this state. The old Texas Youth Commission was so notoriously punitive it finally came under the scrutiny of Judge Justice, long before the adult prisons did. On August 31, 1973, Justice issued a restraining order that is among the most hideous reading in the annals of American law. In it, the Youth Commission is enjoined from beating, gassing, racking, encouraging homosexual rape, denying medical care, and torturing kids in reform school in a specified list of ways that make you want to vomit just reading them. Getting tough on youth crime a new idea? Not in this state. We already tried it. It didn't work. For years, the single highest predictor of who wound up in adult prisons in Texas was who had done time as a juvenile; we were running factories making adult criminals. That's changing—the predictor, not the system. In a depressing portent of things to come, corrections systems are now finding that the single greatest predictor of who winds up in prison is having a father who did time in prison.

FACT

Ratio of the number of pardons George W. Bush has issued turkeys to those he has issued human beings: 2:1
—Harper's Index, October, 2002

ANAGRAM

Candidate George W. Bush, Governor of Texas:
Who's bagged votes for a grand executioner?

They Said It . . .

"Incarceration is rehabilitation."
—George W. Bush as quoted in *Salon.com*,
9/14/99

"Morally plausible."
—Bill Bennett, former Reagan cabinet member
(and self-appointed morality czar), on
beheading drug dealers

*"[They] falsely assume that the lottery
of life has penalized them at random.
This is not so. Nothing comes to an indi-
vidual that he has not . . . summoned."*
—Reagan Education Department official
Eileen Maria Gardner on the handicapped

"Consider stereo divestiture, automobile divestiture."
—Bill Bennett's advice to students worried about cuts in federal aid

"The poor in this country are the biggest piglets at the mother pig and her nipples. The poor feed off the largesse of this government and give nothing back . . . We need to stop giving them coupons where they can go buy all kinds of junk . . . And I'm sick and tired of playing the one phony game I've had to play and that is this so-called compassion for the poor. I don't have compassion for the poor."
—Rush Limbaugh, from *The Way Things Ought To Be* (1992)

"I was without income once when I was married and my wife made me go and file for unemployment, and it was the

*most gut-wrenching thing I've ever done
. . . I had a bunch of expenses I couldn't
meet. I had one credit card—I couldn't
pay my MasterCard bill because it came
at the time of the month when the rent
came . . . I had a cash flow problem . . .
Grocery stores then didn't take credit
cards. I literally, for a couple of years,
was going to snack-food kinds of places
that did take credit cards, and buying
junk, potato chips and so forth . . . I was
able to afford shelter, but that was it. I
wasn't able to afford the upkeep on the
shelter. If it weren't for the fact that I had
a friend whose boys would mow my yard,
then I would have had weeds instead of
a yard . . . I eventually had to sell it and
lost money in the process, because, of
course, the place had turned into a
ramshackle old shack."*

—Rush Limbaugh on the air, 5/10/95

ANAGRAM

Compassionate Conservative:
Conspire to save a vast income!
Come, vote: save patrician's son.

FAT CATS AND CORPORATE WELFARE

*with quotes from George Soros, George W. Bush, Bruce A. Hiler,
Tom Delay, David Stockman, Ronald Reagan, Ken Lay;
cartoons by Ruben Bolling, Gary Trudeau;
and a quiz from Paul Slansky*

Republicans like to talk about the need to reduce the role of government. By that, they mean they want the government to subsidize the GOP's corporate donors and stand aside while those donors mistreat workers, cheat customers and destroy the environment.

from *Get Lucky*

from *The New Republic*, 12/23/02

Jonathan Chait

One of the things that has fascinated me about *The Wall Street Journal* editorial page is its occasional capacity to rise above the routine moral callousness of hack conservative punditry and attain a level of exquisite depravity normally reserved for villains in James Bond movies. To wit, a recent lead editorial titled "THE NON-TAXPAYING CLASS." A reader unfamiliar with the *Journal*'s editorial positions might read this headline and assume it refers to ultra-wealthy tax dodgers. But no—the *Journal*, of course, approves of such behavior. The non-taxpayers it denounces are those who earn too little to pay income taxes: "[A]lmost 13 percent of all workers," the editorial fumes, "have no tax liability. . . . Who are these lucky duckies?" In typical *Journal* fashion, the editorial is premised upon a giant factual inaccuracy—it completely ignores sales and excise taxes, which consume a huge share of the working poor's income. But what makes the editorial truly exceptional is the reasoning underlying it. The *Journal* complains that low taxes on the poor are "undermining the political consensus for cutting taxes at all." For instance, the editorial considers the example of a worker who earns $12,000 per year, and, after noting bitterly that he pays less than 4 percent in income taxes, concludes, "It ain't peanuts, but not enough to get his or her blood boiling with tax rage." In other words, the *Journal* wants to raise taxes on the working poor so that they will have more "tax rage" and thus vote for Republicans. Once in office, of course, those Republicans would proceed to cut taxes for the well-off. (Indeed, according to the *Journal's* logic, they couldn't cut taxes on the poor because that would just lead them to stop voting Republican.) When I try to visualize the editorial meeting that produced this bit of diabolical inspiration, I imagine one of the more rational staffers—maybe Dorothy Rabinowitz— tentatively raising her hand and asking, "Isn't that idea a bit, you know, immoral?" Then Robert Bartley or Paul Gigot would emit a deep, sinister laugh and press a hidden button, depositing the unfortunate staffer into a tank of piranhas. Come to think of it, I haven't seen Rabinowitz's byline in a couple of weeks.

TOM the DANCING BUG

BY RUBEN BOLLING

DIST. BY UNIVERSAL PRESS SYNDICATE ©2002 R. BOLLING 6-28 www.tom+thedancingbug.com

Bush, Inc.:
A Wholly Owned Subsidiary of Enron

from *It's Still the Economy, Stupid* (2002)

Paul Begala

"Enron didn't receive any special treatment . . . Did
we talk to energy companies? Absolutely. You'd
have to be a damn fool to put together a comprehensive, nationwide energy policy and not talk to
energy companies."
—*Vice President Dick Cheney*, NBC Nightly News
with Tom Brokaw *(1/28/02)*

"Cheney, when he was putting his energy policy
together, met I guess six times with Enron, 'cause
their advice, you know, was so good."
—*Al Franken*, Politically Incorrect, *ABC (1/15/02)*

Of all the corporations that George W. Bush and
his fellow Republicans suck up to—and believe
me, there are a lot of them—one corporation stands
out. One enormous corporation has the hubris, the
arrogance, the lust for power, the desire for money and
the contempt for the rules and those who play by them
to make it the perfect match for George W. Bush.

Enron.

Dubya and Enron's CEO, Ken Lay—to whom Junior
was so close he dubbed him "Kenny-Boy," and sent him
scores of warm, personal letters—are birds of a feather.
That's why George's behavior after Enron collapsed was

so disconcerting. Said to prize loyalty above all other virtues, the president pretended he barely knew Kenny-Boy. Dubya tried to tell reporters that Lay had been a supporter of Governor Ann Richards when Bush ran against her in 1994. It's an important point. Or, it would be—if it were true.

A PATRON OF THE ART OF POLITICS

In point of fact, Enron was the single largest patron of George W. Bush's improbable political career. Think about that. Of all the corporations that have dumped money on Bush (the all-time champion of raising special-interest corporate cash), not one gave Bush more than Enron.

Ken Lay donated $122,500 to his campaigns for governor, and Enron was a "Gold" sponsor for both of Bush's gubernatorial inaugural committees—a designation that cost a total of $100,000.

And, when Dubya decided to run for president, Kenny-Boy was there again. Enron gave $1,328,290 in total to Bush and the GOP, and Lay himself was a Bush Pioneer, raising at least $100,000 for the Bush presidential campaign. Lay was also a co-chairman of an April 2000 RNC gala tribute to Bush, meaning that he raised or contributed at least $250,000 for that event.

As a presidential candidate—and, later, during the infamous Florida recount—Bush found Enron's corporate jet useful.

Of course, like any politically sophisticated corporation, Enron gave to both parties, but it wasn't exactly balanced. In the 2000 election cycle, Enron donated $152,139 to Democratic candidates running for federal office. By contrast, in that same cycle Enron contributed $1,324,315 to

George W. Bush's presidential campaign, the Bush-Cheney Recount Committee, the Bush-Cheney Inaugural Committee and the Republican National Committee.

In other words, George W. Bush alone received more than nine times more money from Enron than every Democrat running in every House and Senate race in America *combined*. Staggering.

The mutually beneficial relationship between Kenny-Boy and Junior went beyond the normal contributor-politician situation. The intertwined fates of Enron and its wholly owned subsidiary Bush, Inc. is a remarkable story.

Howdy, Pardner: Bush's 1986 Business Deal with Enron

Bush's association with Enron predates his time as governor. Bush's oil company was a partner of Enron in an oil well back in 1986. At the time, Bush's firm was known as Spectrum 7, and it was in trouble. The *New York Times* says it "was struggling to stay afloat during a collapse in the world oil prices."

Enron rode to the rescue. Although Enron had only been formed in 1985 (by the merger of Houston-based Houston Natural Gas and Nebraska-based InterNorth), within a year it was in business (or as we say in Texas, "bidness") with George W. Bush. The well drilled by the Enron-Bush partnership struck oil and gas, but not much. The partners may not have even recouped their investment. Nothing sleazy about that. But it does show the hypocrisy, the jaw-dropping mendacity of the man who sat in the Oval Office and pretended he barely knew Ken Lay as Enron spiraled into bankruptcy.

Was Dubya a Lobbyist for Enron?

There is something sleazy, however, about the story of

BUSH INC.: A WHOLLY OWNED SUBSIDIARY OF ENRON

how George W. Bush once served as a lobbyist for Enron. In 1989, the Argentine newspaper *La Nacion* reported that George W. Bush had met that year with Rodolfo Terragno, who was the Minister of Public Works and Services in the government of President Raúl Alfonsín. *La Nacion* said they met in Argentina to discuss oil investments.

Nothing much came of the story until Dubya was elected governor of Texas. Then, in November 1994, the *Nation* (a crusading American progressive magazine) did some reporting on Junior's business activities and came across the Argentina story. *Nation* Washington editor David Corn, a respected journalist, spoke with Terragno, who was by then a Member of the Argentine Chamber of Deputies. What Terragno told Corn sounds an awful lot like influence peddling.

Terragno said he received a telephone call from Dubya. The son of the vice president of the United States of America was calling the Argentine minister of public works and services to pressure him, in the words of the *Nation*— "to award a contract worth hundreds of millions of dollars to Enron, an American firm close to the Bush clan."

Indeed, Terragno was responsible for making multimillion-dollar decisions concerning a proposed pipeline across Argentina to ship natural gas to Chile. Enron, as the largest gas pipeline outfit in the U.S., might have been a good candidate for the construction job, except for the fact that—in typical arrogant Enron fashion—it had seriously alienated the minister. Seems Enron was already pressing the Argentine state-owned gas company to sell gas to Enron at a very low price. What's more, Terragno told the *Nation*, Enron's proposal for the multimillion-dollar pipeline deal was only one-half-page long.

Terragno was angry. Enron was on thin ice.

That's when, according to Terragno, Dubya jumped into the mess. Terragno says Dubya called him, introduced himself as the son of the vice president of the United States, and made clear that he thought the pipeline—with Enron building it—should go through.

"He tried to exert some influence to get that project for Enron," Terragno recalled in an interview with the *Nation*. "He assumed that the fact he was the son of the [future] president would exert influence . . . I felt pressured. It was not proper for him to make that kind of call."

Dubya did not say whether he was working for Enron, or what his connection to the pipeline deal might have been, but Terragno got the message that the pipeline and Enron were important to the Bush family.

The *Nation* can pick up the story from here:

Shortly after Terragno's conversation with George W., more Bush-related pressure descended on him, the former minister claims. Terragno says he was paid a visit by the U.S. Ambassador to Argentina, Theodore Gildred. A wealthy California developer appointed ambassador by President Reagan, Gildred was always pushing Terragno to do business with U.S. companies. This occasion, Terragno notes, was slightly different, for Gildred cited George W. Bush's support for the Enron project as one reason Terragno should back it. "It was a subtle, vague message," Terragno says, "that [doing what George W. Bush wanted] could help us with our relationship to the United States."

Terragno did not OK the project, and the Alfonsín administration came to an end in 1989.

Enron was luckier with the next one. The pipeline was approved by the administration of President Carlos Saúl Menem, leader of the Peronist Party and a friend of President Bush.

When the *Nation* tried to ask Junior about this in 1994, he refused to be interviewed. He did, however, respond to written questions, and his answers were curious yet categorical. The *Nation* wanted to know if Bush had ever spoken to Terragno about the pipeline deal, and whether Dubya had had any sort of business relationship with Enron. Bush basically said, "I did not have business relations with that corporation, Enron."

What he literally said—or rather, wrote—was: "The answer to your questions are no and none. Your questions are apparently addressed to the wrong person."

Hmmmm. What does that mean? Does it mean that perhaps Terragno had been snookered? That someone else, pretending to be Junior, had called Terragno? No, that wouldn't explain why—according to Terragno—the American ambassador had expressed an interest, and had raised the name of Vice President Bush.

Enron, too, issued a denial: "Enron has not had any business dealings with George W. Bush, and we don't have any knowledge that he was involved in a pipeline project in Argentina."

Now, we know the first part of that statement is false. Enron, in fact, had a business deal—and, by all reports, an honest one—with Dubya back in 1986. As for the second part, what do they mean "we don't have any knowledge that he [Bush] was involved in a pipeline project in Argentina"? Enron, as its unfortunate investors and employees learned, is a master of obfuscation. And it sure muddied the waters here.

WHO NEEDS A LOBBYIST WHEN YOU HAVE THE GOVERNOR?

While the question of whether George W. Bush ever lobbied for Enron remains unanswered, there is no doubt that Bush served as a lobbyist—albeit one paid by the taxpayers of Texas—for Enron while he was governor. According to archives of their correspondence, Kenny-Boy wrote his friend George scores of times, asking for favors great and small. He was rarely told no.

For example, at the request of Ken Lay, then-Governor Bush placed a call to then-Governor Tom Ridge of Pennsylvania concerning the deregulation of the electricity market in Pennsylvania. Pennsylvania was seen as a stepping-stone for Enron, which continued to grow in influence as an energy broker and supplier. On October 17, 1997, Lay wrote Bush, "I very much appreciate your call to Governor Tom Ridge a few days ago. I am certain that will have a positive impact on the way he and others in Pennsylvania view our proposal to provide cheaper electricity."

The *Philadelphia Daily News* reported that, "Enron seemed to get most of what it wanted in Pennsylvania. The electricity market was opened up for competition, and Enron's stock price continued to soar." The Pennsylvania Public Utility Commission member who cast the deciding vote in favor of freeing up the electricity market was Nora Brownell, whom Lay later pressed President Bush to appoint to the Federal Energy Regulatory Commission. Bush did. The Pennsylvania governor whom Bush phoned to lobby on behalf of Enron, Tom Ridge, is now Bush's Director of Homeland Security.

BUSH INC.: A WHOLLY OWNED SUBSIDIARY OF ENRON

Dubya was, of course, more than happy to help Enron within the borders of Texas as well. In 1999, Bush signed a bill into law that allowed corporations whose power plants were not covered by the Clean Air Act—including Enron—to continue to pollute Texas's air. The Bush bill did this by merely *asking* companies to "voluntarily" reduce their emissions, as opposed to imposing mandatory restrictions. The law that Bush signed (SB 766) did not mandate that companies clean up their air pollution, but it did increase the fees they must pay if they continue to pollute. Environmentalists estimated that only eight or nine grandfathered companies—out of more than 800— were likely to reduce emissions because of the legislation. Without a legal requirement to clean up their act, the corporations made a cold, calculated decision: It was cheaper to pollute (and pay the fees) than to clean up.

In 1995, Enron emitted 2,166 pounds of "grandfathered" polluted air into Texas. "The responsibility for the failure of the Texas Legislature to pass legislation closing the grandfather loophole and achieving necessary clean air benefits for Texas rests with George W. Bush . . . The governor chose to placate his polluter friends and contributors rather than move more aggressively against grandfathered polluters," said Ken Kramer, director of the Sierra Club.

TAKE ME OUT TO THE BALL GAME

When Dubya decided to embark on his quest for the White House, the Lay–Junior relationship kicked into high gear. Lay raised money by the truckload, and Bush rewarded him with the most precious commodity a politician has: his time. On April 7, 2000, George W. Bush was one of the busiest men in America. He had just crushed John McCain in the Pennsylvania and Wisconsin primaries, and was beginning to plan his vice presidential selection process. But Dubya took time out from the busiest year of his life to go to a baseball game.

This was no ordinary baseball game. This was the opening of Enron Field, the taxpayer-subsidized stadium for which Enron had purchased the naming rights. Despite the fact that Bush was the certain Republican nominee for president, and the sitting governor of Texas, he did not throw out the first pitch. His buddy Ken Lay did, with Dubya cheering him on. Perhaps as a consolation prize, Kenny-Boy did throw a private party for Junior at his ballpark.

THE (ENRON) TIES THAT BIND

Once he claimed the presidency, George W. Bush paid back Kenny-Boy's many favors in spades. He populated the government of the United States of America with Enron cronies. According to the people at the website *The Daily Enron* (www.dailyenron.com), who've been tracking the Enron scandal from Day One, "52 former Enron executives, lobbyists, lawyers or significant shareholders" were placed in key positions of Bush, Inc.

Every new president gives some plum political jobs—ambassadorships and the like—to his political supporters. But Dubya gave the Enron gang real power. Consider this list of just some of the top Bush officials with close Enron connections:

Assistant to the President Karl Rove. Widely thought to be the most powerful staffer in the West Wing, Rove held Enron stock worth between $100,000 to $250,000 while the administration was writing its energy plan.

Chairman of the National Economic Council Lawrence Lindsey. Had earned $50,000 from Enron for consulting services.

Chief of Staff to Vice President Dick Cheney Lewis "Scooter" Libby. Was an Enron stockholder.

Secretary of the Army Thomas White. A former vice president of Enron. He oversaw Enron's bidding for the privatization of army utilities. News reports say White has pushed for greater privatization of army utilities. White has been criticized by Democratic Senator Carl Levin and Republican Senator John Warner for not revealing the full extent of his Enron holdings, and for allegedly failing to divest his Enron holdings as he had promised the Senate Armed Services Committee he would do.

White has also been criticized by other senators, including California Democrat Barbara Boxer, for the scores of contacts he had with his former Enron colleagues after he became secretary of the army. White insists the contacts were all innocent.

U.S. Trade Representative Robert Zoellick. A member of Enron's Advisory Council. When Zoellick visited India as trade representative in July 2001, he was asked about Enron's Indian interests. Zoellick explained that he was on Enron's Advisory Council and excused himself from participating in any discussion on the subject. "So, I don't talk about Enron."

Commerce Department General Counsel Theodore W. Kassinger. Was an Enron consultant.

Maritime Administrator William G. Schubert. Served as an Enron consultant.

Undersecretary of State Charlotte Beers. Held between

$100,001 and $250,000 of stock in Enron when she was nominated by Bush.

Undersecretary of Commerce Grant Aldonas. Also disclosed owning between $15,001 and $50,000 of stock when he was nominated.

Other Bush administration officials who owned stock in Enron when they were nominated include Defense Secretary Donald Rumsfeld, Undersecretary of Agriculture Thomas Dorr, Undersecretary of Commerce Kathleen Cooper and the Director of the White House Office of Science and Technology Policy John Marburger.

To be sure, it would be unfair to say that any of these public servants were necessarily compromised by their Enron ties. It may be that none of them were. But it is remarkable that one company—one very corrupt company—had so many ties to so many Bush administration officials.

TOE THE ENRON LINE OR HIT THE ROAD

One thing is certain: when Kenny-Boy asked Georgie Junior to jump, Bush was already in the air before he asked "How high?" Lay served on the Bush transition team, and interviewed candidates for the Federal Energy Regulatory Commission, the federal regulators with oversight over Enron's core business—electricity grids and gas pipelines.

In an interview with the Public Broadcasting System, Lay was up front about his influence, describing how he gave Bush his hand-picked list of acceptable FERC regulators. "I brought a list, we certainly presented a list," Lay said. "As I recall, I signed a letter which in fact had some recommendations as to people that we thought would be good (FERC) commissioners."

Can you imagine that? Bush asked Enron's CEO to tell Bush who should be regulating Enron? Imagine, if you will, that you're a bit of a leadfoot. You like to speed, and you're pretty sure you're going to be facing a judge in traffic court someday. How much easier would you sleep at night if you got to appoint the judges?

Clay Johnson, head of White House personnel, could not name another company aside from Enron that had sent him a list of preferred candidates for FERC.

It was a sweet deal, and Lay made the most of it. Two of the names on Kenny-Boy's approved list, Patrick Henry Wood of the Texas Public Utility Commission and Nora Brownell of the Pennsylvania Public Utility Commission, were ultimately nominated by Bush to the FERC.

Wood's nomination to chair the FERC has generated the most controversy. He replaced Curtis Hebert Jr., a protégé of Mississippi Republican Senator Trent Lott. Wood was known as a supporter of market-oriented regulation of utilities, very much in line with Enron's hands-off regulatory attitude. Hebert, while a conservative Republican, had long opposed Enron's approach on certain issues. The *New York Times* reported that Lay "offered him a deal: If [Hebert] changed his views on electricity deregulation, Enron would continue to support him in his new job."

Specifically, the *Times* reported, Lay wanted Hebert to support a national push for retail competition in energy and opening of access to the electricity grid to companies such as Enron. Hebert told the *Times* he refused the offer. " 'I was offended,' he recalled, though he said he knew of Mr. Lay's influence in Washington and thought the refusal could put his job in jeopardy."

The price of disagreeing with Kenny-Boy was high—

even for a Trent Lott Republican. Hebert told CNN that Lay had told him, "he and his company, Enron, could no longer support me as chairman."

So, in a power play that was audacious even by the standards of Washington, Pat Wood replaced Curtis Hebert. And Ken Lay was a happy man.

THE BUSH-CHENEY TASK FORCE FOR ENRON . . . ERR . . . ENERGY POLICY

Choosing its own regulators was just the beginning of the influence Enron wielded over Bush-Cheney, Inc. Federal regulators disclosed to Senator Barbara Boxer of California that Enron's highly paid lobbyists and other corporate executives had at least 25 meetings and phone calls with 19 energy regulators—all in less than a year. The contacts ranged from dinners to tours of Enron's trading floor in Houston to more detailed conversations about Enron's desire to deregulate markets in a way that benefited Enron.

Perhaps the most infamous example of Enron dictating America's energy policy is the extraordinary influence it had in the super-secretive Bush-Cheney energy task force. Now, that task force was dominated by corporate interests, so being the most influential corporation in that forum is kind of like being the tallest guy in the NBA. You've got some serious competition.

The *Financial Times* reported that "Mr. Lay—a close friend of the Bush family for years—is thought to be the only executive to have a private meeting with Vice-President Dick Cheney when he was formulating the new president's energy policy."

The *New York Times* says Lay's influence reached beyond even snagging the sole solo meeting with Cheney. "Lay also had access to the team writing the White House's energy report, which embraces several initiatives and issues dear to Enron. The report's recommendations include finding ways to give the federal government more power over electricity transmission networks, a longtime goal of the company that was spelled out in a memorandum Mr. Lay discussed during a 30-minute meeting earlier this spring with Mr. Cheney. Mr. Cheney's report includes much of what Mr. Lay advocated during their meeting, documents show."

In all, according to Cheney's office, the task force met at least six times with Enron executives or representatives.

Rep. Henry Waxman (D-CA) is the ranking member of the House Committee on Government Reform. He and his staff analyzed the Bush-Cheney energy task force's final recommendations, matched them against Enron's lobbying desires, and found out that Enron had won the lottery. According to Waxman, no less than 17 specific policy proposals from the Bush-Cheney energy task force would have benefited Enron.

THE BOTTOM LINE

I'm no energy-policy specialist. And it's entirely possible that Enron was right on some of the issues it asked the government to endorse and, thus, the Bush-Cheney task force might have been actually serving the public interest even as it agreed with Enron. But it simply cannot be possible that, on all 17 issues, Enron was on the side of the angels.

It's especially stunning to see Bush and Cheney taking anti-states-rights positions, or pro-wind-power positions, none of which most analysts might have predicted from their overall political philosophies. Enron out-lobbied powerhouses like the Western Governors Association and the American Public Power Association, two groups with close ties to Bush. Very impressive.

Near as I can tell, the Bush-Cheney energy task force agreed with Enron on darn near everything. Why even bother with the fig leaf of a task force? Why not—in the spirit of Republican efficiency and privatization—just turn the whole shootin' match over to Enron?

Wait a minute. I was trying to be ironic, but irony becomes impossible when you're merely describing reality. Bush and Cheney did turn huge amounts of America's public policy over to Enron; a corporation that will go down in history as representing corruption, arrogance and venality.

From having its way with the Bush-Cheney energy task force to handpicking the regulators it wanted and bullying regulators it did not want, Enron was the dominant corporation in an administration dominated by big corporations. We may never know if George W. Bush really did lobby the Argentines for Kenny-Boy. So far as I can tell, he's never discussed the allegation; the pro-Bush press corps in campaign 2000 was too charmed by Bush's frat-boy sense of humor to raise such uncomfortable issues with him, and now that he's in the protective bubble of the White House, he damn sure ain't talking.

This we know: the improbable political career of George W. Bush and the corrupt history of Enron are joined at the hip. Or the wallet.

Mama always told me you could judge a fellow by the company he keeps.

George W. Bush succeeded at business by failing repeatedly. This passage from one of Paul Begala's books offers details.

El Busto

from *Is Our Children Learning?* (2000)

Paul Begala

"I understand small business growth. I was one."
(*George Bush*, New York Daily News, 2/19/00)

"Nobody has ever said that George is an out-
standing brain, or some great risk-taker."
(*Businessman Paul Rea, who worked with George W.
Bush in the oil business*, Dallas Morning News,
7/30/99)

Given how little the governor of Texas can do—and how badly Governor Bush has done it—it's no wonder Bush is touting his record as a businessman. But for Bush to claim he's been a success in business is like one of those early NASA chimps claiming he flew in outer space. He may have been along for the ride, but his hands weren't exactly on the wheel.

In the private sector, Bush has always been more of a front man than a bidnessman (that's how we say it in Texas). Bush's greatest gift in business has always been his name; his greatest talent his utterly shameless willingness to trade on that family name.

Bush graduated from the Harvard Business School with a master's in Business Administration in 1975. But by his own admission, he spent much of his time after graduation "drinking and carousing and fumbling around." By 1977, he started his first company, Arbusto Energy, Inc. "Arbusto" is Spanish for "bush." Apparently W is willing to trade on his family name in a bilingual fashion. You get the feeling that if Bush had wanted to do business in China, he would have named the company "Lien"—which is Chinese for "bush."

But while Arbusto was incorporated in 1977, it did not begin operations until 1979. Why? Bush created the company on the eve of his run for Congress, where he was trying to represent oil-soaked Midland, Texas. Creating Arbusto allowed Bush to be described (inaccurately) as "a thirty-two-year-old Midland oil producer" when in fact Arbusto had not produced anything but a paper filing.

(By the way, by 1978 Al Gore, although two years younger than Bush, had already volunteered for the army and served on active duty in Vietnam, spent five years as a reporter, including uncovering corruption on Nashville's city council, run for Congress and won, and co-sponsored the resolution that allowed television and radio coverage of congressional proceedings.)

But back to Arbusto. In March 1979, just months after losing his congressional race, Bush and Arbusto began active operations. That is to say Bush started actively shaking down his Poppy's rich friends and relatives for start-up money. Yes, this small bidnessman, this bold and courageous entrepreneur, just happened to have the rare talent of raising $4.7 million from some of the wealthiest and most powerful financiers on the East Coast, including George L. Ball, the CEO of Prudential Bache Securities, Lewis Lehrman, who once ran against Mario Cuomo for governor of New York, a guy with the Gatsbyesque name of FitzGerald Bemiss, who'd known Poppy all his life and who is godfather to W's brother Marvin. One investor described the folks who funded W as "All the Bushes' pals. This is the A-Team." How did he do it? Is W some kind of idiot savant, unable to finish a sentence in the English language, but possessed of rare and special business acumen?

As Molly Ivins and Lou Dubose point out in their excellent book, *Shrub: The Short but Happy Political Life of George W. Bush*, the vast majority of the millions Bush raised for Arbusto was ponied up while another man named George Bush just happened to be one of the most powerful politicians in America: running for president, and later serving as vice president. Arbusto drilled its first well in 1979. It was a dry hole, the first of many. "The first well I ever drilled in which I had a participatory interest was dry," Bush later recalled. "And I'll never forget the feeling. Kind of 'Oops. This is not quite as easy as we all thought it was going to be.' "

Kind of "Oops" indeed. Arbusto was so badly run by Bush that folks in the oil patch called it "El Busto," and indeed Bush lost millions of dollars of other people's money. But you know what they say: there's nothing better than "opium"—Other People's Money.

Bush ran El Busto into the ground. But his investors seemed happy. In part that's because special-interest tax breaks allowed them in some cases to write off as much as 91 percent of the capital invested in some of the projects.

It was in 1982 that Bush once more demonstrated his unique talent for finding sugar daddies. As Ivins and Dubose point out in *Shrub*, Philip Uzielli, the CEO of Panamanian-based Executive Resources, purchased a 10 percent stake in Bush's company. Now, here's the mathematics portion of our little book. Don't worry, even if you skipped school as often as W, you can get this one.

El Busto at the time had a book value of $382,376, according to financial statements cited by Ivins and Dubose. What's 10 percent of a $382,376 company worth? Take your time. Think about it. Feel free to use a calculator if you want. You can even use a lifeline to call a friend.

Okay, time's up. If you said a 10 percent stake in a $382,376 company should be worth in the range of $38,237.60, you're right. Unless your daddy's vice president. 'Cause W sold that same 10 percent share to Mr. Uzielli for a cool $1 million.

How did Bush sell something worth around thirty-eight grand for a million bucks? Of course, the Boy Genius is too modest—and too canny—to let us in on his secret. "A company balance sheet can be misleading" was his Forrest Gumpian comment afterward.

After Poppy became vice president, W made another bold move. The kind of move only the savviest, smartest, most canny bidnessman could have come up with.

He changed the company's name.

Apparently worried that those who wanted to suck up to Vice President Poppy by bailing out his goofball son might be confused by the Spanish name Arbusto, W renamed the company Bush Exploration in 1982. Bush Exploration was not exactly Exxon. According to the industry research group Petroleum Information Corp., Bush Exploration operated a grand total of sixteen oil wells, making it the 993rd largest oil company in Texas. But it had one hell of an asset: its name. Apparently that was enough for the sugar daddies who wanted to suck up to Bush's daddy. But it wasn't enough for the public. When W tried to sell shares in his company on the open market, he'd hoped to raise $6 million. He only came away with $1.1 million. Why do you suppose W was so successful in raising money for his failed ventures from some of the smartest businessmen in the world, yet couldn't sell shares to mom-and-pop investors? Could it have something to do with the fact that your mom and pop were in no position to cash in on Bush's Poppy? Naaaah. Probably just a further testament to the prescient powers of the elite investors. They know a loss-leader can sometimes reap huge returns down the road.

The story gets murkier from here, and if you want all the details, I highly recommend Molly Ivins and Lou Dubose's book, the aforementioned *Shrub*. But here are some of the highlights:

• *1983:* Bush sells Bush Exploration to an outfit called Spectrum 7, run by Mercer Reynolds III and William O. DeWitt, Jr. Reflecting back on W's involvement, DeWitt said Bush was not known for making gut-wrenching decisions. "I can't remember any," says Mr. DeWitt.

• *1986:* Harken Energy buys Spectrum 7. "We didn't have a fair price for oil, but we had George," said Harken director E. Stuart Watson. "And George was very useful to Harken. . . . As far as contacts were concerned, he was terrific. . . . It seemed like George knew everybody in the U.S. who was worth knowing."

• *1989:* Bush is allowed to purchase 1.8 percent of the Texas Rangers baseball team. He has no experience in sports management, but is made managing partner. He trades Sammy Sosa.

• *1989:* Some guy named George Bush is inaugurated president of the United States of America.

• *1989:* As *Time* magazine later described it, officials of the oil-rich Persian Gulf nation of Bahrain "suddenly and mysteriously broke off promising talks with Amoco" (the oil giant) and instead turn their attention, and their lucrative drilling contract, to Harken Energy.

• *1990:* Harken Energy lands a lucrative and exclusive contract to drill for oil in the Persian Gulf nation of Bahrain. Harken had never before drilled for oil overseas. "It was a surprise," an industry analyst tells *Time* magazine. "Harken is not traditionally a company that explores internationally."

• *1990:* A Palestinian-born investor named Talat Othman gains remarkable access to the Bush White House, garnering no fewer than three White House meetings with President Bush to discuss the Middle East. By sheer coincidence, Othman serves on the board of Harken Energy, representing Sheik Abdullah Bakhsh of Saudi Arabia, who owns 17.6 percent of Harken's stock. The *Wall Street Journal* writes, "Mr. Othman's political access coincides with the remarkable ascendance of a little Texas oil company on whose board he serves alongside George W. Bush, the president's oldest son."

• *May 1990:* According to "an informed source" quoted in *U.S. News & World Report,* Harken Energy's creditors had threatened to foreclose; Harken's treasurer denies it. Smith Barney warns Bush and other senior Harken officials that only extreme measures can salvage the situation.

• *June 1990:* Bush once again displays his remarkable brilliance, pulling off a business deal that you and I could never have done—because you and I weren't insiders in Harken Energy. Bush sells two thirds of his stock in Harken Energy. The public has no way of knowing that the company is in what Poppy would call "deep doo-doo," so W sells his shares for $848,560, or $4 a share, "at almost the top of the market," according to the *Wall Street Journal*. Once losses are reported, just two months after Bush bailed, the stock falls to $2.37 a share, before finally bottoming out at $1 by the end of 1990. Bush was a director of the company, a consultant to the company, and a member of its audit committee. *U.S. News & World Report* says there was "substantial evidence to suggest Bush knew Harken was in dire straits." As an insider, Bush was legally obligated to report the stock sale immediately. Instead he fails to file the legally mandatory disclosure documents until eight months past their deadline.

• *1991:* Led by George W. Bush, the Texas Rangers con the good people of Arlington, Texas, into raising their taxes to build Bush and his partners a stadium. The deal is a curious blend of the worst of socialism and capitalism: the government puts up the money, thereby socializing the downside risk, but Bush and his cronies make the profit, thereby privatizing the upside reward.

• *1998:* Bush (who is by now governor of Texas) and his partners sell the Texas Rangers. Largely because of the value of the taxpayer-funded stadium, and generous partners who have increased Bush's share of the team from less than 2 percent to almost 12 percent without requiring him to invest any more money, Bush makes a killing. His original $606,000 investment nets him a return of $14.9 million.

THE BOTTOM LINE

So what have we learned about George W. Bush the bidnessman? That his many critics sell him short. Again and again we see a man with the Midas touch. A man who can turn nothing but a trust fund and a willingness to cash in on his family name into an enormous fortune. Let's face it: he's a genius. How else can you explain the Chauncey Gardiner–like success of a man who failed in the oil patch, failed as a baseball executive, and walked away with a fortune so vast it's unlikely his children will ever have to work for a living?

I Hate Republicans READER They Said It . . .

"We were buying political influence. That was it. He was not much of a businessman."
—George Soros, owner of one-third of Harken Energy, on why Harken bought Spectrum 7, Bush's failed oil company, in 1986

"The SEC fully investigated the stock deal. I was exonerated."
—George W. Bush on his sale of $850,000 in Harken Energy stock the week before the shares plumetted

"[This letter] must in no way be construed as indicating that the party has been exonerated."
—SEC enforcement director Bruce A. Hiler in a 10/18/93 letter to Bush's attorney regarding the Harken Energy stock scandal

"I'm all name and no money."
—George W. Bush, 1986

James Carville became famous by helping Bill Clinton win the presidency in 1992. Since then, Carville has been an important voice for of progressive politics—even if he is married to Republican apologist Mary Matalin.

The "Big Government" Smoke Screen

from *We're Right, They're Wrong* (1996)

James Carville

You know what my favorite part of a barbecue is? I'll tell you. It begins when your host pulls out a ten-inch chef's knife and starts slicing up the watermelon that's been chilling all afternoon in the ice cooler. Man, there's nothing better. I always go for one of those middle pieces without a lot of seeds, and then I season it the southern way, with a dash of salt on top. No summer barbecue is complete without it.

Now, if you can make it to that part of the meal without having someone get in your face to spout off nonsense about our "big, bloated, unaccountable government," you're doing something right—or maybe you just forgot your Right Guard. Either way, don't think you're home free. If there is even a single Republican at that barbecue, you're going to have to deal with the subject of "big government." These days it's inevitable. You might just as well be prepared.

Forget about the watermelon for a minute. Walk over to the grill and lift off a nice, juicy medium-rare burger. You can put a sesame seed bun around it, but hold back on the condiments. Ketchup and onions and tomato would diminish the effect we're shooting for here. Good. Now you've got yourself an ideal weapon for the inevitable assault on you and the federal government.

No, you're not going to throw that burger at a Republican. Instead, you're going to use it as a prop. It just so happens that your average backyard barbecue burger is the ideal symbol of how dumb, dangerous, myth driven, and inconsistent these assaults on government really are. Trust me here. You'll see what I'm driving at in just a second.

Three years ago, a couple hundred people in the Pacific Northwest were eating hamburgers like the one in your hand and they got poisoned by a vicious new strain of the common bacteria called *E. coli*. At least three kids died. For good reason, people all across the country were shocked. They expect better than that from our meat supply. They expect that when they make up a hamburger on the grill or pick one up at a fast-food restaurant, the meat won't kill them.

So what went wrong in the Pacific Northwest? Wasn't the meat government inspected? Sure it was. All meat is government inspected. The problem is, the inspection process is outdated—basically, the inspectors just look at the meat and sniff it—and the meat-packers aren't willing to clean up their act on their own. To weed out infected meat, these guys need to bring in new scientific tests and modern laboratories. The old way just doesn't cut it anymore.

Now, some people would look at this situation and say, Let's fix it. That seems like common sense to me. We know the government and the meat producers have the technology to do it right. It might cost us a couple extra cents on a pound of meat. But I, for one, would rather pay $1.59 a pound for something that I knew was safe than $1.56 for something that might kill me.

That's the way the Department of Agriculture saw it,

anyway. Even before the poisonings in the Pacific Northwest, it was working to set higher standards for meat and poultry producers and to modernize the inspection system.

But the Republicans in Congress didn't have much interest in fixing the problem. As you know, they think all new regulations—even regulations to save kids from dying from tainted hamburgers—are too much of a burden for hardworking American big businesses to bear. So the House Republicans voted in June of last year to block the whole USDA overhaul. Sure, the new plan would prevent illness and save lives. But it's just more regulation, they said. And everyone knows that regulation is bad. Case closed.

Now, I should point out that it looks as if the USDA plan is going to go through and we'll get cleaner meat after all. Last summer, the Democrats in the House forced the Republicans to back down. But don't let right-wingers off the meat hook so fast. The Republicans did just about everything they could to trash the system and in the process made it clear that paying off their own campaign IOUs to the meat industry was more important than keeping your burger safe.

So, my friends, you have just seen how your burger can help you make the case that the Republicans' knee-jerk attacks on government can be dangerous. Now it's time to look at how that same juicy burger might help you make the case that these attacks are often based on outright lies.

I admit it: Even if properly inspected, burgers are not the world's healthiest food. In fact, if there are any health-conscious people among the Republicans at your barbecue (they'd be the editorial writers), they'll probably just have a piece of skinless chicken breast on their plates.

That's smart. Too much red meat can eventually lead to heart disease.

Which is a big reason you don't want government red tape keeping any lifesaving cardiovascular medical devices off the market. In 1994, the Speaker of the House of Representatives said he had found just such a case. On *Meet the Press*, Speaker Newt reported that the Food and Drug Administration, the same odious government bureaucracy that wants to steal the cigarettes right out of your children's mouths, had "made illegal" a miraculous new heart pump used in eleven countries that "increases by 54 percent the number of people [who undergo CPR] who get to the hospital and have a chance to recover."

Even I was appalled. The incompetence of it all! The arrogance! The FDA was just fiddling around while people were keeling over and dying!

The story was damaging politically. It had everything in it that the Republicans wanted people to believe about the federal government. Who's not going to hate a big, bad, bloated, regulation-laden government that keeps modern medical devices from hardworking Americans who ate a few too many burgers or who got stressed out at tax time and needed heart resuscitation?

But, lo and behold, Gingrich was dead wrong.

A couple of reporters made some calls and found out the truth about that heart pump: Independent test results showed that the device was of absolutely no benefit, so no one bothered pursuing it. No one had even applied for FDA approval!

Did Newt apologize? What do you think?

The revolution does not stop for apologies.

For our final burger-inspired lesson in "big government,"

here's another look at why these Republican attacks are so pathetically inconsistent.

You'd think if the Republicans were so damn eager to cut down the size of government, even to the point of sacrificing children's nutrition programs, then they'd also first go after every scrap of waste, fraud, and abuse they could find. Well, to put it charitably, they haven't. One of my favorite examples is cattle grazing. That burger in your hand, when it used to be part of a steer, probably spent a good deal of time grazing on federal land out West—in Idaho, Wyoming, or Montana. Now, I don't know how closely you've been following the pipe bombings and other violence in that part of our country, but suffice it to say that cowboys don't take too kindly to the government coming around, meddling in their affairs, giving them all kinds of city-slicker advice about overgrazing and environmental damage.

One thing these rugged individualists don't seem to mind, though, is a big, fat, porky government subsidy for their operations. They've got a mighty fine deal out there in cowboy country. The federal government only charges them about a quarter of what private landowners charge for grazing rights, and the Republicans even tried to sweeten the deal by dropping the fees altogether for some cowboys.

Some people, including the Secretary of the Interior, think this situation is kinda crazy—I mean, taxpayers are handing these people money to ruin our public land! What are we thinking? But when in 1993 the Clinton administration tried to use common sense and raise the grazing fees, the Republicans—and, in fairness, some Democrats—went ballistic and killed the plan. I guess the free market didn't look so good after all.

Right now we're protecting government aid to cows and

at the same time we're cutting nutrition programs for kids. Cattle over kids. What the hell is going on here?

Look, the Republicans have some legitimate gripes about the way our federal government works. So do we Democrats. There's nothing in the Constitution that says we have to settle for third-rate services or $500 toilet seats. We can do something about it. We can set the bar higher and expect more from our government employees. We can bring in private-sector experts to tell us what we're doing wrong. We can drop programs that will never do much good. And, yes, we can ask state governments to do more.

But what we're seeing from the Republicans goes much, much deeper and meaner. We're not talking strategic cuts or increased efficiency; we're talking outright kills. Some would have us kill the Food and Drug Administration, the most important consumer watchdog we have, because the pharmaceutical industry doesn't think it moves fast enough. Some right-wingers would have us kill the Federal Communications Commission because the $350 billion telecommunications industry wants to police itself. Some want to eliminate the Environmental Protection Agency because the big polluters think we should trust industry to do right by our air and water—just like they did in the good old days before the EPA was created. It's not just antigovernment.

It's antiwork.

It's antifamily.

It's anti–common sense.

Republicans will try to convince you that there's some kind of deep philosophical underpinning to their agenda.

Come on! I'd say that there are deeper philosophical underpinnings to a case of indigestion. All they want to do is replace "big government" with big business. That's not philosophy, that's foolosophy. It doesn't take any deep philosophical underpinnings to gut our government. It just takes a willingness to let lobbyists rewrite the legislation that regulates their industries. It takes a willingness to make up regulatory myths when the facts don't say what you believe. It takes a willingness to abandon the federal safety net. It takes a willingness to raze instead of reinvent.

As every child learns in grade school, there is a fine system of checks and balances among the executive, legislative, and judicial branches within our government. What is often forgotten is that our country also depends on having checks and balances to control the power of big business interests. With a crippled federal government, we lose our most important counterweight.

Look, I wish I could say that what's right for big business is always right for America. Sometimes it is, like when a car manufacturer adds thousands of jobs to the economy. But sometimes it isn't, like when that same manufacturer is dead set against air bags, seat belts, and emission controls, or when it doesn't want to recall defective cars. We need a federal government that is powerful enough to take on big business from time to time. We need a federal government that is powerful enough to protect the interests of the powerless. That's what the Founding Fathers had in mind.

And now . . . well, you know the drill.

• • •

FAT CATS AND CORPORATE WELFARE

> I think that we are absolutely bound and deter-
> mined in this new Congress to make the effort to
> restore to states their sovereignty.
> —*Gov. Pete Wilson (R-CA), January 1, 1995*

RAPID RESPONSE The Republicans don't really believe in devolving power to the states. The truth is that they believe in comforting the comfortable and afflicting the afflicted, and where the state is in a better position to do that, they're in favor of states' rights, and where the federal government is in a better position to do that, they're for federal rights.

EXTENDED VERSION Let me give you just a few examples of where the Republican hypocrites voted to take power away from the states. First, there are securities laws, the laws that deal with sales of stocks and bonds. Certain interest groups thought it might be easier if they didn't have to comply with state securities laws, which are usually more strict than federal laws, and the Republicans were all too happy to oblige them and stiff-arm the states. They did the same thing on so-called punitive damages. It seems that big businesses didn't like states making them pay big awards when, through their own negligence, their products hurt their consumers. Not surprising. What was surprising was how quickly the committed devolutionists in Congress tossed aside the state laws and put a federal cap on damages.

> The market is rational and the government is
> dumb.
> —*Rep. Dick Armey, 1995*

RAPID RESPONSE Look, is it rational that the meat industry would let tainted meat out the door, risking a panic that would cost it a huge quantity of business? Is it rational that the fishing industry in the Northeast would deplete the fish stocks and leave itself with nothing but old tires to pull up out of the sea?

EXTENDED VERSION I just do not understand these folks who say that the market is the answer to all our problems. The market does many things well, but it is not always rational. And even when it is, we don't always like what it produces, such as monopolies, pollution, violence on television, and all kinds of short-term decision making.

> Government bureaucracies in general are threats to
> everyday life.
> —*Rep. Newt Gingrich, 1984*

RAPID RESPONSE If you ask me, the biggest threat to our everyday life is Newt Gingrich's mouth.

EXTENDED VERSION If you believe Gingrich, I suggest you address fifty senior citizens and tell them that Social Security and Medicare are a threat to their everyday life. Or maybe you'd prefer to address a group of crime victims and tell them that the Bureau of Prisons is a threat to everyday life. Or perhaps you'd consider telling the folks in Los Angeles who were devastated by an earthquake two years ago that the Federal Emergency Management Agency is a threat to their everyday life. What about the Army Corps of Engineers? The National Institutes of Health? The Centers for Disease Control?

> Both the economic crisis and the moral crisis have
> their roots in the explosion of government.
> —*Sen. Phil Gramm, May 5, 1995*

RAPID RESPONSE Let's get honest here about the so-called explosion of government. Are you aware that President Clinton has cut the federal workforce by more than 200,000 jobs and we now have the smallest federal workforce since Kennedy was President?

EXTENDED VERSION The big increases have been in state governments, which are only going to get bigger before the Republicans are voted out of office. From 1970 to 1992, the number of state employees increased by 65 percent, from 2.8 million to 4.6 million. And here's another interesting little fact: Federal expenditures are a much smaller fraction of the total economy today than they were under Reagan, and they are no larger than they were twenty years ago.

> We believe you can trust the fifty states and the fifty
> legislatures to work together on behalf of the citi-
> zens of their states.
> —*Rep. Newt Gingrich, January 11, 1995*

RAPID RESPONSE Has Newt Gingrich ever seen the Louisiana legislature in action? Take it from me: It's not pretty.

EXTENDED VERSION The Speaker has visited Orange

County, California, where local managers blew billions of taxpayer dollars betting on obscure financial transactions called derivatives. I bet he has—it's solid Republican territory out there. He's surely seen the District of Columbia at work. It's stone-cold broke and begging the feds for money to meet payroll.

Quiz
Paul Slansky

Which headline did not appear in a daily American newspaper in the early days of the George W. Bush presidency?

(a) "FDA TO SUSPEND A RULE ON CHILD DRUG TESTING"

(b) "EPA IS SET TO EASE RULES ON POLLUTING POWER PLANTS"

(c) "U.S. JOBLESS RATE INCREASES TO 6%, HIGHEST IN 8 YEARS"

(d) "EPA PROPOSES TO LET MINES DUMP WASTE IN WATERWAYS"

(e) "WHITE HOUSE CUT 93% OF FUNDS SOUGHT TO GUARD ATOMIC ARMS"

(f) "IN SHIFT, JUSTICE DEPT. PUSHES TO WIDEN RIGHTS TO OWN GUNS"

(g) "CHENEY RETURNS TO U.S. WITH FULL HEAD OF THICK, WAVY HAIR"

Answer: (g)

I Hate Republicans READER They Said It . . .

"Not that I can think of."

—House Majority Leader Tom Delay (R-TX),
when asked if there were any federal regulations he would choose to keep

USA, Inc.:
The Corporate-Government Tapestry
of George W. Bush
(2003)
Michael A. Jewell

O ur republic was created with the knowledge that the centralization of power is a threat to the freedom of individuals. We are committed to our story that in the United States, power lies in our hands, that our three-branch system of government protects us from the tyranny of greed, that our lawmakers represent us—living, breathing, individual persons—and that our domestic and foreign policies are largely driven by the compassion of real persons for real persons.

But for decades we have heard warnings concerning the influence of corporations on national and foreign policy.

As early as 1961, President Eisenhower cautioned: "In the counsels of Government, we must guard against the acquisition of unwarranted influence, whether sought or unsought, by the Military Industrial Complex. The potential for the disastrous rise of misplaced power exists, and will persist. We must never let the weight of this combination endanger our liberties or democratic processes."

USA,INC., the chart on pages 212 and 213, emerged out of an attempt to uncover the actual motivation behind our invasion of Iraq. Although we consistently encounter references to the power that corporations have acquired, the tapestry of corporate-government relationships illustrated by this chart provides stunning insight into the degree to which corporations have become embedded within our government. The story told by this picture is not the story told in our nation's high schools.

Some centralization of power is necessary to maintain cultural stability. Corporations contribute to the efficiency and productivity of our economy. But surely any observer of this picture of corporate-government relationships would be tempted to wonder:

1. Have corporations gained too much influence?

2. Do corporations with board members on governmental organizations (or quasi-governmental organizations such as the U.S. Defense Policy Board) secure unfair leverage in the marketplace?

3. Has corporate influence displaced the voices of citizen voters, thus threatening the integrity of our democracy?

4. Do the agendas of corporations mirror the agendas of individual citizens?

5. How thorough is this weave of relationships between corporations and government?

READING THE CHART

All lines indicate an intimate *and* positive relationship. Like lines on an electronic schematic, they represent flow of power.

Lines between individuals and corporations indicate present or past participation in the company indicated; usually the individual is a member of the company's board of directors.

Lines between individuals indicate an intimate professional history or relevant friendship (for instance, Colin Powell was once a racquetball partner of Ambassador Bandar of Saudi Arabia, while the ambassador's relationship with G.H.W. Bush is so close that he has been called "Bandar Bush" by the ex-president).

Lines between corporations indicate past or present business relationships (for example, the Saudi bin Laden Group's relationship to both Bechtel and Carlyle).

Corporations (enclosed by ovals) surround the chart. For the most part, these corporations are in the energy, defense, and communications industries. Fox News is honored for its ties to the Project for The New American Century (PNAC) and its role as a voice for the conservative right. A small oval indicates a subsidiary company.

Names surrounding corporations indicate board members.

The Defense Policy Board (USDPB) forms the hub location on our chart because it centrally locates and redistributes power between the energy and defense industries and the Defense Department and the White House. The USDPB has gained increased influence in the Bush administration and advises the Secretary of Defense on foreign policy.

Its members are selected by the Defense Department and its meetings are classified. Many of its members are on the boards of companies that stand to earn fortunes from the policies that these members advocate.

The Center for Public Integrity notes that "The board (USDPB) consists of 30 members, at least 9 of whom are linked to companies that have won more than $76 billion in defense contracts in 2001 and 2002." Represented on the board are: Boeing, TRW, Northrop Grumman (through Johnston & Associates), Lockheed Martin, Booz Allen Hamilton, Symantec Corp., Technology Strategies and Alliance Corp., Polycom Inc. and many others.

Members who are particularly influential and/or tied to the defense industry include:

- *Kenneth Adelman*, former aide to Defense Secretary Donald H. Rumsfeld.
- *Richard Allen*, senior counselor to APCO Worldwide, registered lobbyist for Alliance Aircraft, former national security advisor.
- *Barry M. Blechman*, founder and president of DFI International, a consulting firm for government as well as the private sector.
- *Gen. (Ret.) Ronald R. Fogleman*, on the board of several defense-related companies including

Rolls-Royce North America, North American Airlines, AAR Corporation and the Mitre Corp. President and CEO of the Bar J Cattle Company. Chairman and CEO of Durango Aerospace, Inc..

• *Newt Gingrich*, CEO of the Gingrich Group. Former Speaker of the House. Senior fellow at the American Enterprise Institute. Analyst for Fox News. Zealous critic of the Department of State and its propensity for diplomacy and dialogue in foreign relations.

• *Gerald Hillman*, managing director of Hillman Capital Corp. On the board of Trireme.

• *Adm. David Jeremiah*, director or advisor for several corporations that do business with the Defense Department. These corporations have been awarded billions of dollars in contracts with the Pentagon. Has ties with Mitre Corporation and Technology Strategies & Alliances Corporation.

• *Henry Kissinger*, former Secretary of State. Chairman of Kissinger Associates, an international consulting firm. Former consultant to Unocal oil company.

• *Adm. (Ret.) William Owens*, co–chief executive officer and vice chairman of Teledesic LLC. On the board of Symantec. Former president of Science Applications International Corporation.

• *Richard Perle*, (See below.)

• *James Schlesinger*, chairman of the Mitre Corporation. Former director of the Central Intelligence Agency.

• *Gen. (Ret.) Jack Sheehan*, senior vice president of Bechtel, which received one of the largest contracts created by the American invasion of Iraq.

• *Chris Williams*, works for Johnston & Associates, whose clients have included Boeing, TRW, and Northrop Grumman. Works as a registered lobbyist for defense companies.

• *James Woolsey*, vice president of Booz Allen Hamilton. A principal of the Paladin Capital Group. Former Director of the CIA.

• *Richard Perle* earns a central position on our chart because of his pivotal role as both a leading voice in the PNAC and in the U.S. Defense Policy Board (he was recently forced to step down as chairman of the USDPB under allegations of corruption, but remains a member). His experience includes:

> • Board member of Autonomy Corporation, which receives homeland securities contracts from the government.

> • Managing partner of Trireme, a venture-capital company which invests in companies dealing in technology, goods, and services that are of value to homeland security and defense.

> • As a member of Trireme and the PNAC and chairman of the USDPB, Perle secretly met with the Saudi businessmen Adnan Khashoggi and Harb Seleh al-Zuhair in an alleged attempt to secure contracts for Trireme (he denied this motive for the meeting).

> • Subject of a 1983 *New York Times* investigation into allegations that he recommended that the Army buy weapons from an Israeli company from whose owners he had,

two years earlier, accepted a fifty-thousand-dollar fee.

• Member of the Board of Advisors of Foundation for Defense of Democracies (FDD), a Far-Right defense oriented organization. (Other members are William Kristol, Charles Krauthammer, and Gary Bauer).

• Former Assistant Secretary of Defense for international security policy.

• An FBI summary of a 1970 wiretap described Perle discussing classified information with someone at the Israeli embassy. In 1983, newspapers reported that he received substantial payments to represent the interests of an Israeli weapons company. Perle denied conflicts of interest, insisting that, although he received payment for these services after he had assumed his position in the Defense Department, he was between government jobs when he worked for the Israeli firm.

The PNAC (Project for the New American Century), like the USDPB, occupies an important place on the chart. The PNAC is an activist conservative "educational institution" developed in the early 1990s and comprised of corporate board members, CEO's, powerful government employees, and conservative writers. Intimately connected to the religious right, to the USDPB, and to the White House, the PNAC since its inception has lobbied for a United States foreign policy based on preemptive invasion. Throughout the last decade it has been persistent in its cry for an American invasion of Iraq.

Although its policies were rejected by the Clinton Administration, the PNAC has found a friend in George W. Bush. Bush—with Dick Cheney, a PNAC founding member—has cynically exploited a series of attacks on American interests (including the World Trade Towers and the Pentagon) by Saudi Arabian nationals to pursue the PNAC agenda.

Particularly influential past and present PNAC members include:

- *Vice President Dick Cheney,* a PNAC founder and past CEO to Halliburton, who served as Secretary of Defense for Bush Sr.
- *I. Lewis Libby,* Cheney's top national security assistant.
- *Secretary of Defense Donald Rumsfeld,* also a PNAC founding member, along with four of his chief aides including:
  - *Deputy Secretary of Defense Paul Wolfowitz,* served in the Reagan and George H. W. Bush administrations.
  - *Eliot Abrams,* prominent member of Bush's National Security Council, who was pardoned by Bush Sr. after being convicted of withholding information in the Iran/Contra scandal.
  - *John Bolton,* who serves as Undersecretary for Arms Control and International Security in the current Bush administration.
  - *Randy Scheunemann,* President of the Committee for the Liberation of Iraq, Trent Lott's national security aide, and advisor to Rumsfeld on Iraq in 2001.

- *Bruce Jackson*, Chairman of PNAC, past vice president of Lockheed Martin.
- *William Kristol*, noted conservative writer for the *Weekly Standard*, a magazine associated with Fox News Network and owned by conservative media mogul Rupert Murdoch. Kristol also is a political contributor for Fox News.

Saudi Arabia earns a place on our chart because Saudi citizens have been nearly exclusively responsible for terrorism directed toward the United States (including the attacks on 9/11). Therefore to understand why we have invaded Iraq it is necessary to understand why we have *not* invaded Saudi Arabia.

There are no surprises here. The Ambassador of Saudi Arabia ("Bandar Bush") has close personal ties with the Bush family, and was a racquetball partner of Colin Powell. Saudi Arabia has a trillion dollars invested in the American stock market and another trillion dollars in American banks. They hold the major source of emergency oil reserves in the world. And, of course, Saudi companies have close business ties to American corporations. For instance, the Saudi bin Laden Group is a major investor in Carlyle, an employer of George H. W. Bush. (As a leading manufacturer of military hardware, Carlyle is in the position to earn millions of dollars as a result of the decisions that G. H. W. Bush's son makes. And incidentally, George W. used to serve on the board of Caterair, a subsidiary of Carlyle.)

CORPORATIONS, CONFLICTS OF INTEREST, AND THE THREAT TO OUR DEMOCRACY

Ironically, corporations are non corporeal. They are reifications: concepts experienced and treated as concrete entities. And although by law they possess the rights of a person, corporations do not have minds and thus cannot feel compassion. They are not attached to place nor are they imbued with specific content. Staff and management can be replaced, ownership can change hands, office headquarters can be moved, logos can be replaced, subsidiaries can be absorbed and sold—even corporate names can be changed. Yet through all of these incarnations, corporate entities carry on.

Since corporations lack hearts and minds, their goals are limited to maximum profit and maximum growth. And even though corporations are populated by real persons, as employees those persons are expected to represent the agenda of the corporation in which they work. This explains the behavior of tobacco companies, of the Exxon Corporation after the Valdez oil spill, and of Union Carbide after "it" poisoned 200,000 people in Bhopal, India. These companies are presumably managed by responsive and compassionate people who love their relatives, engage in genuine dialogue with others, experience themselves as part of humanity, and function with codes of ethics that recognize the sanctity of life. Yet these companies consistently turn a blind eye to the damage, the suffering, and the death that they cause.

Possessing hearts and minds, individuals behave (and vote) out of a complex fabric of ideological, emotional, selfish, *and* selfless motivations. Most Americans assume that the policies of their government will represent that complex fabric of being. But as mere legal concepts, corporations do not reflect the motives of live individuals and they are not guided by the same ethical and moral standards as are our citizen voters. As corporate influence in our government increases it displaces the influence of our citizens; as domestic and foreign policies increasingly satisfy the wishes of corporations those policies decreasingly reflect the wishes of voters. *Even when consistent with the wishes of voters, policies dictated by corporations are corporate policies and not the policies of citizens.*

The problem with which Americans are now confronted is not party- specific. That our voices have been massively displaced in the media, in the election process and in government by the voice of corporations is a reflection of decades of growing corporate influence. However, the administration of George W. Bush has unabashedly adopted the agendas and the policies of the Project for the New American Century and of defense and energy industry corporations. This neoconservative and corporate juggernaut has had its way with the world and with the American people. That the vice president, the president, the president's father, and nearly the entire team of policy makers in an administration are tied to either the largest defense and energy industry corporations in the world, and/or to an ethnocentric, self-righteous, and militaristic "educational organization" like the PNAC indicates that it is time that voters reevaluate the wisdom of offering mere reifications such enormous power and influence throughout the culture.

The threat that corporations pose to our democracy is clear. The tapestry of government/corporate influence illustrated by *USA, INC.* is not a democracy of the people. It is not the democracy envisioned by our forefathers. It is not the democracy in which we imagine that we live. Rather, this tapestry illustrates an integration of church (of commodity) and state within which our voices are often barely heard.

I am a mountaineering guide and instructor. I researched and designed this chart in less than three months in my spare time. The original version has been edited to fit available space. Thus, the relationships illustrated by the chart are merely "the tip of the iceberg." A thorough treatment of the subject would create a far more complex picture. An enterprising researcher and programmer might consider developing a program that would centralize any of the organizations on the chart (rather than just the USDPB) and then reference the relationships indicated. Such a program would not only illustrate the flow of power in this administration but it would offer an opportunity to compare the flow of power in future administrations and thus track the history and development of corporate influence in our government.

The following chart on pages 212 and 213 was designed by Michael A. Jewell.

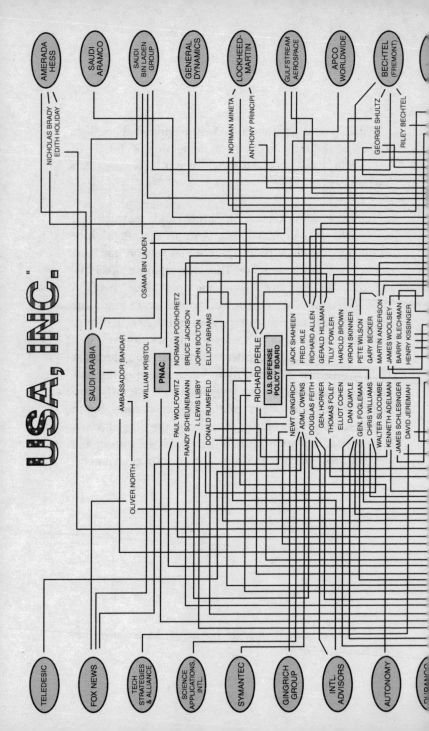

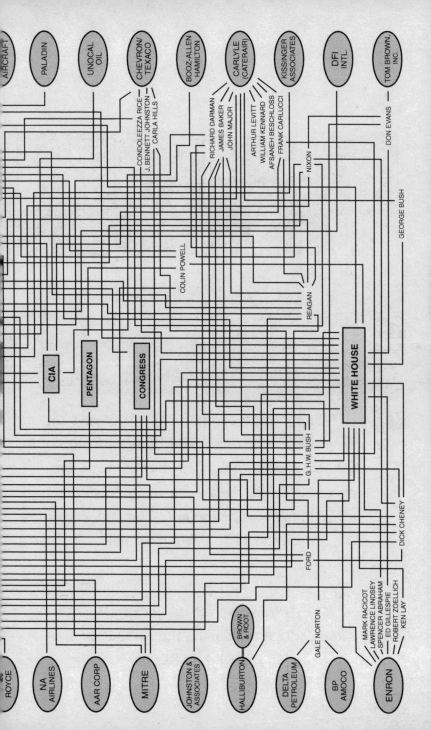

"[Supply-side economics] was always a Trojan horse to bring down the top rate... Do you realize the greed that came to the forefront? The hogs were really feeding."
—David Stockman, Reaagan's Budget Director, on the 1981 Reagan tax bill

"I think we hit the jackpot!"
—Ronald Reagan, signing the bill that deregulated the S&Ls

"He was a supporter of Ann Richards in my run in 1994."
—George W. Bush on Enron ex-CEO Ken Lay, 2002

"I was very close to George W. and had a lot of respect for him, had watched him over the years, particularly with reference to dealings with his father when his father was in the White House and some of the things he did to work for his father, and so did support him."
—Ken Lay on *Frontline* explaining why he supported Bush over Richards in 1994

HATE

*with quotes from Don Toenjas, Thomas Ellis,
Ronald Reagan, James Watt, Jesse Helms;
and quizzes from Paul Slansky*

Many Republicans grew up feeling powerless—imagine Rush Limbaugh or Richard Nixon in high school—which may help explain their ruthless pursuit of power. It also may explain the racist, sexist and homophobic tendencies that are such a strong part of the Republican Party's modern heritage and contemporary culture.

"I have nothing against homosexuals. Being a homosexual is between them and God—and God makes it very clear what he thinks about it. This is their problem."
—Don Toenjas, chairman of the Glenn County, California, Republican party, 2002

"I do not believe in my heart that I'm a racist."
—Reagan appointee Thomas Ellis, 7/26/83. Ellis belonged to an all-white country club, held significant assets in apartheid South Africa (where he recently had been a guest of the government), and had served on the board of a group that funded research about the genetic inferiority of blacks

"A black guy walks into a bar with a parrot on his shoulder. He sits down at the bar and orders a drink. Before long, the bartender, who is quite curious, approaches them and asks, 'Where did you get him?' The parrot answers, 'In Africa!' "
—One of Ronald Reagan's favorite knee-slappers

Quiz
Paul Slansky

Which TV program so offended Nixon that he declared, "I do not think that you glorify on public television homosexuality . . . any more than you glorify, uh, whores."

(a) "All in the Family"
(b) "Rowan and Martin's Laugh-In"
(c) "Love, American Style"
(d) "The Odd Couple"

Answer: (a)

They Said It . . .

"I have a black, a woman, two Jews and a cripple."
—Reagan Secretary of the Interior James Watt on the diversity of his staff, 1983

"We're no longer seeking a token or something."
—Ronald Reagan when asked why there were no women on his commission on Central America, 1983

"Ortega wasn't chosen because she's a woman. She was chosen because she's a Hispanic."
—GOP official at the 1984 Republican Convention, explaining the choice of Katherine Ortega for U.S. Treasurer

Quiz
Paul Slansky

During an Oval Office discussion, a guest made a statement that prompted Nixon to ask, "You believe that?" "Yes, sir," the man assured him. "Oh boy," Nixon said. "So do I. I can't ever say that, but I believe it." What preceded this exchange?

(a) White House adviser John Ehrlichman called J. Edgar Hoover "a little light in the loafers."
(b) The Reverend Billy Graham said that the Jews had a "stranglehold" on the media which "has got to be broken or the country's going down the drain."
(c) Attorney General John Mitchell suggested that it "might not be a bad idea" to "beat the shit out of" some of the "folks on our enemies list."
(d) Vice-President Spiro Agnew complained that the media had "made too much of a fuss about" the My Lai massacre.

Answer: (b)

They Said It . . .

"I'm going to make her cry. I'm going to sing 'Dixie' until she cries."
—Senator Jesse Helms to Republican colleague Orrin Hatch, upon finding himself in an elevator with African-American Senator Carol Moseley-Braun (D-IL). Moseley-Braun's response: "Senator Helms, your singing would make me cry if you sang 'Rock of Ages.'"

from *Hard Right: The Rise of Jesse Helms*
(1986)
Ernest B. Furgurson

Helms's rise to national prominence attracted reporters, and despite his misgivings about "the media," he occasionally invited one to visit him at home. Bill Arthur of the *Charlotte Observer* wrote about how a photographer started to take Helms's picture in his study when the senator pulled an illustration off the wall. "That'll get me in trouble," he said. The picture showed a black man in a rocking chair on the verandah of a plantation, sipping a mint julep and saying, "This is what me and Martin Luther had in mind!"

Earlier, the *Wall Street Journal* reported that Helms had a generic nickname for blacks: "Fred." He told the paper that actually that was not his usage, but perhaps that of two of his former Senate staffers. But an aide said the senator had a habit of saying, in response to a black request, "What does this Fred want?" or "Take care of that Fred." The aide said Helms thought it was funny.

Race was an important factor, perhaps the decisive one, in Helms's hardest Senate race, in 1984. His overall record may have been enough to mobilize the anti-black vote, but Helms and associates did not leave that to chance. He wrangled in the Senate for days against the Martin Luther King holiday bill. He complained early and often of the "bloc vote extremists" aligned against him. He benefited from a huge, organized white backlash against a publicized effort by Jesse Jackson to register black voters. Late in the campaign, he visited the campus of Livingstone College, a black school in Salisbury. There, his speech was boycotted by many students, and he was photographed extending his hand to young blacks who refused to shake it. As he left, Helms suggested the whole thing had been "orchestrated," although he did not say by whom. Asked whether his opponent's camp might be responsible, he said, "I wouldn't be surprised." For him, it was as good as a series of the costly commercials he was broadcasting every night.

Nineteen days later, he won again.

Segregationist giant Strom Thurmond turns 100 in the company of his friends; Trent Lott applauds.
© *Associated Press, AP.*

Trent Lott's Racist Past
(2003)
Nate Hardcastle

Trent Lott in 2002 resigned as Senate Majority Leader after praising Strom Thurmond's segregationist 1948 presidential campaign. But the sentiments behind his remarks were not new: Lott and other Republicans have a long, ugly history of race-baiting and bigotry. (And they call themselves "the party of Lincoln.") Here are a few lowlights from Trent Lott's racist past:

EARLY 1960S

Lott as president of University of Mississippi's inter-fraternity council fights to prevent any chapter of his fraternity, Sigma Nu, from accepting African-Americans. "'Trent was one of the strongest leaders in resisting the integration of the national fraternity in any of the chapters,' recalls former CNN President Tom Johnson, then a Sigma Nu member at the University of Georgia." (CNN.com, 8/12/02)

Lott in 1997: "Yes, you could say I favored segregation then."

1962

Lott, president of his Sigma Nu chapter, runs into trouble when police seize 24 guns while putting down a segregation-related riot at the fraternity.

1980

Referring to Strom Thurmond's anti-integration 1948 presidential campaign at a campaign rally for Ronald Reagan: "If we had elected this man 30 years ago, we wouldn't be in the mess we are today."

1981

Opposes expanding the Voting Rights Act, which imposes penalties for states that don't guarantee voting access to African-Americans. The law, says Lott, is "just not fair."

1983

Opposes creation of the Martin Luther King holiday. Lott: "We have not done it for a lot of other people that were more deserving."

1984

Gives an interview to pro-Confederate magazine *Southern Partisan*, which once sold T-shirts celebrating the assassination of Lincoln. (Other notable Republicans who have appeared in the magazine include Phil Gramm, Jesse Helms, Dick Armey, Thad Cochran and John Ashcroft.) During the interview Lott defends his opposition to the Voting Rights Act and the MLK holiday.

1992

Delivers the keynote address to the Council of Conservative Citizens, a group dedicated to the "preservation" of the white race. Lott says: "The people in this room stand for the right principles and the right philosophy."

DECEMBER 5, 2002

Gives a speech at Strom Thurmond's 100th birthday party; boasts that Mississippi voted for Thurmond's segregationist ticket in 1948, "and if the rest of the country had followed our lead, we wouldn't have had all these problems over the years either." Resigns two weeks later amid massive protests.

Paul Begala's book on then-Texas governor and presidential candidate George W. Bush included this indictment of Dubya's stands on race.

Bush and Race: "Porch Monkeys", Bob Jones, and the Confederate Flag

from *Is Our Children Learning?* (2000)

Paul Begala

"What I am against is quotas. I am against hard quotas. Quotas they basically delineate based upon whatever. However they delineate, quotas, I think vulcanize society. So I don't know how that fits into what everybody else is saying, their relative positions, but that's my position."
(San Francisco Chronicle, 1/21/00)

"That school was based upon the Bible."
(Describing Bob Jones University, Palm Beach Post, 2/4/00)

"I do not agree with this notion that somehow if I go to try to attract votes and to lead people toward a better tomorrow somehow I get subscribed to some—some doctrine gets subscribed to me."
(Trying again to defend his appearance at Bob Jones University, Meet the Press, 2/13/00)

"I don't have to accept their tenets. I was trying to convince those college students to accept my tenets. And I reject any labeling me because I happened to go to the university."
(Trying once more to defend his appearance at Bob Jones University, Today, 2/23/00)

WHEN HATE CAME TO TEXAS, WHERE WAS GEORGE?

When James Byrd, Jr., was brutally murdered—lynched by being dragged from the back of a pickup truck until his body literally came apart—just for being black, it was one of the most shocking crimes in Texas history. The small town of Jasper, Texas, was stunned. Civil rights leaders like the Reverend Jesse Jackson and political leaders like Texas Republican Senator Kay Bailey Hutchison rushed to Jasper to calm the community and comfort the family.

But where was George?

The man who has held so many photo ops with African-American children abandoned his fellow Texans when they needed him most. Bush's absence from Jasper stands in stark contrast to his reaction when seven white Christians were gunned down in a church in Fort Worth. He was campaigning in Minnesota at the time, but Bush flew home to be there.

Why would the governor of Texas fly across the country to comfort white families when he wouldn't drive halfway across the state to comfort black families?

Bush abandoned the African-American community again when the James Byrd, Jr., Hate Crimes Act was before the Texas Legislature. Daryl Verrett, the nephew of James Byrd, Jr., asked Bush to support the legislation. "I asked him personally if he would use his influence to help pass the bill. . . . He told me, 'No.' "

Bush's excuse for opposing the hate crimes legislation is lame. "I've always said every crime is a hate crime. People, when they commit a crime, have hate in their heart. It's hard to distinguish between one degree of hate and another."

Nonsense.

Bush's line of argument shows his facility for the sound

bite ("every crime is a hate crime") and the vapidity of his brain. Of course every crime is not a hate crime. To say so is facile and stupid. Swiping a Christmas wreath from the door of a store as part of a college fraternity escapade, as he did thirty-four years ago, is not a hate crime. It's just a childish prank, easily forgiven. Insider trading (which Bush came perilously close to committing) is not a crime of hate, it's a crime of greed. Killing a man in a barroom brawl is not the same as grabbing an innocent man walking down the street, chaining him to the back of a pickup truck, and dragging him to death. Targeting someone for violence because of their race, religion, gender, disability, or sexual orientation—that's a hate crime.

Bush says, "It's hard to distinguish between one degree of hate and another."

Garbage.

It's called motive, and it is determinative in many other areas of law. If I shoot and kill another man, is it murder? That depends on motive. If my motive in killing an enemy in combat is to do my duty as part of the armed forces, we rightly call that killing a patriotic act. If my motive is self-defense, we rightly call that killing justified. If my motive is to shoot a deer, and I accidentally shoot a man, it may simply be a tragic accident. But if my motive in pulling the trigger is to murder, then it's a crime. And in many states, if my motive for the murder itself is money, or to further some other felony, I can get the death penalty.

The same act, A shooting B, can have five different consequences—all based on motive. Whether I get a medal or the electric chair depends on motive.

We all know in our bones that the punishment for spray-painting "Go Longhorns" on a wall should be less than the punishment for spray-painting "Kill Jews." Both are wrongful acts, but only one is hateful. The motive matters.

When racists in the earlier part of this century lynched black men they were not only murdering, they were also attacking an entire community. And so we all recoil at the suffering of James Byrd, Jr. There were hundreds of murders in Texas in 1998, but that one stands out. Why? Because the racists who did it were trying to send a message of hate to the entire community.

And thus the community of civilized people has a responsibility to send a message as well: if your motive for killing, beating, lynching, or attacking is hatred directed at an entire community, we are going to ensure your swift and certain punishment.

It's a shame that Governor Bush refused to go to Jasper to comfort the Byrd family and heal the community. When character and courage called him to stand against hate—Bush hid.

The conservative philosopher Edmund Burke said, "All that is necessary for evil to triumph is for good men to do nothing." Bush is a good man. He has a good heart—especially on issues of race. And yet when political calculus—and political cowardice—dictated that he do nothing when he was asked to stand against evil, he did nothing.

Shame on him.

BOB JONES UNIVERSITY

On February 2, 2000, Bush made his first campaign stop in South Carolina at Bob Jones University, a school known for its policy banning interracial dating. Bush defended his decision to speak at Bob Jones University two days after speaking there by saying "that school [Bob Jones] was based upon the Bible." Bush wouldn't go to Jasper but he was happy to go to Bob Jones University.

At least W's South Carolina campaign manager was honest enough to admit why. He told *Newsweek* that Bush did not go there to persuade folks to turn away from racial and religious divisions. He went there "to build a wall between McCain and the social conservatives." In other words, to suck up to folks who believe interracial dating should be banned and the pope is an antichrist.

They got the message. And so did we. The message we got was that, while far from prejudiced himself, Bush is shockingly comfortable in the presence of prejudice. As you may know, Bob Jones University has, shall we say, a colorful history:

According to a former student of Bob Jones University, the school president refused to fly the campus flag at half-mast after the Reverend Martin Luther King, Jr., was assassinated, and the president referred to King as an "apostate," one who had abandoned the Christian faith.

The school lost its tax-exempt status in 1970 for refusing to admit African-Americans. The school then changed its policy but still prohibited any interracial dating or marriage.

During a 1982 address in Iowa, then chancellor Bob Jones, Jr., defended Bob Jones University's rule barring interracial dating. Although the school was integrated in the 1970s, in 1982 it had only about a dozen African-Americans. According to Jones, Jr., "blacks aren't attracted to fundamentalism, and they don't like discipline."

In 1983, the U.S. Supreme Court again supported an IRS decision to remove tax-exempt status from the school for its dating policy, which included rules such as "students who date outside their own race will be expelled."

In March 2000, university president Bob Jones III announced that the school had abandoned its interracial dating policy, partially due to the attention the school had received since Bush's visit there. I salute Bob Jones for abandoning—albeit belatedly—its racially discriminatory policy. But the school defiantly continues to preach a rather nasty brand of anti-Catholic bigotry.

The Reverend Bob Jones has called the pope "an antichrist" who "brings a curse wherever he goes." The university's Web site includes a "Message from the President," Bob Jones himself, which describes both the Catholic and Mormon faiths as cults. Bob Jones University Press published a fifth-grade social studies textbook entitled *Heritage Studies for Christian Schools* used by fundamentalist schools around the country. The book describes Catholicism as a "false religion."

All of this was well documented before Bush went there. He knew or should have known about the school. Bush claims he went to Bob Jones not to endorse its message of exclusion, but to tout his message of inclusion. No, W, that's what Alan Keyes did. Keyes went to Bob Jones and spoke as an African-American married to an Indian-American. He spoke as a Catholic. He spoke the truth to power. W, you just kissed butt.

SALUTING THE CONFEDERATE FLAG

We Texans are not especially hung up on the Civil War. My friends from the Deep South call it "the War of Northern Aggression" and see much of their history and heritage through the distorted prism of that tragic experience.

Texans don't identify with losers. The Confederacy lost, and while Texas was a part of it, we did not have any of the crucial battles, nor did we produce any of the Confederacy's key leaders. We went along for the ride, largely, I suspect, because like our Southern neighbors Texas prospered from the sin of slavery. But we Texans haven't spent the last 135 years getting our panties in a wad over honoring the Lost Cause. As I said, we ain't much for honoring losers.

The Texas revolution looms large, and the mythic heroes of the Alamo are still our role models today. (Heck, one of my boys is named after the commander of the Alamo, William Travis, and I have nephews named after Stephen F. Austin and Sam Houston.) We have no need to venerate the racism of the Confederacy; we honor the heroism of the Republic of Texas.

Which is why I was so puzzled and angry over W's gutless performance on the issue of the Confederate flag flying over the state capitol in Columbia, South Carolina. Bush should have called a racist symbol by its name. But he didn't. He dodged and bobbed and weaved. He claimed states' rights. And even when an incredulous MSNBC's Brian Williams put him on the spot by asking him, "So, you have no reaction to the sight, as an American citizen, of that flag?" Bush replied, "No. Not in South Carolina, I do not."

No. Not in South Carolina he doesn't. Bush knew he needed the votes of racists and bigots to stop the reform movement of John McCain. So he hid behind the state's right to offend and insult.

Of course, Bush doesn't believe the state of Oregon has the right to decide whether it can legalize physician-assisted suicide. He doesn't believe any state should have the right to allow legal abortions. So forgive me if I don't buy W's principled support for states' rights on the Confederate flag. Besides, to hear anyone using the states' rights argument to support racism sounds more like George Wallace than George W. Bush.

A Few (Not So) Good Men

In a candid admission of his own lack of ability and experience, W is forever assuring us that he'll have good people around him. (As if a competent, intelligent, experienced leader would not?) So it's fair to look at what some of Bush's "good people" have had to say on the topic of race and equality in America:

"Porch Monkeys," "Black Bastards," and "N***** Charlie"

One of the few powers the governor of Texas has is the power to nominate people to high-level state jobs. So when it came time to appoint someone to take charge of all of the training for the state's law enforcement personnel, the mighty Bush brain swung into action. Of all the people he could have chosen, Bush decided the best man for the job was the police chief of Marshall, Texas, Charles W. Williams. So in November 1999, W elevated Chief Williams to chairman of the Texas Commission on Law Enforcement Standards and Education. A year before W made him chairman, Chief Williams had testified in a discrimination lawsuit that the terms "porch monkeys" and "black bastard" were not racial slurs. "If it's a general statement, no, I don't consider it a racial slur," Williams said.

As recently as April 6 of this year, Williams continued to defend his remarks. When asked by the Associated Press about his comments, Williams said, "You just have to show me where it's a racial slur. It just depends on how it's used and who it's used toward."

And it gets worse. According to the Associated Press,

Williams was asked in the same deposition about the "n-word." He stressed that he only used that word in advising others never to use it. But he also said that as a child fifty years ago in Oklahoma that word was used often, and that black people then didn't mind. "I was born and raised with blacks, and back then we had N***** Charlie and N***** Sam, N***** Joe, and we regarded those people with all the respect in the world. That was their name," said Williams. "They didn't mind. It wasn't any big deal then," he added. "It graduated from that to Negro, then it graduated to black, and now it's African-American. So to me that was not any different than me calling him an African-American today."

Now, I don't know Chief Williams, and I have no interest in judging him. I, too, can remember the n-word being used when I was a kid (and I'm about twenty years younger than the chief). It was never used as a term of respect. It was always used to demean, to denigrate, to dehumanize. I can also remember the side entrance to the Palms Theatre in Sugar Land, Texas. Folks who went through it went straight up to the balcony, while folks who used the front door went through the lobby. I remember asking why. Then someone told me that just above that side door they'd painted over the sign that used to say "Colored Entrance." Those words, those symbols, those insults, were all designed for a purpose. For someone to pretend otherwise is a sin against history.

Kinda makes you nervous about Bush making lifetime appointments, doesn't it?

HISPANICS DON'T CARE ABOUT UNWED PREGNANCIES?

If Chief Williams was the only controversial appointee

Bush had made, you might think I was making too much of it. But then again you probably don't know about Reyn Archer. Dr. William "Reyn" Archer is Bush's appointed health commissioner. He is also the son of Representative Bill Archer, the chairman of the powerful House Ways and Means Committee and the man who succeeded George Herbert Walker Bush in the House of Representatives. (I guess W has a soft spot for the moronic children of powerful politicians.) Dr. Archer is an MD, but he talks like a nutty professor. He once said that one cause of high teenage pregnancy rates in Texas is Hispanics' resistance to the notion that "getting pregnant is a bad thing." Sure, Reyn.

As Ricky Ricardo used to say, you got a lot of 'splainin' to do, Reyn. Here's how he tries to explain it: "Society values pregnancies in teenagers as bad, but certain communities within society may feel differently. I think the Hispanic community generally thinks that pregnancy is a positive thing. They tend to be less judgmental toward a teenager who's pregnant than the Anglo or African-American communities."

Dr. Doofus is also an equal opportunity offender. The *Houston Chronicle* reported that he had also made derogatory comments about African-Americans in a 1998 speech. Archer added that African-Americans were more loyal to each other, that he had seen cultures where loyalty is more important than honesty, and that blacks "don't buy" such cultural and legal institutions as marriage.

Anything else, Doc? Well, yes, frankly, the *Chronicle* also reported that Archer said that loyalty could explain why a black jury thought O.J. Simpson was innocent when most white people do not, or why blacks are loyal to Jesse Jackson when they don't agree with him, and that

"Anglos" were uninvited guests, perhaps, in their attempts to help the black community.

THE BOTTOM LINE

I don't believe for one minute that George W. Bush is a racist. My sense of him is that he doesn't have a prejudiced bone in his body. But he sure seems mighty comfortable in the presence of prejudice. Just like his Poppy was willing to let an independent group exploit the racial angle of the Willie Horton case, Bush is happy to get the support of people who think the pope is an antichrist, or who call black people "porch monkeys," or think Hispanics don't care about teen pregnancy.

Jefferson said slavery in America was like a fire bell in the night. While Bush's heart is in the right place, his sense of political expediency has led him to cover his ears so he can't hear the fire bell.

They Said It . . .

"Mr. Clinton better watch out if he comes down here. He'd better have a bodyguard."
—Senator Jesse Helms (R-NC), quoted in the *New York Times*, 11/23/94, a week after calling the President unfit to be commander-in-chief

INCOMPETENCE

*with quotes from Ronald Reagan, David Stockman, George H. W.
Bush, George W. Bush, Newt Gingrich, Henry Kissinger;
and quizzes from Paul Slansky*

Is it better to be mean or stupid? No worries: These guys are both. Some Republicans look and sound incredibly incompetent all of the time (think Ford, Quayle). Others look and sound incredibly incompetent some of the time (Bush, Bush). But the bottom line is that most Republicans are incompetent most of the time. They make up for it by being greedy and ruthless.

Who introduced George W. Bush at a campaign rally with this anecdote: "At one of these governors' conferences, George turns to me and says, 'What are they talking about?' I said, 'I don't know.' He said, 'You don't know a thing, do you?' And I said, 'Not one thing.' He said, 'Neither do I.' And we kind of high-fived"?

(a) New Mexico Governor Gary E. Johnson
(b) Minnesota Governor Jesse Ventura
(c) Florida Governor Jeb Bush
(d) Former Virginia Governor George Allen

Answer: (a)

What was reported to have led Brazilian President Fernando Henrique Cardoso to observe that Bush is "still learning"?

(a) Bush's unenforceable demand that Israel withdraw from the West Bank.

(b) The Bush administration's clumsy handling of the failed Venezuelan coup.
(c) Bush's policy reversals on steel tariffs and farm subsidies.
(d) Bush's ignorance of the fact that Brazil has the largest black population of any non-African nation, as revealed when he asked Cardoso, "Do you have blacks, too?"

Answer: (d)

They Said It . . .

"I believe that the future is far nearer than most of us would dare hope."
—Ronald Reagan, 1984

"How are you, Mr. Mayor? I'm glad to meet you. How are things in your city?"
—Ronald Reagan addressing his own housing secretary—the only black member of his Cabinet—at a White House reception for big-city mayors, 1981

"None of us really understands what's going on here with all these numbers . . ."
—David Stockman, Budget Director during the first Reagan administration, on the Reagan tax bill, 1981

"Almost every place you can point, contrary to Mr. Mondale's—I gotta be careful here—but contrary of how he goes around just saying everything bad. If somebody sees a silver lining, he finds a big black cloud out there. I mean, right on, whine on, harvest moon!"
—Vice-presidential candidate George H. W. Bush, in a debate with democratic candidate Geraldine Ferraro, 1984

"Facts are stupid things."
—Ronald Reagan, 1988, trying to quote John Adams, who said "Facts are stubborn things"

> *"I'm proud to be his partner. We've had triumphs, we've made mistakes, we've had sex."*
>
> **—Presidential candidate and Vice President George H. W. Bush referring to President Ronald Reagan in a speech at the College of Southern Idaho, 1988**

This passage from Paul Slansky's chronicle of the eighties encompasses the 1988 presidential campaign, which pitted George H. W. Bush and the inimitable Dan Quayle against Michael Dukakis and Lloyd Bentsen.

from *The Clothes Have No Emperor*

(1989)

Paul Slansky

8/14 Bush aides are reported to be talking up Indiana senator Dan Quayle, 41—a darling of the far right—as a possible running mate. Quayle appears on *This Week with David Brinkley*, where he mentions the name "George Bush" 10 times in two minutes. "George Bush is going to make this decision by himself," he says, "and whoever can help George Bush get elected President I'm sure will accept the nod, and that is the goal, because it is so important that we have George Bush as the next President of the United States." He also says the ongoing drought has been hard on the "coyn and sorbean" crops.

•

President Reagan arrives in New Orleans, where he calls the Democrats "liberal" 22 times in his arrival speech. "It's time to talk issues, to use the dreaded 'L' word," he says. "Liberal, liberal, liberal." He is presented with an enormous "Gipper's Gavel" to add to his vast collection of oversized props.

8/15 Russian comic Yakov ("What a country!") Smirnoff opens the Republican convention in New Orleans with the Pledge of Allegiance. Other notable first-day events:

- Bob Dole—who has displayed a perverse eagerness to serve as running mate to a man he despises—fatally damages his cause by describing the vice presidential selection process as "demeaning"
- Al Haig likens the Democratic party to a blind bat "hanging upside down in dark, damp caves up to its navel in guano"
- Nancy Reagan grits her teeth and says, "The time has come for the Bushes to step into the limelight and the Reagans to step into the wings"
- President Reagan delivers his farewell speech to the convention, misstating his catchphrase of the evening, "Facts are stubborn things," as a more-appropriate-for-him "Facts are stupid things."

•

UNDER YOKO'S SPELL
From the explosive new biography of John Lennon, scenes of despair, drugs and domination by his wife
—*People* excerpt from Albert Goldman's necrophiliac exhumation

8/16 After seeing the Reagans off at the airport—where he points out his half-Mexican grandkids as "the little brown ones"—George Bush, finally his own man, announces his first presidential decision: Dan Quayle, a "Man of the Future," will be his running mate. Quayle's youth and alleged good looks—he is billed as a Redford lookalike, though he in fact resembles Pat Sajak—are expected to blind women and baby boomers to his immaturity and hard-right views.

Quayle leaps out of the crowd and up to the podium, bouncing around as he waves his arms and shouts, "Believe me, we will win because America cannot afford to lose!" He grabs Bush's shoulder, almost punching him in the stomach as he brays, "Let's go get 'em!" Bush looks ill.

8/17 George Bush loses the parents-of-mauled-children vote by pledging that he and his running mate will campaign like "pit bulls." Meanwhile, Dan Quayle's debut on the national stage is an inauspicious one, as reporters focus in on several touchy areas. Among them:

• His connection to a 1980 sex scandal involving lobbyist Paula Parkinson—"It's been fully gone into," he says peevishly, "and if you don't know that, you should."
• His neanderthal voting record on civil rights, the environment and other progressive issues
• His embarrassing scholastic record
• His decision, despite vociferous support for the Vietnam War, to avoid the draft by joining the National Guard—"I did not know in 1969 that I would be in this room today, I'll confess"—and the

question as to whether his rich, influential parents pulled any strings on his behalf.

Democratic analyst Robert Squier notes that the GOP "could end up with a ticket [of] Wimp and War Wimp, and that's a tough one to try to campaign with."

8/18 ". . . accept your nomination . . . going to win . . . proud to have Dan Quayle . . . hold my charisma in check . . . don't hate government. . . scandal to give a weekend furlough to a hardened first-degree killer . . . Read! My! LIPS! No! New! Taxes! . . . kinder and gentler nation . . . go ahead, make my 24-hour time period . . . quiet man . . . hear the quiet people others don't . . . I am that man! . . . a thousand points of light . . . I pledge allegiance to the flag of the United States of America . . ."

> —George Bush, who, as did Michael Dukakis a month ago, succeeds in lowering expectations to the point where a competent speech is exalted as a dazzling display of oratorical pyrotechnics

8/19 A mob scene ensues in Dan Quayle's home town of Huntington when campaign aides pipe the sound from a contemptuous press interrogation of the candidate out to a rally of his supporters. Why, he is asked, if no influence was necessary, did he ask his parents to help him get into the National Guard?

"I do—I do—I do—I do what any normal person would do at that age," says Quayle. "You call home. You call home to mother and father and say, 'I'd like to get in the National Guard.'" Despite his barely passing grades, he claims eagerness to pursue his law school education, rather than fear for his safety, led to his decision. The response seems to satisfy his townsfolk, who chant, "BOR-ING! BOR-ING!" at reporters.

8/20 Campaigning with his running mate at the Ohio State Fair, George Bush compares reporters at the Quayle press conference to bluefish. "There was a flurry, there was a feeding flurry in the water out there," he says. "Have you ever seen them when they are just squirming all around and feeding in a frenzy. That's exactly what was happening."

Quayle, who warns that the US is "naked, absolutely nude to attack" by the Soviets, faces his first hecklers, who chant, "Quayle, Quayle called his mom/Everybody else went to Nam." They also shout "Chicken!" as hundreds of live fowl can be heard squawking nearby.

8/21 After coming face to face with a furious World War II vet who snarls, "You're a draft dodger," Dan Quayle is sent home for a crash course in campaigning, or, as the press dubs it, "Vice President school."

•

"This was a PR outfit that became President and took over the country."

> —Former Reagan press aide Leslie Janka,
> as quoted by Mark Hertsgaard in *On Bended Knee: The Press and the Reagan Presidency*, a book that convincingly points up the media's inadequacies and is therefore poorly reviewed by said media

8/22 "He did not go to Canada, he did not burn his draft card and he damn sure didn't burn the American flag! And I am proud to have him at my side!"

> —George Bush assuring a Veterans of Foreign Wars convention in Chicago that his running mate is innocent of a series of unmade charges

"My National Guard unit was never called up to active duty, but after the last 72 hours no one can say I never faced combat."

> —Dan Quayle, making amends with the Veterans of Foreign Wars by trivializing their experiences

•

"Don't let him fool you, America. He's about as close to Ronald Reagan in the area of national security as Winnie the Pooh is to Refrigerator Perry in the area of bears."

> —George Bush attacking Michael Dukakis in Chicago

•

FOREST FIRES RAGE IN WESTERN PARKS:
YELLOWSTONE HAS ITS WORST DAY—ARMY SENDING TROOPS
> —*The New York Times*

8/23 "If the Vice President is saying he'd sign an unconstitutional bill, then in my judgment he's not fit to hold the office."

> —Michael Dukakis, trailing in post-GOP convention polls, but confident that this is all he has to say to put an end to that pesky Pledge of Allegiance issue

•

Playboy reveals that Paula Parkinson told lawyers seven years ago that Dan Quayle "said he wanted to make love" and "flirted a lot and danced extremely close and suggestively" during that 1980 golf weekend in Florida. Quayle stages a taking-out-the-trash photo op to demonstrate what he thinks of such stories, demanding "some respect and dignity for things I did not do."

Meanwhile, James Quayle says his son Dan's main interests in school were "broads and booze."

8/25 "I don't know what his problem is with the Pledge of Allegiance. . . . His fervent opposition to the pledge is symbolic of an entire attitude best summed up in four little letters: ACLU. . . . He says—here's an exact quote—he says, 'I am a card-carrying member of the ACLU.' Well, I am not and I never will be."

> —George Bush, uncowed by his opponent's
> cries of "Unconstitutional!"

•

Dan Quayle cites, among his qualifications to be President, his eight years on the Senate Armed Services Committee, where his work with cruise missiles involved "getting them more accurate so that we can have precise precision."

Asked by a farmer about a local pork issue, Quayle says, "Whatever you guys want, I'm for," explaining that he knows "quite a bit about farm policies" because "I come from Indiana, a farm state." And what, then, is his message to farmers? "My message?" says Quayle, looking confused. He smiles and says nothing.

•

THE WORLD IS RUN BY C STUDENTS

"He was as vapid as student as I can ever recall. . . .
Nothing came out of his mouth that was worth
remembering."
> —Dan Quayle's political science professor,
Robert Sedlack, who said he would "inevitably think of
Dan Quayle" when he heard the phrase, "The World is
run by C students."

"Girls, golf and alcohol."
> —Dan Quayle's classmate describing his majors

"Dan Quayle was one of the few people able to get
from the Deke house to the golf course without
passing through a classroom."
> —Dan Quayle's English professor

"He received a D in political science, which was his
major, and his record was pretty much Cs."
> —Robert Sedlack

Right-wing Idaho senator Steve Symms claims to have
heard that there are photographs of Kitty Dukakis
"burning the American flag" in the '60s, though he, of
course, has not actually seen them.

8/26 Though the release of school records is a normal requirement for any number of positions, Dan Quayle—seeking to place himself a chicken bone away from the Presidency—refuses to divulge his. He concedes that his resume contains an inflated description of his job with the Indiana attorney general's office, though the error is blamed, oddly enough, on his staff.

8/27 "Although in public I refer to him as Mr. Vice President, in private I call him George. When he called, when I talked to him on the phone yesterday, I called him George rather than Mr. Vice President. But in public, it's Mr. Vice President because that's who he is."

> —Dan Quayle explaining the "intra-personal" relationship he has developed with George Bush

8/28 Asked what qualifications he would bring to the role of anti-drug czar, should he be so assigned, Dan Quayle claims to be familiar with the National Narcotics Border Interdiction System "in a general sense." He is asked who runs it. "Who is the head of it? I don't know who the head of it is," says Quayle. The answer? George Bush.

8/29 Michael Dukakis serenely embarks on a two-day tour of his home state, as if wresting the "Wimp" label away from George Bush hasn't just cost him 15–20 points in the national polls.

●

Jessica Hahn, the first celebrity to parlay a nude spread in *Playboy* into a radio job, starts work at Phoenix's KOY-FM as the "Morning Zoo Y95 Weather and Prize Bunny." One of the first listeners to phone in calls her a "slut."

8/30 Dan Quayle addresses a convention of fire chiefs, where he holds a fireman's hat over his head for cameras, but doesn't actually put it on, lest he disturb his coiffure.

8/31 Sen. Orrin Hatch calls the Democrats "the party of homosexuals," then denies he said it. A radio station produces the comment on tape.

●

At a Lake Erie campaign stop, George Bush declares, "I am an environmentalist," a statement Michael Dukakis finds so patently absurd that he sees no need to make sure the voters understand how truly Orwellian it is.

9/1 George Bush arrives in Boston for a ferry ride in what he calls "the dirtiest harbor in America"—a devastating invasion of their home turf that Dukakis aides have known about for days yet failed to combat. A local poll shows that the governor of Massachusetts has blown a 14-point lead in his home state.

9/2 "My opponent expressing concern about the environment is like George Steinbrenner expressing concern for managers."

—George Bush campaigning at a New Jersey beach

"Eeek! Eeek! Eeek!"

—George Bush being nipped repeatedly as he

empties traps aboard a Delaware crab boat,
after which he claims the Democrats remind
him of "what I brought out of that river—
blue crabs"

•

"There's two men running for President. . . . Michael
Dukakis [is] a liberal, and he doesn't want to admit it. . . .
George Bush [is] a pure opportunist, who's pretending
he's an arch-conservative. . . . They're the Duke and the
Dauphin, the two characters in *Huckleberry Finn*. . . . These
are guys who are charlatans. Neither one of them is telling
the truth."

—Political analyst Christopher Matthews

•

With a growing sense of doom settling on his campaign, Michael Dukakis rehires manager John Sasso, who
says—because what else can he say?—"I think the campaign is going incredibly well." Adds Dukakis campaign
chairman Paul Brountas, "The fact is, this campaign is in
excellent shape."

9/4 "Perestroika is nothing more than refined Stalinism."
—Dan Quayle displaying his unrefined
comprehension of the Soviet political system

9/5 Tammy Faye Bakker describes her last night in her
PTL mansion before being evicted by Jerry Falwell. "As I
lay on the floor in the dark, empty room," she says, "Tuppins, my puppy, licked at the tears running down my face.
'Oh, Tuppins,' I sobbed. 'Why has God forsaken me?'"

•

With both candidates fond of fish metaphors, George

Bush officially kicks off his campaign by struggling to fillet a freshly caught bass, while his tie dips into a bin of seafood. Afterward, he attacks his opponent's defense positions, claiming, "He thinks a naval exercise is something you find in Jane Fonda's workout book."

Meanwhile, at the Statue of Liberty, Dan Quayle's mind-numbing word-by-word analysis of the Pledge of Allegiance is interrupted by angry protesters who hoist hostile signs and shout, "40,000 dead from AIDS—where was Dan?" Says Quayle uneasily, "Who are these folks?"

9/6 "Dan Quayle's idea of a naval exercise is getting golf balls out of a water hazard."

—Dukakis aide Mark Gearan

9/7 "Today, you remember—I wonder how many Americans remember—today is Pearl Harbor Day. Forty-seven years ago to this very day we were hit and hit hard at Pearl Harbor. . . . Did I say September 7th? Sorry about that. December 7th, 1941."

—George Bush, who twice called Memorial Day "Veterans Day," promising voters a very special kind of continuity

9/8 "I could have been an atheist. I could have been a polygamist. I could have been anything else and questions wouldn't have been asked."

—Bush campaign worker Jerome Brentar, fired when his oft-voiced doubts about the existence of the Holocaust come to light

•

The two campaigns reach an agreement on debates: there will be two (Dukakis wanted three or four), the first will be September 25th (Dukakis wanted September 14th), the second will be October 13th or 14th (Dukakis wanted the end of October) and both will be general in subject matter (Dukakis wanted the first devoted solely to foreign policy).

Says Paul Brountas of the pact, "I'm pleased with it."

•

After the taping of a *Geraldo* about violent men and the battered women who kill them, a feminist and a wife-beater get into a brawl. "I see why your wife shot you!" screams the feminist. "You deserve to be shot in the head!" shouts the wife-beater. Rivera locks himself in his dressing room and drinks a gin and tonic until police arrive.

•

Believing himself to be at his best off the cuff, Dan Quayle dismays his advisers by abandoning his prepared text and delivering a rambling, incoherent speech that leaves his Chicago audience baffled. Among the highlights: his citing of the Tom Clancy novel *Red Storm Rising* as justification for building an anti-satellite weapon, and his citing of the philosophy of basketball coach Bobby Knight to support increased defense spending. Says an aide of this ad-libbing, "We didn't think he would deviate that far."

On the domestic front, he declares that Republicans "understand the importance of bondage between parent and child," though, of course, he means "bonding."

•

Dan Quayle's toothy, retro-coiffed wife, Marilyn, observes six times in the course of a single plane ride that she's "not getting paid" for serving as her husband's chief adviser. "Well, I'm working, but I'm still not getting paid," she says. "I'm still a lawyer, I'm just not paid." "I have no different role for Dan than his administrative assistant. It's just I don't get paid." Etc.

She also defends her spouse's much-maligned intellect, claiming that he "really is the studious sort" who "tries to read Plato's *Republic* every year" (though she does not reveal if he has ever succeeded), and points out that "Franklin Roosevelt was a lousy student. He failed the bar exam seven times." In fact, FDR took the test once, as a second-year law student, and passed.

9/9 Surrendering to Republican pressure, Jim Wright announces that the Pledge of Allegiance will be recited in the House twice a week.

•

Addressing a sweaty, T-shirted audience at an Ohio steel plant, a suit-clad Dan Quayle declares, "I can identify with steelworkers. I can identify with workers that have had a difficult time." He claims to have defended steel quotas in a face-to-face encounter with President Reagan, looking him "right across the eyes." Says one worker of Quayle's appeal, "It's a long way off yet."

•

"I got into law school fair and square. Nothing improper was done and no rules were broken."

> —Dan Quayle responding to a report that his college grades were so low that his entry into law school was dependent on a special "equal opportunity" program primarily intended to increase minority admissions

continued on page 259

......

THE QUAYLE WIT

"I understand you have a balloon festival here. Well, you ought to invite Michael Dukakis. He's got a lot of hot air."

—Dan Quayle campaigning in Albuquerque

"I can understand why Michael Dukakis doesn't fit in too well down here. He thinks a longhorn is something you play in the Boston Symphony."

—Campaigning across Texas

"The only thing that zigs and zags more than the Rio Grande is our opponent's positions on the issues."

—Campaigning in El Paso

"He thinks an oilman is someone who just went swimming in Boston Harbor."

—Campaigning in Wisconsin

"His idea of farm production is growing flowers in Harvard Yard."

—On the agricultural policies of Michael Dukakis

"You have even more snow here than comes out of the mouth of the man from Massachusetts."

—Campaigning at an Ohio ski lodge

......

from page 257

9/11 Bush campaign aide Fred Malek resigns after the resurfacing of a previously reported revelation that, in 1971, he followed President Nixon's orders and compiled a list of Jews at a government bureau.

9/12 Six more Bush campaign advisers quit amid charges of anti-Semitism.

•

TV PREMIERE: *USA Today: The Television Show*—a daily TV version of the newspaper that set out to be a print version of TV. "We're taking television into the next decade," says producer Steve Friedman. "Twenty-five years from now, people will look back at this show and call it one of the most influential shows in television."

9/13 Touring the General Dynamics plant in Michigan, Michael Dukakis puts on an enormous green helmet and rides around in the turret of an M-l Battle Tank, evoking unhelpful media comparisons to Snoopy and Rocky the Flying Squirrel. Explains an aide, "He said he wanted to hear what the other guys in the tank were saying. Fine. But he looked like an idiot."

•

"Want to hear a sad story about the Dukakis campaign? The governor of Massachusetts, he lost his top naval adviser last week. The rubber duck drowned in his bathtub."
                            —Dan Quayle campaigning in Milwaukee

9/14 "Back under the previous Administration, things were rough in the flag business. . . . Well, since we began restoring pride in the United States of America, business has been booming. Flag sales have taken off."

—George Bush campaigning in Orange County

•

Landslide: The Unmaking of the President: 1984–88, by White House correspondents Jane Mayer and Doyle McManus, reveals that Reagan was so detached during the Iran-contra scandal that aides signed his initials to documents without his knowledge. Says an aide to Howard Baker of Reagan's underlings, "They told stories about how inattentive and inept the President was. . . . They said he wouldn't come to work—all he wanted to do was to watch movies and television at the residence."

9/15 Howard Baker confirms that when he became chief of staff, there was some concern about the President's ability to remain in office. But, he says, he instantly found Reagan to be "the most presidential man I've ever known," and that was that.

Says the President of the *Landslide* report, "No truth at all." In other words, fiction.

•

Asked about the Holocaust during a rare news conference, Dan Quayle calls it "an obscene period in our nation's history." Reminded that the Holocaust did not take place in America, he explains that "in this century's history" is what he meant to say. "We all lived in this century," he says, adding cryptically, "I didn't live in this century."

9/16 Defending his campaign against charges of ethnic prejudice, George Bush says, "I hope I stand for anti-bigotry, anti-Semitism, anti-racism." He goes on to mis-quote, of all things, the Pledge of Allegiance: "And to the liberty for which it stands, one nation under God with freedom and justice for all."

Meanwhile, Dan Quayle repeatedly calls Belgian endive "Belgium endive."

●

The 1988 Summer Olympics begin in Seoul, South Korea. Among the highlights:

- US middleweight Anthony Hembrick is eliminated when his coaches misread the schedule and he arrives 12 minutes late for his match
- Greg Louganis smashes his head on the diving board but goes on to win a gold medal
- A referee is attacked in the ring by the coaches of a losing South Korean boxer
- Two US gold-medal swimmers are arrested for stealing a marble lion's head from a hotel
- Canadian track star Ben Johnson is stripped of his gold medal for using steroids.

NBC broadcasts a numbing 179½ hours of competition—less a considerable chunk for commercials—which, given the serious lack of interest among US viewers, is overkill of a high order.

9/17 "There's a lot of things we can refer to the man from Massachusetts as. We can call him 'Mr. Tax Increase.' We can call him 'Mr. Polluter.' We can call him 'Mr. Weak on National Defense.' But let me tell you something. Come November 8th, there's one thing we'll never call the governor of Massachusetts, and that is 'Mr. President.' "

> —Dan Quayle, described by an adviser as
> "the future standing right up there"

9/19 MICHAEL JACKSON'S PLASTIC FACE IS MELTING—
SAYS SURGEON

—Star

•

A CRY FOR HELP

Fearing for her life, friends of Robin Givens leak a frightening story of Mike Tyson's private violence and his threat to kill them both.

—People

•

Bobby McFerrin's "Don't Worry, Be Happy"—adopted, with no irony, as the Bush campaign's theme song—begins two weeks as the nation's Number One song.

9/20 "I've never been to a flag factory!"

—George Bush in New Jersey,
visiting his first one

"Wouldn't working here lift your spirits?"

—Senate candidate Pete Dawkins to Bush as
they leave the actually quite grim workplace

"We took it exactly one day too far."

—Bush aide responding to the "Enough with
the flag, already!" stories on all three
network newscasts

9/21 "Go back and tell George Bush to start talking about the issues."

—Barry Goldwater stunning Dan Quayle
at an Arizona campaign stop

THE QUOTABLE QUAYLE

"The real question for 1988 is whether we're going to go forward to tomorrow or past to the—to the back!"

"We will invest in our people, quality education, job opportunity, family, neighborhood, and yes, a thing we call America."

"We'll let the sunshine come in and shine on us, because today we're happy and tomorrow we'll be even happier."

"We're going to have the best-educated American people in the world."

"This election is about who's going to be the next president of the United States!"

9/23 Michael Deaver gets three years in prison (suspended), 1,500 hours of community service, and a $100,000 fine. "It was a very fair sentence," he says, "if I had been guilty."

•

An MTV poll finds that by a 42%–27% margin, its viewers think Michael Dukakis would be the "most fun on a cross-country road trip." Dukakis also ekes out a 37%–36% victory on the question of who "would throw the best parties," though more viewers [43%–36%] want to have dinner at George Bush's house.

9/25 Billy Carter, 51, dies of pancreatic cancer in Plains, Georgia.

•

Marilyn Quayle and her parents are reported to be followers of Col. Robert B. Thieme, Jr., a far, far right-wing preacher who has been known to wear his Air Force uniform in the pulpit. His specialty is Armageddon.

•

At their first debate in Winston-Salem, North Carolina, Michael Dukakis:

> • Unconvincingly claims to "resent" the slurs on his patriotism
> • Attempts to soften his "Zorba the Clerk" image by emotionlessly declaring, "I care deeply about people, all people"
> • Finds himself laughed at when he says he's "very tough on violent crime"
> • Can be seen smirking toothily whenever his opponent speaks.

George Bush, meanwhile:

> • Says "there's plenty" of weapons systems he opposes, naming three that have already been cut
> • Complains about the cocaine scene in *Crocodile Dundee* and refers to a drug addict as "a narcotics-wrapped-up guy"

• Refers to Dukakis as the "Ice Man"
• Admits he has not yet "sorted out" what the penalties should be if abortion is again made illegal, leaving open the possibility that he would jail women who have them.

9/26 James Baker says that after the debate George Bush decided that women shouldn't go to jail for having abortions after all, but maybe the doctors who perform them should.

•

Time runs a photo of Dan Quayle with a fly resting between his eyebrows.

9/27 "Bush skitters like a waterbug on the surface of things, strewing fragments of thoughts, moving fast lest he linger so long that he is expected to show mastery of, or even real interest in, anything."
                    —Columnist George Will on the debate

"What also came through . . . is the utter banality of Bush's intellect. His mind is organized like a factory-outlet store—everything scattered around and nothing worth more than $49.95."
                    —Columnist Ross K. Baker

"The debate sharpened the choice . . . a man who can't express his thoughts or a man who can't express his feelings."
                    —Columnist Mary McGrory

•

"I would think very exciting."
                    —Lloyd Bentsen on what life would be like
                    under President Quayle

9/28 Country singers Loretta Lynn, Crystal Gayle and Peggy Sue travel on George Bush's bus tour across central Illinois. "He's country and I love him," Lynn tells a crowd. "George Bush. Phew!" And just how much does she dislike Michael Dukakis? "Why, I can't even pronounce his name!"

9/29 No longer taken for granted, the space shuttle *Discovery* is the center of attention as it blasts off without blowing up, ending a 32-month US absence from space.

•

"Hello, everybody, I'm Dan Quayle."

> —Robert Redford campaigning with Michael Dukakis in New Jersey

•

Fawn Hall's agent says she's writing her autobiography.

•

The Nobel Peace Prize, which the First Lady was known to covet as the perfect going-away present for her husband, goes to the UN peacekeeping forces. Says one former Reagan aide, "They had very, very high hopes. Nancy must be wearing black."

9/30 Delivering his standard speech in Texas, Michael Dukakis suddenly refers to his father as "my daddy."

•

The Dukakis campaign begins broadcasting "The Packaging of George Bush," an incomprehensible series of ads purporting to depict cynical Bush aides thinking up ways to manipulate the voters. Observes one political consultant, "It took me 10 seconds before I realized it wasn't a Bush spot."

•

"He had a great time. I didn't think we were ever going to get him out of the booth."

> —Marlin Fitzwater on President Reagan's visit to Wrigley Field, where he did the play-by-play of the first inning of a Cubs-Pirates game, taking the opportunity to tell some of his favorite sportscasting stories

•

Mike Tyson sits calmly beside wife Robin Givens as she tells Barbara Walters that he's a violent manic depressive and life with him is "torture . . . pure hell . . . worse than anything I could possibly imagine." Two days later police are called to their New Jersey estate after the champion begins throwing large objects through the windows. Givens files for divorce within days.

10/3 BRUCE'S NEW LOVE

Here's the lowdown on Springsteen's mystery woman, Patti Scialfa, the 35-year-old Jersey Girl who displaced actress Julianne Phillips, 29, and brought the Boss back to his roots

> —*People*

10/4 The Bush campaign begins airing a stark black-and-white spot featuring prisoners going through a revolving door. An ominous voice-over talks about "weekend furloughs to first-degree murderers" while misleading statistics about Dukakis' record on crime are flashed on the screen.

•

"The liberal governor of Massachusetts—I love calling him that!"

> —George Bush campaigning in Albuquerque

"You are such a weenie."

> —University of Pennsylvania student
> greeting Dan Quayle

•

Stephen Mernick, an Orthodox Jew, buys PTL for $115 million.

10/5 On the morning of his debate with Lloyd Bentsen, Dan Quayle visits the Omaha Civic Auditorium to check out the debate site. "You're going to see Dan Quayle as he really is," he tells reporters. Inside, an ABC camera crew catches him rehearsing with Bush media adviser Roger Ailes. "Hey, Roger," he says nervously, "does . . . on, on this, you know, if I'm gonna, if I, if I decide on my gesture over there . . . is that all right . . . you don't mind?"

Leaving the hall after a sound check, he declares, "The mike works. That's very important to make sure the mike works and ours is working well."

•

Asked three times at the debate what he would actually do if he suddenly became President—and three times robotically reciting his meager qualifications—Dan Quayle testily observes, "I have as much experience in the Congress as Jack Kennedy did when he sought the Presidency."

"Senator," says Lloyd Bentsen somberly, delivering what is instantly recognized as the sound bite of the night, "I served with Jack Kennedy. I knew Jack Kennedy. Jack Kennedy was a friend of mine. Senator, you're no Jack Kennedy."

"That was really uncalled for, Senator," whimpers Quayle, affecting the look of a wounded fawn.

"*You're* the one who was making the comparison, Senator," Bentsen shoots back, "and I'm one who knew him well. And frankly I think you're so far apart in the objectives you choose for your country that I did not think the comparison was well taken."

•

"After seeing Quayle, I could not vote for Bush."
>   —Toledo carpenter Greg Kretz, a member of
>   the national 2-1 majority that thinks Lloyd
>   Bentsen wiped the floor with his opponent

"When you think about what might have happened, we have to be pretty happy."

>   —Campaign chief James Baker
>   assessing the Quayle performance

10/6 "I think that remark was a cheap shot unbecoming a senator of the United States."
>   —President Reagan—who not too long ago
>   called Michael Dukakis an "invalid"—
>   complaining about Lloyd Bentsen's assault on
>   Quayle

•

"Clint Eastwood's answer to violent crime is, 'Go ahead, make my day.' My opponent's answer is slightly different. His motto is, 'Go ahead, have a nice weekend.' "
>   —George Bush campaigning in Texas

10/7 Michael Dukakis travels to a Missouri automotive parts plant to decry foreign ownership of American businesses, blissfully unaware that the plant is owned by Italians. "Maybe the Republican ticket wants our children to work for foreign owners and owe their future to foreign owners," he declares, "but that's not the kind of future Lloyd Bentsen and I want for America." Crowd response is muted.

•

Dan Quayle, whose handlers are struggling to fool people into thinking he's not an immature brat, sprays water on reporters during a campaign stop. "This is for all the articles you've written about me," he says.

•

"Dan Quayle can no longer be dismissed as a public man incapable of enlarging his stature. On Wednesday afternoon, he was only a vague misfortune for the Republicans, and overnight, he swelled himself close to the proportions of a disaster."

—Murray Kempton

10/10 Dan Quayle is again asked what he would do if he had to assume the Presidency. "Certainly, I know what to do," he says angrily, "and when I am Vice President—and I will be—there will be contingency plans under different sets of situations and I tell you what, I'm not going to go out and hold a news conference about it. I'm going to put it in a safe and keep it there! Does that answer your question?"

10/12 Humiliated by Bush aides who describe their job as having to "potty train" him, Dan Quayle declares his independence from his handlers. "Lookit," he says, "I've done it their way this far and now it's my turn. I'm my own handler. Any questions? Ask me. . . . There's not going to be any more handler stories because I'm the handler. . . . I am Doctor Spin." Speculation begins instantly that his handlers told him to say this.

•

On the eve of the second Bush/Dukakis debate, ABC's evening news devotes more than half its broadcast to a new poll showing George Bush with a virtually guaranteed electoral vote landslide.

DANNY, WE HARDLY KNEW YE

"I've had that stigma since I first ran for the Senate. It's stuck ever since. I think I have a feeling of what Jack Kennedy went through."
—Dan Quayle on his resemblance to Robert Redford

"I'm very close to the same age as Jack Kennedy when he was elected, not Vice President, but President."
—Dan Quayle campaigning in Boonville, Missouri

"I would point out that he has held elective Federal office for 12 years, virtually the same as John F. Kennedy when he ran for President."
—Dan Quayle's dad writing in *The New York Times*

"I've had 12 years of service, the same years of service that John Kennedy had before he ran for President, and I'd be glad to compare my legislative accomplishments . . . with his accomplishments."
—Dan Quayle

10/13 Scientific tests prove that the Shroud of Turin—believed by Catholics to be Christ's burial cloth—was a fake created no earlier than the mid-13th century.

"Most alarming is his staunch refusal to inform the public about his performance in college and law school—or to provide his academic and his disciplinary records. He has admitted 'mediocre grades,' but he won't release the records. If he has nothing to hide, why has he permitted rumors to persist, not only about poor grades, but disciplinary actions for plagiarism and the hiring of surrogates to take his exams?"

—Full-page ad in major US newspapers demanding, "RELEASE DAN QUAYLE'S COLLEGE RECORDS NOW"

•

"It's everything he's ever done, basically."

—UCLA anti-Bush protester Liela Rand explaining her distaste for the candidate

•

Michael Dukakis arrives at UCLA with one goal for the second debate: act like a normal human. He wastes no time demonstrating his inability to do so, answering Bernard Shaw's unusually blunt first question—"If Kitty Dukakis were raped and murdered, would you favor an irrevocable death penalty for the killer?"—with a bloodless recital of his opposition to capital punishment and the importance of fighting drugs. The race is understood to be over.

For his part, Bush again reminds viewers that Dukakis "equated the President to a rotting *fish!* He said that!" Afterward, Dukakis quickly scurries off stage, leaving Bush alone to bask in his triumph.

10/14 Welcoming the crew of the space shuttle *Discovery* to the White House, President Reagan wonders aloud how long it will be before "the children of America turn to their parents and say, 'Gee, Mom and Dad, can I borrow the spaceship tonight?' " No one hazards a guess.

•

NOW PLAYING: *The Accused*, starring Jodie Foster as a gang-rape victim. St. Elizabeths does not suggest a field trip for John W. Hinckley, Jr.

10/15 "I'm picking up Bush vibrations/He's the best guy to lead this nation."

> —Beach Boys Mike Love and Bruce Johnston
> serenading Bush rallies in California

•

NUCLEAR HAZARDS AT OHIO WEAPON PLANT WERE ALLOWED BY U.S. FOR DECADES

> —*The New York Times*

10/16 "Now, I'm having trouble with these questions, because they are putting me beyond where I want to be. . . . I am focusing on November 8th, and I don't want to be dragged beyond that."

> —George Bush taking reporters' questions
> for the first time in 18 days, annoyed that
> they keep asking what he'd do as President

•

DUKAKIS PLOTS STRATEGY TO WIN WITH 18 STATES: CAMP SEEKS TO DISPEL NOTION BUSH HAS WON

> —*The Washington Post*

10/17 Michael Dukakis meets with a supporter in a Cleveland diner. "Let's kick some ass out there, okay?" the man says. "Okay," says Dukakis dully. "Very good. We'll do it."

"I hope this means our liberal congressional friends are dropping their nostalgia for the 'do your own thing in your own time, baby' 1960s."

>—President Reagan on efforts to pass a bill
>mandating the death penalty for drug
>kingpins

○

Lisa Marie Presley

LOVE ME TENDER

Elvis's little girl, now 20 and pregnant with his first grandchild, comes out of the shadows to marry her Scientologist boyfriend.

>—*People*

○

Elaine Crispen confirms that, despite her 1982 announcement that she would not do it anymore, Nancy Reagan has continued to receive free designer clothing over the past six years. "She made a promise not to do this again and she broke her little promise," says Crispen, who points out—as Reagan aides so often seem to do—that no actual laws were broken.

10/18 "Our hearts are with you."

>—President Reagan, whose tolerance for the
>suffering of poor humans is boundless,
>phoning the Alaskan National Guard to offer
>his support in the effort to rescue three
>whales trapped under ice

○

"I am the future."

>—Dan Quayle

○

THE CRITICS ON DAN QUAYLE

"He doesn't have the greatest smarts in the world."
—James Quayle, Dan's dad

"He is not a ruminating creature. His nesting place is the mindless crowd, and his native woodnote the barbaric yawp. . . . The back of Dan Quayle's head is beginning to bald and his pale eyes sit upon a balcony of crow's feet and there is the alarming suspicion that he will too soon be wrinkled and yet still be callow and too early grown old before he has really grown up."
—Murray Kempton

"He has a smile that can be as unctuous as Jerry Falwell's, and too lean and hungry a look much of the rest of the time."
—Tom Shales

Children's Express reporter Suki Chong, 11, interviews Dan Quayle for a PBS show about the candidates. "Let's suppose I was sexually molested by my father and I became pregnant," she begins. "Would you want me to carry that baby to term?"

"My answer would be yes," says the visibly uncomfortable candidate, who looks younger than his inquisitor.

"But, don't you think this would *ruin my whole life?*" asks the girl.

"I would just like to see the baby have an opportunity."

"So," says Chong, with a directness infuriatingly lacking in her older colleagues, "although you're not actually killing me, you would sacrifice my prospects for the future for that baby."

"See, I've gotten to know you just a little bit," says Quayle, "and you're a very strong woman. You're a strong person. And . . . though this would be a traumatic experience that you would never forget, I think that you would be very successful in life."

Later, she asks Bush campaign manager Lee Atwater if the message the choice of Quayle sends is that "kids should get average grades in schools." Atwater claims Quayle "wasn't an average student." Replies Chong contemptuously, "Of course he was."

10/19 "Friends, this is garbage. This is political garbage."
—Michael Dukakis finally fighting back,
attacking an Illinois GOP flier claiming, "All
the murderers and rapists and drug pushers
and child molesters in Massachusetts vote for
Michael Dukakis"

10/20 "For a public official's spouse to be 'on the take' is wrong, plain and simple. Nancy Reagan knew it, hid it for years, lied when caught, and now seeks to have a flock of taxpayer-paid press agents explain her ethical lapse away . . ."
—William Safire on the First Lady's inability
to just say no when it comes to her clothing
addiction

•

"We have gold and yellow and some red and, believe

me, those are Republican colors. Bold colors, bright colors, future colors! You know what our opponents' colors are? Gray and dark gray!"

> —Dan Quayle talking about the fall colors in rural Ohio

•

NBC agrees to pull an ad for *Favorite Son*, a six-hour miniseries about kinky sex in Washington, after Bush campaign aides complain that the promotional copy—"He's a handsome, charismatic young senator. He's campaigning for a place in the White House. But something in his past could cost him the election"—could reflect badly on Dan Quayle.

10/21 "If I'm elected President, if I'm remembered for anything, it would be this: a complete and total ban on chemical weapons. Their destruction forever. That's my solemn mission."

> —George Bush, who cast several tie-breaking votes in the Senate to resume production of nerve gas

•

"George Bush says he hears the quiet people other's don't. I have a friend in Los Angeles who hears the quiet people others don't, and he has to take a lot of medication for it."

> —Albert Brooks campaigning for Michael Dukakis

10/24 Convicted killer John Wayne Gacy objects to his name being used "to scare people into voting for George Bush" in a campaign flier claiming he'd be eligible for weekend furloughs if he'd committed his 33 murders in Massachusetts.

•

Dan Quayle is asked whether he'd want his wife to have the baby if she were raped and became pregnant. In the event of such a "tragic" situation, he says, he would hope that she "would have the child." And how he would feel about raising, say, Willie Horton's child? He is not asked.

•

Okay, our focus: Are Babies Being Bred for Satanic Sacrifice? Controversial, to say the least. Unbelievable, to say the least. Disgusting, to say the least. We'll be right back."

> —Geraldo Rivera cutting to a commercial
> on his daily talk show

10/25 ". . . Drinking blood . . .grave robbing . . . mutilated animals . . . drinking her 15-year-old victim's blood . . . gouged out his victim's eyes . . . butchered his mother . . . cut the ears off . . . drinking his own blood. . . . The acts . . . are so horrible that the question could fairly be raised again: why are we doing this broadcast?"

> —Geraldo Rivera presenting his first—and last—NBC
> special, *Devil Worship: Exposing Satan's Underground*,
> which *The New York Times* calls "pornography mas-
> querading as journalism"

"What must it be like to a father to think that his own son was disposed of in bits and pieces and thrown in the garbage?"

> —Geraldo to the parent of a victim, needing to know

"That man is so repugnant. All of these satanic murderers are."

> —Geraldo making it clear that, though he loves

to recycle excerpts from his interview with "today's top satanic celebrity," Charles Manson, personally he can't stand him

"Geraldo should be arrested for exposing himself."
—Former NBC News president Reuven Frank
on the Rivera oeuvre

•

"What is it about the Bush campaign that has absolutely nailed you to the wall?"
—Ted Koppel to Michael Dukakis during a stultifying appearance on *Nightline*, where the candidate uses his precious time to remind voters why his election is even more unthinkable than Bush's

10/27 Continuing his free media blitz, Michael Dukakis tells Dan Rather that he might not have responded to Bush's attacks "as quickly as I should have."

•

"I would guess that there's adequate low-income housing in the country."
—Dan Quayle offering a very uneducated guess about the homeless situation

10/28 *The Philadelphia Daily News* says it "could have endorsed the 1979–80 George Bush," but not the 1988 version "who pretends, despite all the evidence, that J. Danforth Quayle is not a callow moron."

continued on page 281

....

WHAT'S QUAYLE'S SIGN?

Among the placards and banners greeting the candidate on the campaign trail:

"Quayle: Intensely Mediocre"

"War Hero? Rich Boy"

"VPs Should Be Better than C Students"

"Honk if you're smarter than Dan Quayle"

"Did your daddy get you this job, too?"

"Spoiled Rich Sissy"

"Dan, Call Me!" (girl w/phone number on sign)

"Definition of a Quayle: Two right wings and no backbone"

"Dan, who took your law exam for you?"

"Vote for Quayle or Manson gets out of jail"

"Quayle's no J.F.K."

"He's not Quayleified."

"Dan Quayle is an Awesome Dude"

....

from page 279

10/29 "My only hope for those whales is that they don't end up in Boston Harbor."

> —George Bush doing shtick about the two surviving creatures, who are heading back to the open sea

10/30 DUKAKIS MAY BE STAGING COMEBACK:
LONGTIME DEMOCRATS IN KEY BIG STATES LEAVE BUSH AS POLLS SHOW GAP CLOSING

> —*Los Angeles Times*

•

"I'm a liberal in the tradition of Franklin Roosevelt and Harry Truman and John Kennedy."

> —Former moderate technocrat Michael Dukakis discovering the joys of populism as he goes into the last full week of the campaign 10 points behind

10/31 "Miracle of miracles! Headlines! Read all about it! My opponent finally, after knocking me in the debate, called himself the big 'L,' called himself a liberal."

> —George Bush, reverting to hysteria as the clock runs out

•

The Islamic Jihad releases a taped statement by Terry Anderson—held in Lebanon since March 1985—in which he accuses the US of blocking efforts to free him and the other hostages. "I don't think that was Terry speaking," says President Reagan. "I think he had a script that was given to him. When I was given a script, I always read the lines."

•

Dan Quayle crashes through a paper pumpkin at a Halloween rally in a Michigan high school.

11/1 Campaigning in California, President Reagan quotes that well-known character "Huckleferry Binn."

11/2 "It seemed like he appeared on every television show except *Wheel of Fortune*. You see, he was afraid that Vanna might turn over the 'L' word."

> —George Bush attacking Michael Dukakis
> for going on TV

> "If he's Harry Truman, I'm Roger Rabbit."
>> —President Reagan, attacking Dukakis while
>> demonstrating that when it comes to inane
>> pop-culture references, he still has no peer

•

Asked if the woman raped by Willie Horton should have had his baby if she'd become pregnant, Dan Quayle says yes. He goes on to display his continuing gynecological ignorance, claiming that rape victims wouldn't need to worry about abortions if they'd just submit to the "normal medical procedure" of a "D & C" (dilation and curettage) right afterward. In fact, uterus scraping is never part of post-rape care, since a fertilized egg takes several days to enter the womb.

11/3 "I only play the Terminator in my movies. But let me tell you, when it comes to the American future, Michael Dukakis will be the real Terminator!"

> —Arnold Schwarzenegger campaigning for George Bush

•

"Respond to the attacks immediately. Don't let them get away with a thing."
> —Michael Dukakis revealing what he's learned from the campaign, though not explaining why he needed to learn it again, having been beaten by a similar campaign 10 years earlier

•

Geraldo Rivera gets a long-overdue comeuppance during the taping of a sweeps-month segment on "Teen Hatemongers" when talk show brawler Roy Innis, with the host's blessing, attempts to throttle a white supremacist. During the resulting melee—the logical culmination of a year of increasingly confrontational TV programming—a chair lands in the sensation-mongering host's face, demolishing his nose.

11/4 Oklahoma prison inmate Brett Kimberlin, who has been trying to call a press conference to claim that he used to sell marijuana to Dan Quayle, is placed in solitary confinement.

•

'VIRUS' IN MILITARY COMPUTERS DISRUPTS SYSTEMS NATIONWIDE: EXPERTS CALL IT THE LARGEST ASSAULT EVER ON THE NATION'S SYSTEMS
> —The New York Times

11/5 AUTHOR OF COMPUTER 'VIRUS' IS SON OF N.S.A. EXPERT ON DATA SECURITY
> —The New York Times

•

"If you ask me, as Robert Palmer has been singing recently, you are simply irresistible."
> —President Reagan responding to cheers
> from college students

11/6 George Bush rejects poll results showing most voters blame him for the negative tone of the campaign, citing instead "those personal attacks night after night on me, on my character at that idiotic Democratic convention."

•

"He's slipping and sliding, we're rocking and rolling."
> —Michael Dukakis, ending his campaign
> with a marathon 48-hour, nine-state blitz

•

"In the primaries . . . it was enough for him then not to be Jesse Jackson, and he seems to have taken it for granted that it would be enough thereafter not to be George Bush. Not being Jesse Jackson worked but not being George Bush apparently hasn't, and now he must try to arise and say in thunder just who Michael Dukakis is, and the gifts of nature and the allotment of time look too small to equip him for that job."
> —Murray Kempton on Michael Dukakis

11/7 "So, if I could ask you one last time, tomorrow, when mountains greet the dawn, will you go out there and win one for the Gipper?"
> —President Reagan making his last campaign
> appearance on behalf of George Bush, whose
> half-hour election-eve TV ad omits any men-
> tion of a Mr. Dan Quayle

11/8 Dan Quayle celebrates Election Day with a bizarrely ritualistic visit to the dentist. Though he and George Bush are elected by a 54%–46% margin, polls show that Quayle cost the ticket at least 2% of the vote. The Democrats win 10 states and 112 electoral votes, their best showing since 1976. Voter turnout—50.16%—is the lowest since 1924.

11/9 George Bush names campaign chief James Baker Secretary of State.

11/10 John Mitchell, the only US Attorney General to do time in jail, dies of a heart attack at 75.

11/14 "As we sat in front of our TV set, we realized that something had changed. No longer did the programming include, at regular intervals, footage of violent criminals going through revolving doors, recitations of the horrors that might be visited on peace-loving Americans if a 'card-carrying member of the ACLU' became President, or bursts of talk about Boston Harbor and 'Taxachusetts.' George Bush was not even President yet, and the United States was already a kinder and gentler place, because the Bush campaign was over."

—*The New Yorker's* Talk of the Town

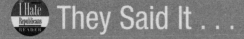

"A tax cut is really one of the anecdotes to coming out of an economic illness."
—George W. Bush, 2000

"And so, in my State of the—my State of the Union—or state—my speech to the nation, whatever you want to call it, speech to the nation—I asked Americans to give 4,000 years—4,000 hours over the next—the rest of your life—of service to America. That's what I asked—4,000 hours."
—George W. Bush, 2002

Quiz
Paul Slansky

Complete this quote by Ron Reagan: "The big elephant sitting in the corner is that George W. Bush is simply unqualified for the job. What is his accomplishment?

(a) That he decided that he would never again brand someone with a hot metal coat hanger?"
(b) That he managed to stonewall the media on the coke thing?"
(c) That he's learned not to make fun of people he's executed?"
(d) That he's no longer an obnoxious drunk?"

Answer: (d)

Quiz
Paul Slansky

Complete this quote by the *Times* columnist Gail Collins: "If Dan Quayle looked like a deer caught in the headlights when he was in front of the cameras, [George W.] Bush sometimes resembles

(a) a proud lion, fiercely defending his positions as if they were his cubs."

(b) a salmon struggling to swim upstream."

(c) a raccoon pawing through the empties behind the frat house."

(d) a possum cornered in the garage—hunched over, tense, eyes darting worriedly."

Answer: (d)

They Said It . . .

"I believe the results of focusing our attention and energy on teaching children to read and having an education system that's responsive to the child and to the parents, as opposed to mired in a system that refuses to change, will make America what we want it to be—a literate country and a hopefuller country."
—George W. Bush, 2001

"You teach a child to read, and he or her will be able to pass a literacy test."
—George W. Bush, 2001

"This is the Democratic Machine's reces-sion, and each one of them will be held personally accountable."
—Newt Gingrich, 1993, during the second year of an eight-year economic boom

"They want the federal government con-trolling Social Security, like it's some kind of federal program."
—George W. Bush, 2001

Satire:

Bush: 'Our Long National Nightmare of Peace And Prosperity Is Finally Over'

from *The Onion* (2000)

Washington, DC—Mere days from assuming the presidency and closing the door on eight years of Bill Clinton, president-elect George W. Bush assured the nation in a televised address Tuesday that "our long national nightmare of peace and prosperity is finally over."

"My fellow Americans," Bush said, "at long last, we have reached the end of the dark period in American history that will come to be known as the Clinton Era, eight long years characterized by unprecedented economic expansion, a sharp decrease in crime, and sustained peace overseas. The time has come to put all of that behind us."

Bush swore to do "everything in [his] power" to undo the damage wrought by Clinton's two terms in office, including selling off the national parks to developers, going into massive debt to develop expensive and impractical weapons technologies, and passing sweeping budget cuts that drive the mentally ill out of hospitals and onto the street.

During the 40-minute speech, Bush also promised to bring an end to the severe war drought that plagued the nation under Clinton, assuring citizens that the U.S. will engage in at least one Gulf War–level armed conflict in the next four years.

"You better believe we're going to mix it up with

somebody at some point during my administration," said Bush, who plans a 250 percent boost in military spending. "Unlike my predecessor, I am fully committed to putting soldiers in battle situations. Otherwise, what is the point of even having a military?"

On the economic side, Bush vowed to bring back economic stagnation by implementing substantial tax cuts, which would lead to a recession, which would necessitate a tax hike, which would lead to a drop in consumer spending, which would lead to layoffs, which would deepen the recession even further.

Wall Street responded strongly to the Bush speech, with the Dow Jones industrial fluctuating wildly before closing at an 18-month low. The NASDAQ composite index, rattled by a gloomy outlook for tech stocks in 2001, also fell sharply, losing 4.4 percent of its total value between 3 P.M. and the closing bell.

Asked for comment about the cooling technology sector, Bush said: "That's hardly my area of expertise."

Turning to the subject of the environment, Bush said he will do whatever it takes to undo the tremendous damage not done by the Clinton Administration to the Arctic National Wildlife Refuge. He assured citizens that he will follow through on his campaign promise to open the 1.5 million acre refuge's coastal plain to oil drilling. As a sign of his commitment to bringing about a change in the environment, he pointed to his choice of Gale Norton for Secretary of the Interior. Norton, Bush noted, has "extensive experience" fighting environmental causes, working as a lobbyist for lead-paint manufacturers and as an attorney for loggers and miners, in addition to suing the EPA to overturn clean-air standards.

Bush had equally high praise for Attorney General nominee John Ashcroft, whom he praised as "a tireless champion in the battle to protect a woman's right to give birth."

"Soon, with John Ashcroft's help, we will move out of the Dark Ages and into a more enlightened time when a woman will be free to think long and hard before trying to fight her way past throngs of protesters blocking her entrance to an abortion clinic," Bush said. "We as a nation can look forward to lots and lots of babies."

Continued Bush: "John Ashcroft will be invaluable in healing the terrible wedge President Clinton drove between church and state."

The speech was met with overwhelming approval from Republican leaders.

"Finally, the horrific misrule of the Democrats has been brought to a close," House Majority Leader Dennis Hastert (R-IL) told reporters. "Under Bush, we can all look forward to military aggression, deregulation of dangerous, greedy industries, and the defunding of vital domestic social-service programs upon which millions depend. Mercifully, we can now say goodbye to the awful nightmare that was Clinton's America."

"For years, I tirelessly preached the message that Clinton must be stopped," conservative talk-radio host Rush Limbaugh said. "And yet, in 1996, the American public failed to heed my urgent warnings, re-electing Clinton despite the fact that the nation was prosperous and at peace under his regime. But now, thank God, that's all done with. Once again, we will enjoy mounting debt, jingoism, nuclear paranoia, mass deficit, and a massive military build-up."

An overwhelming 49.9 percent of Americans responded enthusiastically to the Bush speech.

"After eight years of relatively sane fiscal policy under the Democrats, we have reached a point where, just a few weeks ago, President Clinton said that the national debt could be paid off by as early as 2012," Rahway, NJ, machinist and father of three Bud Crandall said. "That's not the kind of world I want my children to grow up in."

"You have no idea what it's like to be black and enfranchised," said Marlon Hastings, one of thousands of Miami-Dade County residents whose votes were not counted in the 2000 presidential election. "George W. Bush understands the pain of enfranchisement, and ever since Election Day, he has fought tirelessly to make sure it never happens to my people again."

Bush concluded his speech on a note of healing and redemption.

"We as a people must stand united, banding together to tear this nation in two," Bush said. "Much work lies ahead of us: The gap between the rich and the poor may be wide, be there's much more widening left to do. We must squander our nation's hard-won budget surplus on tax breaks for the wealthiest 15 percent. And, on the foreign front, we must find an enemy and defeat it."

"The insanity is over," Bush said. "After a long, dark night of peace and stability, the sun is finally rising again over America. We look forward to a bright new dawn not seen since the glory days of my dad."

"When you meet the President you ask yourself, 'How did it ever occur to anybody that he should be governor, much less President?'"

—Henry Kissinger, who did not know that a reporter was present, on Ronald Reagan, 1986

NATURE LOVERS

*with quotes from James Watt, George W. Bush;
and a cartoon by Ruben Bolling*

*When a Republican takes a walk in the woods,
he's usually looking for something to kill. That's
because Republicans don't like to admit that
they're part of nature; instead, they see the
world around us as a collection of resources to
be exploited for short-term financial gain—
which explains why Republican presidents
appoint people like James Watt and Gale
Norton to "protect" the environment.*

They Said It . . .

> *"I do not know how many future generations we can count on before the Lord returns."*
> —Reagan Secretary of the Interior James Watt, 1981, when asked if natural resources must be preserved for future generations

It's not that Republicans don't like the great outdoors—they just like money more.

The Nexus vs. the Environment
from *Pigs at the Trough* (2003)
Arianna Huffington

How have President Bush and his corporate backers worked to undermine the environment? Let me count the ways. . . . Um, I better go get my calculator.

Since January 2001, the president and his energy-industry-friendly appointees (an understatement akin to calling mosquitoes "blood-friendly") have trashed the environment through dozens of actions. They have (take a breath, through a gas mask, if you've got one) abandoned a campaign promise to regulate carbon dioxide emissions, suspended an executive order preventing repeat polluters from obtaining government contracts, proposed reversing a ban on road building in 60 million acres of national forest, canceled a deadline for automakers to develop prototypes for high-mileage cars, rolled back safeguards for storing nuclear waste, shifted Superfund hazardous-waste cleanup costs from polluters to taxpayers, blocked a program to stem the discharge of raw sewage into America's waters, undermined protections for national parks and national monuments, and put forward a plan to reduce the likelihood of forest fires by allowing the timber industry easier access to federal lands in order to chop down trees. And that's just a partial list.

From arsenic in our water to carbon dioxide in our air; from undermining Kyoto to promoting drilling in Alaska; from refusing to raise auto mileage standards to handing the keys of our energy policy over to corporate interests, this administration has done exactly what Big Business wanted it to do.

Nowhere is this more evident than in the president's flip-flop on carbon dioxide.

During his run for the White House, candidate Bush made an unequivocal pledge to—read my lips—"require all power plants to meet clean air standards in order to reduce emission of sulfur dioxide, nitrogen oxide, mercury and carbon dioxide."

But soon after assuming office, responding to pressure from energy industry lobbyists, the president removed a line about carbon dioxide and the importance of clean air from his maiden speech to a joint session of Congress. The question became: Was this merely a rhetorical concession or a preview of a full-scale surrender to anti-environmental zealots?

The answer became all too clear when it was revealed there was an e-mail circulating among members of the energy crowd's "Cooler Heads Coalition" high-fiving themselves on this "famous victory"—i.e. convincing the president to abandon his one major pledge on the environment.

The president claimed that in executing his CO_2 flip-flop he was "responding to realities" and taking care "not to take actions that could harm consumers." But there in black and white in the e-mail was the "reality" he was actually responding to: "President Bush and Vice President Cheney have made the right decision . . . with *a little good advice from their friends.*"

The gloating was nauseating, but not nearly as nauseating as the vice president's claim that Bush's campaign position on carbon dioxide was a mistake because carbon dioxide isn't really a pollutant. By way of a reply, one can't do better than quote David Doniger of the Natural Resources Defense Council: "If carbon dioxide isn't a pollutant, maybe ketchup is a vegetable after all."

It's worth noting that when faced with a similarly vociferous campaign of opposition from the energy industry, the president's father had the guts to resist and do the right thing, signing an acid rain program into law as part of the Clean Air Act of 1990. But where "41" stood firm, "43" caved. The younger Bush's enemies might say it's the difference between a decorated WWII pilot and an AWOL Air National Guardsman. But others know it's simply the fact that campaign contributions from the energy industry to the Grand Old Party have amounted to an astounding $185,022,044 since 1989.

The assault on the environment continued. Limits on arsenic cramping your profitability? No problem. Gone. No more arsenic limits. Regulations about how to dispose of toxic waste putting a dent in your annual report? Say no more. Toss it wherever you'd like. That handy river, for instance.

This president's record, both in Austin and in Washington, clearly demonstrates that he puts the profits of industry ahead of the health and safety of people—no matter how devastating and long-term the consequences. Just talk about how the science "isn't conclusive," cite a few "experts" on the industry payroll, and mention jobs a lot. Besides, the consequences of such policies—you know, leukemia, brain tumors, auto-immune diseases, workplace accident rates—probably won't show up until after the next election.

As governor of Texas, Bush signed an "audit privilege" law that allowed companies to "keep secret all information about toxic chemical releases, spills and other environmental problems"—even from state regulators and citizens trying to sue. If it's the people's air, water, and health, how can one possibly assert "privilege" in violating them? But, then, Bush and his cronies are used to taking privilege for granted.

If California had had an audit privilege law, then the thousands of people poisoned in the case made famous by Erin Brockovich could never have sought and received legal redress. In Los Angeles, Chromium 6—the same carcinogenic chemical that had a starring role in the film—was detected in the water system at levels that spurred scientific debate over safety limits. The Brockovich case involved hundreds of victims; those affected by contaminated water in the L.A. Basin could number in the hundreds of thousands.

That's why the public's right to know is so fundamental—and so strenuously resisted by the chemical industry.

When a group in Ohio, for instance, spent $150,000 trying to pass a right-to-know ballot measure in 1992, Big Chemical poured in $4.8 million to defeat it. Such victory-at-any-price tactics have proved extremely effective—the last right-to-know initiative to pass was in California in 1986.

Of course, if they're not doing anything wrong, why would they care so much if the public, through its regulatory agencies, double-checked? I guess "trust but verify" doesn't apply domestically. More like "trust and drink up."

The industry has been equally effective at preventing government regulation of any kind for all but a small fraction of the 80,000 synthetic chemicals that have been created in the last 50 years. Instead, we rely on the industry's "self-regulation." The problem is, the honor system never works with people who have no shame.

To try to keep profits soaring, the chemical industry has stepped up its toxic contributions to our political class. After all, the right to pollute our air and water system isn't free. It requires that you first pollute our public policy system. A 1980 industry memo fretted over the polluters' "political muscle, how much we've got, and how we can get more." Clearly, they found out. Since then, the industry has doled out $122 million in political contributions—and has been flexing its political muscle since dollar one.

In March 2001, Bill Moyers, one of the Fourth Estate's preeminent defenders of true democracy, produced *Trade Secrets*, an explosive PBS documentary that used a million pages of internal chemical industry documents to expose the long-term cover-up of the poisonous effects of various chemicals on unsuspecting workers and consumers. Most of these chemicals are still unregulated.

Obtained by lawyers representing Elaine Ross, whose

husband died of brain cancer at the age of 46 after working at a chemical plant in Louisiana for 23 years, the documents—many of them stamped "secret" and "strictly confidential"—conjured up a terrifying moral universe in which deadly hazards to human life were nothing more than impediments to ever healthier bottom lines. Unfortunately, it's also the universe our political and corporate leaders are forcing most of us to live in, whether we want to or not.

The Chemical Papers, as the documents at the heart of *Trade Secrets* were called, are the toxic twin to the infamous Tobacco Papers. With any justice, they should have turned the chemical companies they've exposed—including Dow, DuPont, Shell, Conoco, and B.F. Goodrich—into the political pariahs that tobacco companies have become. But justice is the one thing the industry has been happy to ban.

Consider a 1959 Dow Chemical memo which conceded that extended exposure to one of the company's products was "going to produce rather appreciable injury," then shockingly added: "As you can appreciate, this opinion is not ready for dissemination yet, and I would appreciate it if you would hold it in confidence." In other words, this stuff causes cancer—but keep it under your hat.

When I met with Moyers shortly after the documentary was aired, he spoke with authority and passion about the "vast chemical experiment" being shamefully conducted on our children.

"I was walking in Central Park with my grandson," Moyers told me back then, "and he asked, 'How old are you, Pa?' I told him that I was 66. Then he looked up at the sky and asked: 'What is the world going to be like when I'm 66?' And the truth is, I couldn't tell him. We just don't know." And we even have to fight for the *right* to know.

But what we do know is that breast cancer, brain cancer in kids, testicular cancer in teens, infertility, and learning disabilities are all on the rise. And that this isn't just a coincidence. We also know that if we ended the noxious collusion between the chemical industry and our political overlords, Bill Moyers' grandson would have a better chance of getting to see what the world will be like when he's 66.

And these anti-environmental zealots are no longer just throwing cash in from the outside, influencing policy from industry-sponsored think tanks. They're now directing policy much more comfortably—from right inside the administration. Take Lynn Scarlett. Before being tapped by Bush for assistant secretary at the Department of the Interior, she was CEO of the Reason Foundation, a think tank promoting less regulation. Before becoming an environmental regulator, Ms. Scarlett described environmental regulations as a form of "Green punishment." It's unclear whether "green" means "environmental" or "monetary." Although to Ms. Scarlett the two are probably one and the same.

Then there's John Graham, named to head the Office of Information and Regulatory Affairs after a heroic career dedicated to fighting public health and safety rules. As head of the Harvard Center for Risk Analysis, he argued against the EPA's efforts to regulate dioxin. And pesticides. And radon. And second-hand tobacco smoke. And, of course, asbestos. His arguments have invariably been based on a perverse cost-benefit analysis that somehow "proves" that everything that is bad for you is actually good. (Though I wonder how many asbestos milk shakes or radon-laced cookies Mr. Graham whips up for his own children.)

And the president apparently believes it, too. What else

can explain the front-page stories in April 2001, trumpeting the Bush administration's decision to end mandatory testing for salmonella in hamburger meat served in federal school lunch programs? Such was the outpouring of indignation and incredulity that, within 24 hours, the decision was reversed and blamed on—who else?—a subordinate at the Department of Agriculture. "Somebody made a mistake," said department spokesman Kevin Herglotz.

But even in the incredibly unlikely event that it was just "a mistake," it was a revealing one. And it was entirely in keeping with this administration's ethos that perceives all environmental and public health regulations as government coercion designed to interfere with the free market. Why else would you even consider abandoning a policy that saw a 50% drop in salmonella contamination in the ten months before Bush decided to reverse it? And why else would you target the Environmental Protection Agency for a $300 million budget cut?

This decision didn't happen in a vacuum. There was one other factor: intense lobbying by the meat industry to ditch the testing—even though salmonella causes 1.4 million illnesses and 600 deaths a year. The industry's business-friendly alternative included irradiating the beef to kill the bacteria—which would have put a whole new spin on that cafeteria classic, "mystery meat." Today's special: Nuke Burgers and Toxic Joes.

THE ENERGY TASK FORCE

Then, of course, there's the sorry excuse for administration outreach known as Dick Cheney's Energy Task Force. In early 2002, after more than a year of stonewalling by the administration, the membership of the task force was finally disclosed. It was instantly clear that it was the oil, coal, and gas lobby that had been doing all the thinking, taking over both long-term policy-making and day-to-day environmental decisions. The result has been a massive regulatory rollback and juicy profits for industry fat cats. Cheney effectively privatized the nation's energy policy.

Along with doing everything in its considerable power to find a way to realize its obsessive dream of drilling in the Arctic National Wildlife Refuge, the Bush administration, cheered on by an all-star team of lobbyists, has also worked tirelessly to promote an energy plan that is long on building new power plants but pathetically indifferent, even hostile, to the idea of conservation. It doesn't even address the single most obvious and effective step we can take to conserve energy: increasing auto fuel-efficiency standards.

Instead of supporting the effort by senators John Kerry (D-Mass.) and John McCain (R-Ariz.) to gradually increase fuel standards over the next 13 years, in March 2002 the White House and 62 senators joined in an unholy alliance with carmakers and autoworker unions to kill the plan, which would have saved about 2.5 million barrels of oil a day. That, roughly, is the amount we currently import from the entire Middle East. Isn't the terrible cost of our oil dependency on the Middle East obvious enough to justify standing up to the auto industry?

Remember the wide-eyed walk the president took in 2001 through a Department of Energy showcase of energy-saving devices, including that triumph of American ingenuity, a state-of-the-art cell-phone charger? After the tour, he grandly announced over $85 million in grants to encourage the development of renewable-energy technologies. Sure, it sounded good, but it was classic Bush zero-sum grandstanding—it simply restored the $85 million in funding for renewable energy the president had previously recommended cutting. It was like a carjacker wanting the key to the city for returning one of the two cars he just boosted.

It was also a drop in the bucket when compared to the roughly $1 billion in tax incentives, credits, and other deductions handed out to the president's buddies in the oil, coal, nuclear, and gas industries since he took office. To announce those, by the way, there was no press conference.

It's more than a little ironic that, in his private life, President Bush is actually a leader in consumer conservation. His Crawford, Texas, ranch has been described as "an environmentally sensitive showplace" designed with "state-of-the-art energy efficiency." The house is filled with energy-saving devices, while the lawn and orchard are irrigated with recycled water.

Isn't it time that Bush starts preaching to the nation what he practices back at the ranch? And isn't it time that the members of Congress who betrayed the health and safety of their country are punished? On election day, voters have the opportunity to elbow aside the lobbyists. If Washington insists on importing its thinking, we need to make sure the ideas aren't stamped "Made by Big Business."

*The infamous James Watt had nothing on our current Secretary
of the Interior, Gale Norton.*

Unwise Use:
Gale Norton's New Environmentalism

from *The Progressive* (6/03)

David Helvarg

In his State of the Union address, President Bush called
for investing in hydrogen-powered cars. After initial
reluctance, the Administration has also implemented
Clinton-era proposals to reduce arsenic in drinking water
and air pollution from diesel trucks and tractors. And it
ordered General Electric to clean up PCB contaminants in
the Hudson River. Reporting on what this Administration
has done for the environment not only makes for a suc-
cinct paragraph but avoids the tedious listing process now
required when invoking the ways in which the White
House is rolling back a generation of environmental laws,
regulations, and treaty commitments.

So when George Bush refers to environmentalists as
"Green Green Lima Beans," it's a safe bet he's not engaged
in any deep rethinking of policy. Still, as a politician he
knows he has to at least appear committed to environmental protection, which is why his political brain, Karl
Rove, recently claimed Bush is following in Teddy Roosevelt's environmentalist tradition. That would be the
same Roosevelt who condemned "the landgrabbers and
great special interests"—the coal, timber, and oil cartels.
"The rights of the public to the nation's natural resources
outweigh private rights," said T.R.

UNWISE USE: GALE NORTON'S NEW ENVIRONMENTALISM

While the media has portrayed EPA Administrator Christine Todd Whitman as Bush's token environmentalist, Secretary of the Interior Gale Norton has been his real point-woman in promoting "common-sense solutions to environmental policy"—the Republican rhetoric that functions as a pretext for pillage.

When George Bush stood in front of a giant sequoia in California on Earth Day two years ago and spoke of "a new environmentalism for the twenty-first century" that would "protect the claims of nature while also protecting the legal rights of property owners," Norton was by his side nodding approvingly. A veteran of the small but influential "Wise Use" movement, Norton helped Bush through his environmental tutorial as a Presidential candidate, providing the intellectual arguments that deregulation, devolution, and free markets are the best ways to achieve environmental goals.

Two decades after Ronald Reagan's Secretary of the Interior James Watt used these same arguments to push for the privatization and industrialization of federal lands (among his quotes, "We will mine more, drill more, cut more timber"), Watt's agenda has again become government policy. "Twenty years later it sounds like they've just dusted off the old work," confirms Watt from retirement.

The 1988 Wise Use agenda was written by Watt biographer Ron Arnold, who is executive vice president of the Center for the Defense of Free Enterprise. It called for opening the Arctic National Wildlife Refuge (ANWR) to oil drilling, gutting the Endangered Species Act, opening wilderness lands to energy development, logging, and motorized recreation, and giving management of national parks over to private firms like Disney.

As early as October of 2001, Norton was arguing that

opening ANWR to drilling would provide the equivalent of eighty years of Iraqi oil imports (pre-invasion) to the United States. She's also pursuing energy development, logging for "forest health" and motorized recreation on public lands, mountain-top removal for coal mining in Appalachia, and captive breeding of endangered species in lieu of habitat protection. She's reversed a plan that would have banned snowmobiles from Yellowstone and Grand Teton National Parks, she is limiting the amount of land set aside for wilderness protection, and she is moving forward with a plan to begin "outsourcing" National Park Service jobs to private firms.

"I wish we could take credit for that but we can't," admits Ron Arnold. "Sometimes you just put something out there long enough and it gets picked up, despite what you do."

There was a brief moment, in the earliest days of the Bush Administration, when it appeared the White House might balance its thirst for oil with a nod toward wilderness protection by naming John Turner as Secretary of the Interior. Former head of the U.S. Fish and Wildlife Service under Bush Senior, Turner is also a Wyoming fly-fishing buddy of Dick Cheney's. He comes from the clipped moderate wing of the Republican Party that sees conserving nature as part of the conservative tradition.

But before Turner's name could be put forward, the White House was flooded with angry faxes and e-mails organized by the American Land Rights Association's Chuck Cushman, a Wise Use firebrand who maintains an e-mail action list of thousands of property rights, mining industry, and National Cattlemen's Beef Association members. He warned his listserv, "Turner's longstanding relationships with the Rockefeller

Family Foundation and their financing of the environmental left" would lead to a green takeover of the Department of the Interior by "Land-Grabber Turner."

Backstopped by his Washington lobbyist Mike Hardiman at the American Conservative Union, Cushman and the Wise Use fringe were able to do what they do best: sabotage a potentially eco-friendly initiative, in this case by scaring the Bush White House into thinking it might lose some of its core constituents on the hard right.

"They caved. They blinked. Cheney's probably angry at us but who cares," says Arnold. "Norton is a friend."

And an old one at that. Norton got her start at Watt's Mountain States Legal Foundation in Denver, which billed itself as the "litigation arm of Wise Use." While there, she argued that the government should pay financial compensation whenever environmental laws limited a developer's real or potential profits.

This argument is based on the Fifth Amendment, which states, "No person shall be . . . deprived of life, liberty, or property, without due process of the law: nor shall private property be taken for public use without just compensation." Today, when the government condemns land to build a highway (or a Texas baseball stadium) the Fifth Amendment guarantees that the landowner be paid market value for his or her lost property.

Yet, in 1887, when a Kansas beer brewer argued a prohibition law in his state was also a takings under the Fifth Amendment, the Supreme Court ruled against him, stating that, "a government can prevent a property owner from using his property to injure others without having to compensate the owner for the value of the forbidden use."

But Norton has argued for a major shift in the takings

jurisprudence. "We might even go so far as to recognize a homesteading right to pollute or to make noise in an area. This approach would eliminate some of the theoretical problems with defining a nuisance," she wrote in the *Harvard Journal of Law and Public Policy* back in 1990. She later recanted her "right to pollute" phrase during her Senate confirmation hearing.

In 1998 Norton became co-chair of the Coalition of Republican Environmental Advocates. Dedicated to "free market environmentalism," the coalition included auto, coal mining, and developer lobbyists. Traditional Republican environmentalists like the late Senator John Chafee of Rhode Island refused to join.

In 1999 Norton, now working as a lawyer representing the lead industry, became part of the team advising candidate Bush on developing a conservative "environmentalism for the twenty-first century." Among those working with her was David Koch of Koch Industries, which in 2000 paid a $35 million fine for oil pollution in six states, as well as Lynn Scarlett from the libertarian Reason Foundation of Los Angeles. Scarlett was also a senior fellow at Montana's Foundation for Research on Economics and the Environment (FREE), which lived up to its acronym by holding a series of all-expenses-paid property-rights "seminars" for federal judges at a Montana dude ranch.

Norton also spent time as a fellow at the Political Economy Research Center (PERC), Montana's other property-rights think tank. David Koch is a major funder of both FREE and PERC. With his family's $23 billion fossil fuel fortune, Koch also bankrolls a hornet's nest of D.C.-based free market think tanks, including the Heritage Foundation, the Cato Institute, the Competitive Enterprise

Institute, and Citizens for a Sound Economy, which all advocate for the "new environmentalism" of deregulation.

"The last three decades is what I call the old environmentalism," Scarlett says. Scarlett is now Norton's assistant secretary for policy, management, and budget, and since Norton likes to keep a low profile, Scarlett has become Norton's emissary to the public.

"The old environmentalism tended to rely on the four 'P's: prescription, telling you how you're supposed to do things; process, a focus on the permit you need to 'pass go' rather than the result; punishment, as a way to motivate action; and a piecemeal approach to air, land, and water," Scarlett explains. "We're not getting rid of regulation, but shifting the emphasis, extending a hand to work with, not against, landowners. We think real sustainability has to be about what we call Cooperative Conservation, about engaging people."

The Department of the Interior is now packed with people previously engaged in the employ of industry. The department's Deputy Secretary Steve Griles is a former mining and oil lobbyist. The Senate, before confirming him, made him sign an agreement that he wouldn't meet with his former clients. Nevertheless, Griles has gone on to meet with his former clients to discuss new rules that allow the dumping of coal mining waste in Appalachian rivers and a massive coal-bed methane drilling project in Wyoming, according to *The Washington Post*. On April 7, Senator Joe Lieberman, Democrat of Connecticut, asked the Interior Department's inspector general to investigate Griles following a report by the Associated Press that Griles also attended meetings on offshore leases in which his former clients had significant interests.

"These reports raise numerous, troubling questions about whether the deputy secretary has successfully avoided conflicts of interest, or the appearance of conflicts," said Lieberman.

Eric Ruff, director of communications at the Department of the Interior, disputes the facts of *The Washington Post* account and says Griles "has followed the highest ethical standards of the department."

Norton's special assistant on Alaska is a former oil lobbyist, her assistant secretary for water and science is a former mining lawyer who has called for the abolition of the Endangered Species Act, and her solicitor is from the Cattlemen's Beef Association, where he lobbied for cheap grazing fees on Interior lands.

With those kinds of built-in conflicts of interest, even Norton's collaborative rhetoric and her attempts at outreach (including a letter to actor/environmentalist Robert Redford in which she pitched their shared love of zoo-bred condors) haven't been enough to prevent a series of in-house scandals.

Ironically her biggest controversy is an inherited one, the century-old accounting mess at the Bureau of Indian Affairs. American Indians claim the federal government has squandered billions in oil, gas, and timber royalties from their lands and are suing to reclaim the money.

A more recent scandal that has also angered California Indian tribes involves the death of more than 35,000 salmon on the lower Klamath River, attributed to low water flows after the U.S. Bureau of Reclamation diverted water north to Oregon farmers.

In the spring of 2001, alfalfa, hay, and potato farmers marched through the streets of Klamath Falls, Oregon, and illegally opened dam gates to protest a federal decision cutting their irrigation water to guarantee protection for endangered suckerfish and coho salmon runs. Like the snail darter and spotted owl before it, the suckerfish quickly became the poster-animal for anti–Endangered Species Act pundits from talk radio's Rush Limbaugh to the editorial writers at *The Wall Street Journal.* What few of these conservative critics were willing to acknowledge was that the water crisis was precipitated by the worst drought to hit the Northwest in over a century, a drought that, like the region's forty-six shrinking glaciers, is likely linked to fossil-fuel-enhanced climate change. "1994 was the last substantial rain we had," Ryan Kliewer, a young fourth-generation farmer who marched in the protests, told me.

Under pressure from the White House, Norton's Bureau of Reclamation slashed the river flow, returning much of the water to the irrigators, despite a report from a team of federal scientists warning this would place the coho salmon in serious jeopardy (along with the commercial fishermen and Indian tribes who depend on them). Last October, Representative Mike Thompson and a group of California protesters dumped 500 pounds of dead, rotting Klamath salmon on the front steps of the Department of the Interior, accusing Norton of a massive cover-up.

This wasn't the first time Norton's been accused of ignoring or suppressing government scientists.

In the fall of 2001, she had to explain why, in a letter to the Senate Committee on Energy and Natural Resources, she'd altered scientific data to make it appear that oil operations in ANWR would not harm hundreds of thousands of migratory caribou, when her own Fish and Wildlife Service had provided her with data suggesting they would.

"We did make a mistake. We will take steps to clarify and correct that," she told reporters in explaining one of the numerous discrepancies.

Norton also concluded that drilling the Arctic wouldn't violate an international treaty that protects polar bears. The Fish and Wildlife Service, which has twice issued reports stating that drilling poses a threat to the bears, was directed "to correct these inconsistencies" (in line with Norton's position).

Bush also signed off on an Army Corps of Engineers proposal that makes it easier for developers and mining companies to dredge and fill America's wetlands through a "general permitting" process that is rarely if ever challenged. Again, Norton failed to forward comments from her Fish and Wildlife Service to the Army Corps, even though the service had written that the proposed policy change would result in "tremendous destruction of aquatic and terrestrial habitat."

Norton's top aides are now actively monitoring career staffers to make sure that scientific assessments don't conflict with their pro-business political goals, according to whistleblowers within the department who've been in touch with reporters and environmental groups. As a result, morale among Interior field scientists is said to be falling faster than a wing-shot condor.

The latest suppressed study (which surfaced in *The New York Times* on January 31) came from the National Park Service. Today, the largest constituency organized to open up parks and wilderness areas to roads and development is no longer Wise Use loggers and resource industry employees but suburban owners of motorized dirt bikes, ATVs, snowmobiles, and personal watercraft. While millions of Americans are having a love affair with fast, loud off-road vehicles, their owners are creating major user conflicts with tens of millions of other outdoor recreationists who enter wilderness areas believing they've left the noise and pollution of the freeway behind.

Air pollution from winter snowmobilers and harassment of buffalo and other wildlife got so bad in Yellowstone National Park that the Park Service decided to phase out the activity. But Norton's Department of the Interior—in response to a suit from the International Snowmobile Manufacturers Association—announced it would reassess the rule-making process, this despite 360,000 e-mails and letters, 80 percent of which supported banning the machines.

"I think the national environment groups have turned on recreation with a vengeance now that they've driven the commodity users off the [public] lands," argues Bill Horn, Washington counsel for the Snowmobile Manufacturers. "Our conversations with the Secretary [of Interior Norton] show her greater appreciation of public recreation on public lands. We need these places for everyone's enjoyment—not just to have these scientists go in there and create biospheres under glass."

In November, the Bush Administration proposed a cap of 1,100 snowmobiles a day, up from the present average of 815, arguing that a new generation of machines will be quieter and less polluting. At the same time, according to the *Times*, the Park Service concluded an internal report (not made public) that found banning the machines was the best way to protect the park's air quality and wildlife and the health of visitors and employees. Still, thousands of snowmobiles continued to make their runs through Yellowstone and Grand Teton this winter and will continue to do so, at least for the remainder of the Bush Administration.

The next big push at the Interior Department is likely to be the privatization of thousands of National Park Service jobs, including the entire corps of park scientists. The government-wide "competitive sourcing" initiative, being promoted by Bush and his Office of Management and Budget, targets as many as 850,000 jobs in the largely unionized federal workforce to be replaced by private contractors, including up to 11,524 out of 16,470 National Park Service jobs.

Fran Mainella, director of the Park Service, sent an e-mail to her employees at the end of January assuring them that while 70 percent of their jobs were being studied to see if they were "inherently governmental" functions, that "70 percent has never been used as a measuring stick for privatizing National Park Service jobs." Under present plans, 15 percent of Park Service jobs will be outsourced by 2004, which will, according to Scarlett, "help tap professional tools with better delivery of services to the public, and new skills and technologies and discipline."

"The plan is designed to meet ideologically set goals and will rip apart the fabric of the agency," counters Jeff Ruch, executive director of Public Employees for Environmental Responsibility, a Washington-based activist organization that's represented a number of Park Service workers. Ruch claims that replacing park scientists will lead to "private consulting firms telling the Park Service what it wants to hear in order to get their contracts renewed."

With the Department of the Interior also promoting recreational user fees, corporate sponsorship of park activities, and partnerships for bio-prospecting (companies looking to develop new drugs from microbes, plants, and animals) in the parks, one can start to imagine Smokey the Bear recast as ComCast Bear, Arches National Park as Golden Arches National Park, or hip ads promoting Yellowstone washed jeans. Certainly the Wise Use vision of park management given over to private firms, "with expertise in people-moving such as Walt Disney," seems consistent with Norton's policies.

As does the end of wilderness itself. On the evening of Friday, April 11, after Congress had recessed for spring break, the Department of the Interior quietly released a statement announcing that, after almost forty years of scenic and biologically important habitat protections under the Wilderness Act, it would no longer seek any additional wilderness designations on public lands. This potentially opens up some 250 million acres of federal rangelands and Western mountains to mining, drilling, road construction, and other forms of development.

Still, by keeping a low profile and being a team player, by talking about her love of hiking, condors, and conservation while promoting the White House energy plan to open millions of acres of public lands to mining and drilling, by choosing her audiences and never second-guessing her boss, Norton has remained a relatively non-controversial figure in the Administration. Despite her early portrayals by environmentalists as "James Watt in a skirt," she has shown far more political acumen than the man who once bragged of a commission on which he had a black, a woman, "two Jews, and a cripple."

Rather then openly attack environmental laws like the Endangered Species Act (which she has argued is unconstitutional), Norton has used the regulatory process to ease up on industry and the administrative process to crack down on agency professionals who disagree with her.

Of course, with the Republicans now in charge of both the White House and Capitol Hill, the impulse to overreach and go for a more fundamental realignment of broadly popular environmental laws may prove highly tempting.

For environmentalists to move beyond a purely defensive posture, however, it will take more than waiting on a Republican gaffe or alarmed direct mail solicitations showing nursing caribou on the tundra.

The environmental movement has to address the links among oil, energy, climate change, landscape, and security. This will mean dealing with the Middle East wars, as well as Norton's drilling permits in the Gulf of Mexico and Alaska. It will mean committing to a level of national and global politics that could prove highly partisan, complex, and intense.

They Said It . . .

I Hate
Republicans
READER

"There are some monuments where the land is so widespread, they just encompass as much as possible. And the integral part of the—the precious part, so to speak—I guess all land is precious, but the part that the people uniformly would not want to spoil, will not be despoiled."
—George W. Bush, 2001

BIG BROTHER

with a quote from Ed Meese;
a cartoon by Ruben Bolling;
and a quiz from Paul Slansky

Republicans love to wrap themselves in the flag, but they don't care much for the freedom it represents. They rejoice in programs that promote spying on citizens, and they are quick to stifle free speech when it calls attention to their morally and intellectually bankrupt policies at home and abroad.

Quiz
Paul Slansky

What kind of rights did George W. Bush say are given to the American people in the Declaration of Independence?

(a) "Unalienable"
(b) "Inalienable"
(c) "Uninalienable"
(d) "Securitized"

Answer: (c)

The run-up to war in Iraq was accompanied by a clamp-down on public discourse—led by mercenary lapdogs who dominate the cable "news" and talk shows. This piece by Stanley I. Kutler struck a different tone.

There Will Absolutely Be No Dissension
from *The Chicago Tribune* (3/18/03)
Stanley I. Kutler

As we march to war, the Bush administration's interest is to discredit, even foreclose, dissent.

Passivity and a sense of powerlessness are pervasive everywhere. Tabloids and cable channels refer to the "treason" of celebrities who oppose President Bush. Our political leaders march in lockstep with the president. The so-called "opposition" hedges its bets, "patriotically" supporting Bush's actions, but ever hopeful he will stumble on the economy and give them the opportunity of 1992 all over again.

The freedom and diversity we so cherish for others is strikingly lacking in our public discourse. We must not forget our traditions of challenge and dissent. For openers, we can invoke the injunctions of Theodore Roosevelt, the most red-blooded and manly of our presidents—if that is to be the litmus test for strong leadership. In 1918, ex-President Roosevelt challenged Woodrow Wilson's sweeping crackdown against dissent after the American entry into World War I. "To announce that there must be no criticism of the president, or that we are to stand by the president, right or wrong," Roosevelt said, "is not only unpatriotic and servile, but is morally treasonable to the American public."

Abraham Lincoln more pointedly serves the present, critical need. Challenging President James Polk's dubious response to alleged Mexican aggression against the United States, Congressman Lincoln voted to censure the president in 1848—while the war against Mexico still raged. He contended that the president's justification for war was "from beginning to end the sheerest deception." Polk would have "gone further with his proof if it had not been for the small matter that the truth would not permit him." Lincoln threw down the gauntlet: "Let him answer fully, fairly and candidly. Let him answer with facts and not with arguments. . . . Let him attempt no evasion, no equivocation." Lincoln more than suspected that the president was "deeply conscious of being in the wrong."

Today, as we prepare to go to war, will the qualities of democracy, diversity, and the open society President Bush so ardently desires for the nation-building he will do for the Iraqis be available at home? The chorus for unanimity is rising, usually in the name of support for our troops in harm's way. Hardly a new ploy for presidential behavior. Once he commits troops abroad, the argument goes, then we must have a moratorium on criticism.

Again, Lincoln can help us. He realized that he had to distinguish between the role of the military and the policies of President Polk. The army had done its work admirably, Congressman Lincoln noted, but the president had "bungled" his. Polk, he feared, was "a bewildered, confounded and miserably perplexed man. God grant he may be able to show there is not something about his conscience more painful than all his mental perplexity."

Our "loyal opposition" at this moment borders on the comic. Most Democratic leaders desperately try to walk both sides of the line, keeping their options open, and say little to criticize or restrain the president in his headlong rush for war. Notably, ex-President Jimmy Carter and Sen. Robert Byrd (D-W.Va.) have spoken out.

Carter rests his opposition to Bush's policy on Christian principles of a just war. We have not exhausted all non-violent options, Carter argues; we plan no distinctions between combatants and civilian non-combatants; and we face a strong prospect that war will only destabilize Iraq and the Middle East, and increase opportunities for terrorism. Carter also has noted that the war will not be sanctioned by the international community the United States professes to represent. George Bush's "alliance of the willing" apparently is a very exclusive club.

Sen. Byrd has pointedly challenged the president's recital of slogan, and his paucity of facts and evidence. Byrd is a powerful man within congressional boundaries, but he is readily dismissed as a caricature of sorts in the media, and elsewhere. Those anxious to discredit him resurrect his youthful membership in the Klan, a fact which he has decisively repudiated—unlike Sen. Strom Thurmond (R-S.C.), and others like him, who never, never publicly disowned or repudiated their support for segregation, then or forever. But the passivity of the media is most striking in giving President Bush an open field.

Bush's March 6 press conference was not, in the minds of many observers, a particularly forceful or articulate moment for him. His answers seemed repetitious. Commentators suggested that many questions might have been planted, and that the president carefully limited his attention to friendly reporters. Planted questions? Favored softball questioners? How shocking; how surprising. Meanwhile, chattering commentators shortchanged their audience with little or no attention to the substance, or lack thereof, of his performance. Omission is the weapon of choice for the media's passivity.

The Sunday TV programs ignored the revelations of the executive director of the International Atomic Energy Agency, demonstrating that a document purporting to show an Iraqi purchase of uranium from Niger had been forged. That document was a key element in a British intelligence report, which the United States in turn had used to build its case against Iraq.

Even more lamentable has been the ongoing refusal of the American media to acknowledge a March 2 *London Observer* story detailing "an aggressive surveillance operation" against UN delegates, including the interception of home and office telephone calls and e-mails. The information came from a leaked memo from the National Security Agency. The targets were uncommitted

UN delegations, including Angola, Cameroon, Chile, Mexico, Guinea and Pakistan.

The pro-war, Murdoch-owned *London Times* called it an "embarrassing disclosure."

American officials quietly labored to discredit the report, suggesting it was a forgery. Well, the British government has announced an arrest of someone in its National Security Administration counterpart, who is charged with leaking the memo. The *New York Times* did not print it because it could not get confirmation, although it had been confirmed in a variety of ways by the English press. Several days later, the *Washington Post* downplayed the story by noting that it was not particularly alarming, and the *Los Angeles Times* said American spy activities were "longstanding."

No one could quite bring themselves to acknowledge the obvious: It was true, however longstanding and commonplace such practices may have been.

And now, on CNN, Richard N. Perle, chairman of the Defense Policy Board and the president's "minister without portfolio" labeled Seymour M. Hersh a "terrorist"—"the closest thing American journalism has to a terrorist." And why? Because "he [Hersh] sets out to do damage." In a recent *New Yorker* magazine article, Hersh exposed how Perle's venture-capital firm invests in "companies dealing in technology goods and services that are of value to homeland security and defense."

CNN talk show host Wolf Blitzer sat silently through Perle's tirade and dutifully asked him if the opponents of war were "sending a mixed message to Saddam Hussein and giving him some comfort in suspecting that if he plays out this game, he's going to be able to get his way."

Perle almost smiled.

More satire.

Bill of Rights Pared Down to a Manageable Six

from *The Onion* (12/18/02)

Washington, DC—Flanked by key members of Congress and his administration, President Bush approved Monday a streamlined version of the Bill of Rights that pares its 10 original amendments down to a "tight, no-nonsense" six.

A Republican initiative that went unopposed by congressional Democrats, the revised Bill of Rights provides citizens with a "more manageable" set of privacy and due-process rights by eliminating four amendments and condensing and/or restructuring five others. The Second Amendment, which protects the right to keep and bear arms, was the only article left unchanged.

Calling the historic reduction "a victory for America," Bush promised that the new document would do away with "bureaucratic impediments to the flourishing of democracy at home and abroad."

"It is high time we reaffirmed our commitment to this enduring symbol of American ideals," Bush said. "By making the Bill of Rights a tool for progress instead of a hindrance to freedom, we honor the true spirit of our nation's forefathers."

The Fourth Amendment, which long protected citizens' homes against unreasonable search and seizure, was among the eliminated amendments. Also stricken was the Ninth Amendment, which stated that the enumeration of certain Constitutional rights does not result in the abrogation of rights not mentioned.

"Quite honestly, I could never get my head around what the Ninth Amendment meant anyway," said outgoing House Majority Leader Dick Armey (R-TX), one of the leading advocates of the revised Bill of Rights. "So goodbye to that one."

Amendments V through VII, which guaranteed the right to legal counsel in criminal cases, and guarded against double jeopardy, testifying against oneself, biased juries, and drawn-out trials, have been condensed into Super-Amendment V: The One About Trials.

Attorney General John Ashcroft hailed the slimmed-down Bill of Rights as "a positive step."

"Go up to the average citizen and ask them what's in the Bill of Rights," Ashcroft said. "Chances are, they'll have only a vague notion. They just know it's a set of rules put in place to protect their individual freedoms from government intrusion, and they assume that's a good thing."

Ashcroft responded sharply to critics who charge that the Bill of Rights no longer safeguards certain basic, inalienable rights.

"We're not taking away personal rights; we're increasing personal *security*," Ashcroft said. "By allowing for greater government control over the particulars of individual liberties, the Bill of Rights will now offer expanded personal freedoms whenever they are deemed appropriate and unobtrusive to the activities necessary to effective operation of the federal government."

Ashcroft added that, thanks to several key additions, the Bill of Rights now offers protections that were previously lacking, including the right to be protected by soldiers quartered in one's home (Amendment III), the

BILL OF RIGHTS PARED DOWN TO A MANAGEABLE SIX

guarantee that activities not specifically delegated to the states and people will be carried out by the federal government (Amendment VI), and freedom of Judeo-Christianity and non-combative speech (Amendment I).

According to U.S. Sen. Larry Craig (R-ID), the original Bill of Rights, though well-intentioned, was "seriously outdated."

"The United States is a different place than it was back in 1791," Craig said. "As visionary as they were, the framers of the Constitution never could have foreseen, for example, that our government would one day need to jail someone indefinitely without judicial review. There was no such thing as suspicious Middle Eastern immigrants back then."

Ashcroft noted that recent FBI efforts to conduct investigations into "unusual activities" were severely hampered by the old Fourth Amendment.

"The Bill of Rights was written more than 200 years ago, long before anyone could even fathom the existence of wiretapping technology or surveillance cameras," Ashcroft said. "Yet through a bizarre fluke, it was still somehow worded in such a way as to restrict use of these devices. Clearly, it had to go before it could do more serious damage in the future."

The president agreed.

"Any machine, no matter how well-built, periodically needs a tune-up to keep it in good working order," Bush said. "Now that we have the bugs worked out of the ol' Constitution, she'll be purring like a kitten when Congress reconvenes in January—just in time to work on a new round of counterterrorism legislation."

"Ten was just too much of a handful," Bush added. "Six civil liberties are more than enough."

They Said It . . .

"You don't have many suspects who are innocent of a crime . . . If a person is innocent of a crime, then he is not a suspect."
—Reagan Attorney General Ed Meese, 1985

George W. Bush's stand on civil liberties became evident during his tenure as Texas governor.

George W. Bush
from *The Dirty Truth: George W. Bush's Oil and Chemical Dependency* (2000)
Rick Abraham

On August 30, 2000, a state District Court ruled against Governor Bush after he asked to be dropped from a lawsuit brought by citizens who were arrested for peacefully protesting outside the Governor's mansion. The judge's ruling was based on his belief that the Texas Governor has a general responsibility to ensure that the State police enforce the law and act in a lawful manner. Governor Bush, who appoints the commissioners of the state police, claimed to have no such responsibility. The lawsuit was filed in 1999 after citizens were arrested, strip searched, and jailed. The head of the Governor's "Protective Detail," after meeting with Governor Bush, enacted the "new policy" leading to the arrests. Governor Bush then publicly supported the policy and the jailing of citizens.

For years, the public sidewalk outside the fence surrounding the Governor's mansion has been a traditional site of public protest. This has been true under Democratic and Republican governors alike. Even the state police officers testified they were aware of no previous arrests of peaceful protestors. Historically, citizens have gathered outside the mansion to freely express their views—at least until Governor Bush began to campaign for the Presidency.

In early 1999, when Governor Bush began entertaining an entourage of political leaders and media representatives, unwritten "new rules" were adopted governing the public's use of the sidewalk. Governor Bush and the head of his Protective Detail met and discussed the "new" rules. After this discussion, citizens were arrested. Governor Bush then publicly approved of the new rules and the arrests.

Lieutenant Escalante, who heads Bush's Protective Detail, says he can remember nothing about his discussion with the Governor. Governor Bush refused to testify under oath about his discussion with Escalante and others concerning the rules and the arrests.

Governor Bush says he had nothing to do with the policy or the arrests. However, few people believe that highly publicized arrests in front of the Governor's Mansion, initiated by the Governor's own Protective Detail, would have taken place without the Governor's approval.

One officer testified that the Governor was informed whenever a demonstration took place.

The Governor and his "Protective Detail" failed to follow the required process for approval of "new rules" governing the use of the public sidewalk. They also selectively enforced the rules, allowing some protesters to stay on the sidewalk while others were forced to leave under threat of arrest. The judge, who denied the Governor's motion to be dismissed from the lawsuit, was shown photographs of protesters waving the Confederate flag and protesting that it be flown over the Capitol. The Confederate protesters were *allowed* to do the same thing, in the same place, that landed environmentalists in jail.

All of the environmental protesters were focusing attention on Bush's environmental policies and campaign contributions from big business polluters. Dierdra Tinker, a PTA mother, was handcuffed and placed in the back seat of a patrol car. Mrs. Tinker was arrested, apparently because she did not move fast enough (off the sidewalk) to satisfy the demands of the state trooper threatening her with arrest. She was released only after her companions pleaded that she needed to pick her children up from daycare. Along with other citizens from the organization "Downwinders at Risk," she had driven several hours from the Dallas area to protest a hazardous waste-burning cement kiln near her home. The continued burning was allowed by Bush's environmental agency appointees.

A little over two weeks later, on March 29, 1999, about 50 people from across the state met at the Governor's mansion sidewalk to peacefully protest Bush's role in a "voluntary" pollution reduction program for some of the largest industrial polluters in the state. All protesters were ordered off the sidewalk, including women, children, and mothers pushing baby carriages. They were directed further away from the mansion to a public sidewalk across the street. Every protestor except one did as ordered for fear of being arrested. They didn't want to miss the chance to testify at a legislative hearing.

Texans United Education Fund Director Rick Abraham (the author), was left alone on the sidewalk with the Governor's Protective Detail and state troopers. For the atrocity of carrying a sign that read, *"Air Pollution Kills,"* Abraham was arrested, handcuffed, strip searched, and jailed for twelve hours. He was charged with "blocking an entrance." In fact, the entrance to the Mansion was closed and no one was present to be blocked.

A CITIZEN SPEAKS AND THE GOVERNOR REFUSES TO LISTEN

The following letter was sent to Governor Bush, received by his office, and marked with a notation that a response was not necessary.

April 10, 1999

Dear Governor Bush,

On Monday March 29, approximately 50 citizens from around the state held a news conference and protest rally outside our Governor's mansion. We held the event at the mansion, your home, because you are advocating legislation that would allow more pollution in the homes of average Texas families. You want to continue the legal loophole for "grandfathered" industrial polluters that exempts them from full permits and modern pollution controls. Representatives from envi-

ronmental, labor, and citizen organizations attended the protest rally to publicly express opposition to your legislation.

When citizens first gathered on the public sidewalk adjacent to the mansion, a representative from the Governor's Protection Detail of the Capitol Police came and demanded to see identification. He threatened citizens with arrest if they did not move to the sidewalk across the street. The entrance to the mansion was closed and the sidewalk was not being blocked. Even so, I was arrested, charged with "blocking an entrance," and jailed overnight.

Since there was a hearing on pollution legislation that same afternoon, most citizens did not want to take the chance of being arrested. They attended the hearing in large numbers and it lasted into the early hours of the next morning. Citizens should not have had to choose, as I did, between exercising their right to protest and testifying at the hearing.

Others have been arrested for protesting outside the Governor's mansion, including a PTA mother who dared to speak out against pollution several weeks earlier. You must speak out against these illegal arrests. It is wrong to allow powerful corporate polluters to avoid pollution laws at the same times citizens' rights to protest pollution are being violated. Our first amendment rights, like our pollution laws, should not be selectively enforced on the basis of who gives you money and support.

This letter is to ask you to inform those associated with your "protection" detail that the constitutional rights of citizens do not end at the public sidewalk in *front of our Governor's mansion. Protecting you from public criticism is not a proper function of the Capitol Police who are paid with public funds.*

We respect your right to advocate the programs you choose and we certainly expect you to respect the rights of Texans to oppose those programs. Lawful public protest is a part of the process by which public policy is debated and decided. We hope you will remember this as our Governor— and never forget it should you become President.

Citizens will no doubt hold other lawful demonstrations outside the Governor's mansion. We can only hope that you will recognize and support our first amendment rights with the same level of enthusiasm that you support "grandfathered" corporate polluters. We would appreciate a copy of your letter to the Capitol Police regarding this matter.

Sincerely,
Rick Abraham
Executive Director
Texans United Education Fund

The letter was received by the Governor's office and a decision was made not to answer it. After the letter was received by the Governor's office, the arrests continued.

On April 19, 1999, a third environmental protest was held outside the Governor's mansion on the public sidewalk. This time four people were arrested while standing on the edge of the sidewalk far from the entrance to the Governor's mansion. They stood with their backs against a brick wall to make sure there was room for pedestrians to pass, even though no pedestrians were present.

Among those arrested were Michael Covington and Karen Sloan, two refinery workers from Crown Central Petroleum, a notorious polluter, and a heavy contributor to Governor Bush's election campaigns. Also arrested were Roger Baker, a member of the Green Party, and, for a second time, Texans United's Rick Abraham. This arrest came after the Governor had received and decided not to respond to Abraham's letter. All of those arrested, including Karen Sloan, were again charged with "blocking an entrance." They were jailed, strip-searched, and made to sleep on the floor in overcrowded jail cells.

Later, on the same day, after the third set of arrests were made, Teighlor Darr, a reporter for Austin radio station KJFK-FM, went back to the Governor's Mansion sidewalk. She also carried a sign. Her sign simply read "I like Bush." When approached by the Governor's Protective Detail, she explained that her action was a "support" and not a "protest." She then was freely allowed, for two hours, to walk up and down the exact same sidewalk. This occurred on the same sidewalk where the environmental protesters had been arrested only hours before. She was neither jailed, nor strip-searched. Her use of the public sidewalk to voice "support" for the Governor went unchallenged— even as the protesters of Bush's environmental policies sat behind bars.

On May 25, 1999, environmental protesters returned to the Governor's Mansion sidewalk, this time joined by Frances "Sissy" Farenthold, a former state legislator and a candidate for Texas Governor in the 1970s. This time only Jim Baldauf, a Texans United board member, was arrested. Mr. Baldauf, as was the case with others who had been arrested before, was walking on the sidewalk alone. No one was near him who would be inconvenienced in any way. However, rather than arrest Ms. Farenthold, who continued to walk on the sidewalk in the presence of news media, the police decided to forgo any more arrests.

Jim Baldauf, who was arrested for doing exactly what Ms. Farenthold and others were allowed to do, was handcuffed, strip-searched, and jailed for 24 hours—without ever being charged. The other protesters arrested in March and April of 1999 were never prosecuted. The Travis County Attorney determined there was insufficient evidence. Videotapes of the arrests clearly show that citizens were doing nothing more than peacefully exercising their constitutionally protected rights.

GOVERNOR BUSH: KEEPER OR SLAYER OF THE FIRST AMENDMENT

In August of 1999 Texans United and others filed a lawsuit against the Department of Public Safety (state police) and Governor George W. Bush. The lawsuit challenges the constitutionality of the new, unwritten policy and seeks to restore free speech rights to the public sidewalk outside the Governor's Mansion. To date, both Governor Bush and the Department of Public Safety (state police) have chosen to maintain and defend their unwritten policy against protests.

Following the arrests on April 19, Governor Bush held a news conference with visiting New York Mayor Rudolph Giulliani. He said he approved of the policy governing the use of the sidewalk and the arrests of the protesters. The Governor said, "People have just gotta understand what the rules are." However, as of September 2000, the "rules" are still not in writing and seem subject to different interpretations. According to citizens' Attorney David Kahne, "the courts have previously held that such unwritten rules are unconstitutional because they give 'unbridled discretion' to authorities who can use them to silence their critics."

AVOIDING RESPONSIBILITY AND DODGING SWORN TESTIMONY

Governor Bush's deposition was requested to determine the extent of his role in establishing the unconstitutional policy. If he played no such role, his sworn deposition could have gone far to establish his innocence. Instead, Governor Bush refused to be deposed and avoided having to answer questions under oath. He did so even though he criticized President Clinton for attempting to do the exact same thing.

"Governor Bush thinks he's above the law," said Jim Baldauf, one of the arrested citizens. "Governor Bush brags about 'leadership' and preaches about 'personal responsibility' and then says, 'I'm not responsible.' According to Baldauf, who was jailed for 24 hours without being charged, "He refused to testify under oath in the 'Funeral-gate' case, he refused to give a sworn deposition in our case and he's refused to answer specific questions about his military record and his drug and alcohol use."

The citizens who dared to file the lawsuit against Governor Bush and the state police were grilled by the Governor's lawyers about previous arrests that may have occurred over their lifetime—including any related to drug and alcohol use. Governor George W. Bush, who so freely approved of the citizens being jailed, could rightfully be asked if he knows what it's like to be deprived of his freedom. Has *he* ever been arrested? How many times, and what for? Some people speculate that the fear of being asked such questions is one reason he refused to testify.

Not only has Governor Bush and the Department of Public Safety, headed by Bush's appointees, sought to deny the right to free speech and peaceable assembly, they have also tried to undermine citizens' rights to freedom of association. The state's lawyers have tried to obtain the lists of all members of Texans United—and the names of its contributors. Some members and contributors actually work for industrial polluters and/or government agencies. If the names of the members employed by polluters were disclosed, these people would almost surely face recriminations. Forcing the names of members and contributors of private organizations to be made a matter of public record could have a chilling effect on citizen participation. The courts historically have recognized this risk and have routinely protected this information from forced disclosure.

Rather than using the power of his office to ensure citizens' free speech rights are protected, Governor Bush has used law enforcement officers, paid by taxpayer dollars, to curtail free speech and jail his more vocal critics. He apparently forgot that public debate on his and every politician's records, is at the heart of this country's freedom.

Even *if* Bush didn't cook up the new rules for protesters, he did not *object* to them. Neither has he objected to his lawyers prying into the memberships of private organizations. This says he doesn't understand constitutional rights, or he doesn't believe in them. Either prospect is frightening.

AMERICAN
EMPIRE

*with quotes from Ronald Reagan, George H. W. Bush, Oliver
North, George Shultz, Richard Perle;
a quiz from from Paul Slansky;
and an anagram*

Republicans love war. War gives them an excuse to call their political opponents traitors. War helps them to reward campaign donors with fat government contracts to make weapons and rebuild cities they destroy with those weapons. War distracts Americans' attention from recessions, bear markets and federal deficits. War lets Republicans give unctuous speeches to real soldiers—who may not know that the beady-eyed little bantam in the flight jacket pulled every string in the book to avoid the Vietnam draft.

Quiz
Paul Slansky

True or false:

George W. Bush's nickname for Russian President Vladimir Putin is Vlad the Impaler.

Answer: False—he calls him Pootie-Poot.

They Said It . . .

"My fellow Americans: I'm pleased to tell you today that I've signed legislation that will outlaw Russia forever. We begin bombing in five minutes."
—Ronald Reagan, testing a microphone before a radio broadcast, 1984

"We love your adherence to democratic principle."
—George H. W. Bush in a toast to Philippine dictator Ferdinand Marcos, 1981

"I thought using the Ayatollah's money to support the Nicaraguan resistance . . . was a neat idea."
—Oliver North, former staff member of the National Security Council, 1987, discussing the diversion of funds from arms sales to Iran

Some of our smartest journalists live abroad these days, because much of their work is too controversial for the mainstream American media. Chris Floyd lives in England. He did manage to publish this piece in The Bergen Record *(Bergen County, NJ) a few weeks before the United States invaded Iraq.*

American Dominance
from *The Bergen Record* (2/23/03)
Chris Floyd

SUNDAY, FEBRUARY 23, 2003

An attack on Iraq. Vast increases in military spending. Planting new American bases all over the world, from the jungles of South America to the steppes of Central Asia. Embracing the concept of preemptive war and unilateral action as cornerstones of national strategy.

These policies may seem like reactions to the changed world confronting America after the Sept. 11 terrorist attacks. But in fact, each one of them—and many other policies now being advanced by the Bush administration—was planned years before the first plane ever struck the doomed Twin Towers.

They are the handiwork of an obscure but influential conservative group called Project for the New American Century, whose members—including Vice President Dick Cheney and Defense Secretary Donald Rumsfeld—now sit at the highest reaches of power. The papers they produced during the 1990s are like a roadmap of the course that America is following—a course that PNAC hopes will lead to an utterly dominant America in world affairs.

PNAC was formed in 1997, with a roster of conservative heavy-hitters, many of whom are now major players in the Bush administration. In addition to Cheney and Rumsfeld, the lineup included Paul Wolfowitz (now deputy defense secretary), Lewis Libby (Cheney's chief of staff), Zalmay Khalilzad (special emissary to Afghanistan), John Bolton (undersecretary of state for arms control), and Elliot Abrams, who was convicted of lying to Congress in the Iran-Contra scandal but was pardoned by George H. W. Bush (now White House director of Middle East policy).

Other influential participants included publisher Steve Forbes, conservative Christian activist Gary Bauer, former Secretary of Education William Bennett, former Vice President Dan Quayle, and Jeb Bush, brother of the president-to-be and now governor of Florida.

PNAC fired its first shot across the bow in 1998, with letters to President Clinton and congressional leaders calling for regime change in Iraq, by force if necessary, and the establishment of a strong U.S. military presence in the region. Then in September 2000, just months before the disputed election that brought George W. Bush to power, the group published a highly detailed, 90-page blueprint for transforming America's military—and the nation's role on the world stage.

The document, "Rebuilding America's Defenses," advocated a series of "revolutions" in national defense and foreign affairs—all of which have come to pass, in a very short time, since the Sept. 11 terrorist attacks.

The measures proposed in PNAC's 2000 report included:

Projecting American dominance with a "worldwide network of forward operating bases"—some permanent, others "temporary access arrangements" as needed for various military interventions—in the Middle East, Asia, and Latin America. These additions to America's already-extensive overseas deployments would act as "the cavalry on the new American frontier"—a frontier that PNAC declared now extended throughout the world.

Withdrawing from arms control treaties to allow for the development of a global missile shield, the deployment of space-based weapons, and the production of a new generation of battlefield nuclear weapons, especially so-called "bunker-busters" for penetrating underground fortifications.

Raising the U.S. military budget to at least 3.8 percent of gross domestic product, with annual increases of tens of billions of dollars each year.

Developing sophisticated new technologies to "control the global commons of cyberspace" by closely monitoring communications and transactions on the Internet.

Pursuing the development of "new methods of attack—electronic, non-lethal, biological . . . in new dimensions, in space, cyberspace, and perhaps the world of microbes."

Developing the ability to "fight and decisively win multiple, simultaneous major theater wars." This means moving beyond the two-war standard of preparedness that has guided U.S. strategy since World War II in order to account for "new realities and potential new conflicts." It lists countries such as Iraq, Iran, Syria, North Korea, and Libya as targets for those potential new conflicts, and urges Pentagon war planners to consider not merely containing them or defeating them in battle, but "changing their regimes."

Oddly enough, although regime change in Iraq was still clearly a priority for PNAC, it had little to do with Saddam Hussein and his brutal policies or his aggressive tendencies. Instead, removing Hussein was tied to the larger goal of establishing a permanent U.S. military presence in the Persian Gulf in order to secure energy supplies and preclude any other power from dominating the vital oil regions of the Middle East and Central Asia.

The PNAC report puts it quite plainly: "The United States has for decades sought to play a more permanent role in Gulf regional security. While the unresolved conflict with Iraq provides the immediate justification, the need for a substantial American force presence in the Gulf transcends the issue of the regime of Saddam Hussein."

Many critics say this is why the Bush administration has offered a constantly shifting menu of rationales for the impending attack on Iraq: because the decision to remove Hussein was taken long ago as part of a larger strategic plan, and has little to do with any imminent threat from the crippled Iraqi regime, which is constantly bombed, partially occupied (with U.S. forces already working in the autonomous Kurdish territories), and now swarming with United Nations inspectors. If the strategic need for the attack "transcends the issue of the regime of Saddam Hussein," then almost any rationale will do.

Perhaps due to the presence of Washington insiders like Cheney and Rumsfeld, the PNAC report recognized that thorny political difficulties could stand in the way of implementing the group's far-reaching designs. Indeed, in one of the most striking and prescient passages in the entire 90-page document, PNAC acknowledged that the revolutionary changes it envisaged could take decades to bring about—unless, that is, the United States was struck by "some catastrophic and catalyzing event—like a new Pearl Harbor."

That new Pearl Harbor did come, of course, in the thunderclap of Sept. 11, 2001. And the PNAC alumni now in government were quick to capitalize on this catalyzing event.

All of the PNAC recommendations listed above were put into place, with almost no debate from a shellshocked Congress and a populace reeling from the unprecedented assault on American security.

In the very first days following the attack, Rumsfeld urged the Bush Cabinet to make "Iraq a principal target of the first round in the war against terrorism," despite the lack of any proof connecting Baghdad to the terrorist atrocity, according to Bob Woodward's insider account, *Bush at War*.

But Rumsfeld was overruled by Colin Powell, who counseled that "public opinion has to be prepared before a move against Iraq is possible."

The "war on terrorism" was launched initially against Afghanistan, where the Taliban regime was harboring the Saudi terrorist Osama bin Laden and his band of international extremists. The attack on Afghanistan was accompanied by the construction of new American bases and "temporary access arrangements" throughout Central Asia, giving America a military "footprint" in the strategically vital region for the first time.

At the same time, new U.S. forces were dispatched to East Asia, to the Philippines, for example, where just last week American troops were ordered into direct combat against Muslim insurgents, and to South America, to help Colombia fight "narco-terrorists" and to protect that nation's vital oil pipelines.

Meanwhile, at home, military budgets skyrocketed to

deal with the "new realities and potential new conflicts." As it had earlier indicated it would, the Bush administration withdrew from the landmark ABM arms control treaty and began construction of missile defense facilities. It provided new funds for the militarization of outer space (dubbed "Full Spectrum Dominance"), and the development of "non-lethal" biochemical weapons. Pentagon technicians, led by another convicted Iran-Contra figure, John Poindexter, began the development of Internet data-mining and monitoring technology (which, despite some recent congressional restrictions, continues today).

And the U.S. announced a new nuclear strategy, including the willingness to use tactical nuclear weapons— a move supported by the Republican-led House of Representatives, which approved Pentagon plans to develop the bunker-buster nukes specifically recommended by PNAC. And just this month, Rumsfeld told Congress that he has asked the president for a special waiver that will allow American forces to use non-lethal chemical arms in subduing enemy armies—and enemy populations. The long-standing international treaties banning combat use of chemical weapons have "tangled us up so badly," Rumsfeld testified.

Finally, much of the PNAC philosophy was enshrined as official U.S. policy last September when Bush proclaimed a new National Security Strategy. Bush even adopted some of the same language found in the PNAC reports. He stated that no global rival would be allowed even the "hope of surpassing or equaling the power of the United States" and pledged that America would maintain its "global leadership" through "the unparalleled strength of the United States armed forces and their forward presence" around the world.

Bush pledged the United States to PNAC's cherished principle of preemptive war, saying the nation will act not only against imminent threats but also "against emerging threats before they are fully formed." Bush called this "the path of action—the only path to peace and security." He declared that America would use its power of global leadership to promote the "single sustainable model of national success"—a free enterprise system that Bush describes in some detail, including low taxes, little government regulation of business, and open markets for international investors.

The existence of PNAC and its influence on the Bush administration is not some sinister conspiracy theory. It follows a pattern frequently seen in American history: A group of like-minded people band together in think tanks, foundations, universities, and other institutions, where they lay out their vision for America's future. And when they at last have access to the levers of power, they try to make that vision a reality. In that sense, the PNAC group is not so different from the academics and activists behind Lyndon Johnson's Great Society programs, for example.

What is different now is that the Sept. 11 attacks have given this particular group an unprecedented amount of political capital—not to mention cold, hard federal cash—to put their long-held dreams into practice, virtually without opposition. What is also different is the essential goal of that vision: the establishment of what might almost amount to an American empire.

This empire would be different from the old Roman or British models, of course. It would not entail direct occupation of foreign lands, but instead offer paternal protection and guidance—albeit backed up with strategically placed military bases and "temporary access arrangements" for the inevitable "constabulatory duties" required to enforce PNAC's longed-for "Pax Americana."

However, the intent is not conquest or plunder, but the

chance to bring "the single sustainable model of national success" to all the world, to set people, and their markets, free—as long as no "regional or global challenges to America's leadership" arise, of course.

But there will be costs to taking up what Thomas Donnelly, the principal author of the PNAC blueprint, calls "the free man's burden." Donnelly, a former journalist and legislative aide, wrote in the journal *Foreign Affairs* last year that America should look to its "imperial past" as a guide to its future.

Reviewing *The Savage Wars of Peace*, a pro–American dominance book by journalist Max Boot, Donnelly cites approvingly the "pacification" of the Philippines by American forces in 1898–1900, in which at least 100,000 Filipinos were killed in a bid for independence. He also points to the U.S. Army's success in subduing the Native American tribes in a series of small wars, and, closer to our time, the efficient "constabulatory operation" in Panama, which was invaded by the first President Bush in 1989.

Similar "savage wars of peace"—pacifications, counterinsurgencies, police actions, invasions—will be required to maintain American dominance, says Donnelly.

And here, too, George W. Bush has clearly echoed the thinking of the PNAC members who now surround him in the White House. Speaking at a Republican fund-raiser last August, the president seemed keenly aware of the heavy price in blood and treasure the nation will have to pay to maintain its imperium in the New American Century:

"There's no telling how many wars it will take to secure freedom in the homeland."

Wallace Shawn is an actor and playwright.

from *Fragments from a Diary*

from *The Nation* (3/31/03)

Wallace Shawn

You can say that Bush and his colleagues would like to conquer Iraq in order to possess a secure source of oil and to begin a process of controlling the world, but that may not fully account for the strength of their motivation, the evident fervor of their commitment.

Why are we being so ridiculously polite? It's as if there were some sort of gentlemen's agreement that prevents people from stating the obvious truth that Bush and his colleagues are exhilarated and thrilled by the thought of war, by the thought of the incredible power they will have over so many other people, by the thought of the immensity of what they will do, by the scale, the massiveness of the bombing they're planning, the violence, the killing, the blood, the deaths, the horror.

The love of killing is inside each one of us, and we can never be sure that it won't come out. We have to be grateful if it *doesn't* come out. In fact, it is utterly wrong for me to imagine that Bush is violent and I am not, that Bush is cruel and I am not. I am potentially just as much of a killer as he is, and I need the help of all the sages and poets and musicians and saints to guide me onto a better path, and I can only hope that the circumstances of my life will continue to be ones that help me to stay on that path. But we can't deny that Bush and his men, for whatever reason, are under the sway of the less peaceful side of their natures. From the first days after the World Trade Center fell, you could see in their faces that, however scary it might be to be holding the jobs they held, however heavy the responsibility might be for steering the ship of state in such troubled times, they in fact were loving it. Those faces glowed. You could see that special look that people always have when they've just been seized by that most purposeless of all things, a sense of purpose. This, combined with a lust for blood, makes for particularly dangerous leaders, so totally driven by their desire for violence that they're almost incapable of hearing anyone else's pleas for compromise or for peace.

Why do they want this war so much? Maybe we can never fully know the answer to that question. Why do some people want to be whipped by a dominatrix? Why do some people want so desperately to have sex with children that they can't prevent themselves from raping them, even though they know that what they're doing is wrong? Why did Hitler want to kill the Jews? Why do some people collect coins? Why do some people collect stamps?

We can't fully understand it. But it's clear that Bush and his group are in the grip of something. They're very far gone. Their narcissism and sense of omnipotence goes way beyond self-confidence, reaching the point that they're impervious to the disgust they provoke in others, or even oblivious to it. They've made very clear to the people of the world that they value American interests more than the world's interests and American profits more than the world's physical health, and yet they cheerfully expect the people of the world to accept their leadership in the matter of Iraq. They're so unshakable in their belief that everyone will like them that they happily summoned the world, a year ago, to observe what they'd done to the people they'd taken as prisoners, proudly exhibiting them on their knees in cages, under a ferocious sun, with their faces hooded and their bodies in chains. In other words, the only thing you can really say about them is that like all of those who for fifty years have sat in offices in Washington and dreamed of killing millions of enemies with nuclear weapons and chemical weapons and biological weapons, these people are sick. They have an illness. And it's getting to the point where there may be no cure.

Meanwhile, I read my *New York Times*, and it's all very calm. The people who write there seem to have a need to believe that their government, while sometimes wrong, of course, is not utterly insane, and must at least be trusted to raise the right questions. These writers just can't bear the thought of being completely alienated from the center of their society, their own government. Thus, although they themselves would have considered a "pre-emptive" invasion of Iraq two years ago to be absurd and crazy, they now take the idea seriously and weigh its merits respectfully and worry gravely about the danger posed by Iraq, even though Iraq is in no way more dangerous than it was two years ago, and in every possible way it is less dangerous.

In fact, the dispassionate tone of the "debate" about Iraq in the *New York Times* and on every television screen seems psychotically remote from the reality of what will happen if war actually occurs. We are talking about raining death down on human beings, about thousands and thousands of howling wounded human beings, dismembered corpses in pools of blood. Is this one of the "lessons of Vietnam" that people have learned—that the immorality of this unspeakable murdering must never be mentioned?

That the discussion of murder must never mention murder, and that even the critics of murder must always criticize it because it turns out not to be in our own best interest? Must these critics always say that the murders would come at too high a price for *us*, would be too expensive, would unbalance the budget, hurt the economy, cause us to stint on domestic priorities; that it would lose us our friends, that it would create new enemies? Can we never say that this butchering of human beings is horrifying and wrong?

Yesterday I walked through a neighborhood of shabby apartment buildings on shabby streets, and I ate lunch in a lousy restaurant. The bread a bit hard, and the lettuce was rather stiff and resistant. But the thing was, honestly, it wasn't that bad. I could survive some lousiness, some uncomfortableness, some decline. Back on the street, I kept walking for a while and wondered what would happen if we allowed some of the fossils to simply lie there under the sand, if we decided not to try to dominate the world. We'd have no control over what would happen. We'd let go and fall. How far would we sink? How far? How far? Sure, it's been great, the life of comfort and predictability. But imagine how it would feel if we could be on a path of increasing compassion, diminishing brutality, diminishing greed—I think it might actually feel wonderful to be alive.

They Said It . . .

"Why don't we give him AIDS?"
—Ronald Reagan's Secretary of State George Shultz, 1986, on what to do with Libyan President Moammar Qadaffi

"First, we would not accept a treaty that would not have been ratified, nor a treaty that I thought made sense for the country."
—George W. Bush, 2001, on the Kyoto Treaty on global warming

Senator Robert Byrd (D-WV) was a lonely voice on the Senate floor during the months leading up to the invasion of Iraq. His courage stood in stark contrast to the craven and self-serving flag-waving of Senators such as Richard Shelby (R-AL) and Larry Craig (R-ID).

We Stand Passively Mute
(2/21/03)

U.S. Senator Robert Byrd

To contemplate war is to think about the most horrible of human experiences. On this February day, as this nation stands at the brink of battle, every American on some level must be contemplating the horrors of war.

Yet, this Chamber is, for the most part, silent—ominously, dreadfully silent. There is no debate, no discussion, no attempt to lay out for the nation the pros and cons of this particular war. There is nothing.

We stand passively mute in the United States Senate, paralyzed by our own uncertainty, seemingly stunned by the sheer turmoil of events. Only on the editorial pages of our newspapers is there much substantive discussion of the prudence or imprudence of engaging in this particular war.

And this is no small conflagration we contemplate. This is no simple attempt to defang a villain. No. This coming battle, if it materializes, represents a turning point in U.S. foreign policy and possibly a turning point in the recent history of the world.

This nation is about to embark upon the first test of a revolutionary doctrine applied in an extraordinary way at an unfortunate time. The doctrine of preemption—the idea that the United States or any other nation can legitimately attack a nation that is not imminently threatening but may be threatening in the future—is a radical new twist on the traditional idea of self-defense. It appears to be in contravention of international law and the UN Charter. And it is being tested at a time of world-wide terrorism, making many countries around the globe wonder if they will soon be on our—or some other nation's—hit list. High level Administration figures recently refused to take nuclear weapons off of the table when discussing a possible attack against Iraq.

What could be more destabilizing and unwise than this type of uncertainty, particularly in a world where globalism has tied the vital economic and security interests of many nations so closely together? There are huge cracks emerging in our time-honored alliances, and U.S. intentions are suddenly subject to damaging worldwide speculation. Anti-Americanism based on mistrust, misinformation, suspicion, and alarming rhetoric from U.S. leaders is fracturing the once solid alliance against global terrorism which existed after September 11.

Here at home, people are warned of imminent terrorist attacks with little guidance as to when or where such attacks might occur. Family members are being called to active military duty, with no idea of the duration of their stay or what horrors they may face. Communities are being left with less than adequate police and fire protection. Other essential services are also short-staffed. The mood of the nation is grim. The economy is stumbling. Fuel prices are rising and may soon spike higher.

This Administration, now in power for a little over two years, must be judged on its record. I believe that that record is dismal.

In that scant two years, this Administration has squandered a large projected surplus of some $5.6 trillion over the next decade and taken us to projected deficits as far as the eye can see. This Administration's domestic policy has put many of our states in dire financial condition, under funding scores of essential programs for our people. This Administration has fostered policies which have slowed economic growth. This Administration has ignored urgent matters such as the crisis in health care for our elderly. This Administration has been slow to provide adequate funding for homeland security. This Administration has been reluctant to better protect our long and porous borders.

In foreign policy, this Administration has failed to find Osama bin Laden. In fact, just yesterday we heard from him again marshaling his forces and urging them to kill. This Administration has split traditional alliances, possibly crippling, for all time, international order-keeping entities like the United Nations and NATO. This Administration has called into question the traditional worldwide perception of the United States as well-intentioned peacekeeper.

This Administration has turned the patient art of diplomacy into threats, labeling, and name calling of the sort that reflects quite poorly on the intelligence and sensitivity of our leaders, and which will have consequences for years to come.

Calling heads of state pygmies, labeling whole countries as evil, denigrating powerful European allies as irrelevant—these types of crude insensitivities can do our great nation no good. We may have massive military might, but we cannot fight a global war on terrorism alone. We need the cooperation and friendship of our time-honored allies as well as the newer found friends whom we can attract with our wealth. Our awesome military machine will do us little good if we suffer another devastating attack on our home-land which severely damages our economy. Our military manpower is already stretched thin and we will need the augmenting support of those nations who can supply troop strength, not just sign letters cheering us on.

The war in Afghanistan has cost us $37 billion so far, yet there is evidence that terrorism may already be starting to regain its hold in that region. We have not found bin Laden, and unless we secure the peace in Afghanistan, the dark dens of terrorism may yet again flourish in that remote and devastated land.

Pakistan as well is at risk of destabilizing forces. This Administration has not finished the first war against ter-rorism and yet it is eager to embark on another conflict with perils much greater than those in Afghanistan. Is our attention span that short? Have we not learned that after winning the war one must always secure the peace?

And yet we hear little about the aftermath of war in Iraq. In the absence of plans, speculation abroad is rife. Will we seize Iraq's oil fields, becoming an occupying power which controls the price and supply of that nation's oil for the foreseeable future? To whom do we propose to hand the reigns of power after Saddam Hussein?

Will our war inflame the Muslim world resulting in devastating attacks on Israel? Will Israel retaliate with its own nuclear arsenal? Will the Jordanian and Saudi Ara-bian governments be toppled by radicals, bolstered by Iran which has much closer ties to terrorism than Iraq?

Could a disruption of the world's oil supply lead to a world-wide recession? Has our senselessly bellicose language and our callous disregard of the interests and opinions of other nations increased the global race to join the nuclear club and made proliferation an even more lucrative practice for nations which need the income?

In only the space of two short years this reckless and arrogant Administration has initiated policies which may reap disastrous consequences for years.

One can understand the anger and shock of any President after the savage attacks of September 11. One can appreciate the frustration of having only a shadow to chase and an amorphous, fleeting enemy on which it is nearly impossible to exact retribution.

But to turn one's frustration and anger into the kind of extremely destabilizing and dangerous foreign policy debacle that the world is currently witnessing is inexcusable from any Administration charged with the awesome power and responsibility of guiding the destiny of the greatest superpower on the planet. Frankly many of the pronouncements made by this Administration are outrageous. There is no other word.

Yet this chamber is hauntingly silent. On what is possibly the eve of horrific infliction of death and destruction on the population of the nation of Iraq—a population, I might add, of which over 50 percent is under age 15—this chamber is silent. On what is possibly only days before we send thousands of our own citizens to face unimagined horrors of chemical and biological warfare—this chamber is silent. On the eve of what could possibly be a vicious terrorist attack in retaliation for our attack on Iraq, it is business as usual in the United States Senate.

We are truly "sleepwalking through history." In my heart of hearts I pray that this great nation and its good and trusting citizens are not in for a rudest of awakenings.

To engage in war is always to pick a wild card. And war

must always be a last resort, not a first choice. I truly must question the judgment of any President who can say that a massive unprovoked military attack on a nation which is over 50 percent children is "in the highest moral traditions of our country." This war is not necessary at this time. Pressure appears to be having a good result in Iraq.

Our mistake was to put ourselves in a corner so quickly. Our challenge is to now find a graceful way out of a box of our own making. Perhaps there is still a way if we allow more time.

Here's another of Senator Byrd's speeches to the Senate.

The Arrogance of Power
(3/19/03)

U.S. Senator Robert Byrd

I believe in this beautiful country. I have studied its roots and gloried in the wisdom of its magnificent Constitution. I have marveled at the wisdom of its founders and framers. Generation after generation of Americans has understood the lofty ideals that underlie our great Republic. I have been inspired by the story of their sacrifice and their strength.

But, today I weep for my country. I have watched the events of recent months with a heavy, heavy heart. No more is the image of America one of strong, yet benevolent peacekeeper. The image of America has changed. Around the globe, our friends mistrust us, our word is disputed, our intentions are questioned.

Instead of reasoning with those with whom we disagree, we demand obedience or threaten recrimination. Instead of isolating Saddam Hussein, we seem to have isolated ourselves. We proclaim a new doctrine of preemption which is understood by few and feared by many. We say that the United States has the right to turn its firepower on any corner of the globe which might be suspect in the war on terrorism. We assert that right without the sanction of any international body. As a result, the world has become a much more dangerous place.

We flaunt our superpower status with arrogance. We treat UN Security Council members like ingrates who offend our princely dignity by lifting their heads from the carpet. Valuable alliances are split. After war has ended, the United States will have to rebuild much more than the country of Iraq. We will have to rebuild America's image around the globe.

The case this Administration tries to make to justify its fixation with war is tainted by charges of falsified documents and circumstantial evidence. We cannot convince the world of the necessity of this war for one simple reason. This is a war of choice.

There is no credible information to connect Saddam Hussein to 9/11. The twin towers fell because a worldwide terrorist group, Al Qaeda, with cells in over 60 nations, struck at our wealth and our influence by turning our own planes into missiles, one of which would likely have slammed into the dome of this beautiful Capitol except for the brave sacrifice of the passengers on board.

The brutality seen on September 11th and in other terrorist attacks we have witnessed around the globe are the violent and desperate efforts by extremists to stop the daily encroachment of Western values upon their cultures. That is what we fight. It is a force not confined to borders. It is a shadowy entity with many faces, many names, and many addresses.

But, this Administration has directed all of the anger, fear, and grief which emerged from the ashes of the twin towers and the twisted metal of the Pentagon towards a tangible villain, one we can see and hate and attack. And villain he is. But, he is the wrong villain. And this is the wrong war. If we attack Saddam Hussein, we will probably drive him from power. But, the zeal of our friends to assist our global war on terrorism may have already taken flight.

The general unease surrounding this war is not just due to "orange alert." There is a pervasive sense of rush and risk and too many questions unanswered. How long will we be in Iraq? What will be the cost? What is the ultimate mission? How great is the danger at home? A pall has fallen over the Senate Chamber. We avoid our solemn duty to debate the one topic on the minds of all Americans, even while scores of thousands of our sons and daughters faithfully do their duty in Iraq.

What is happening to this country? When did we become a nation which ignores and berates our friends? When did we decide to risk undermining international order by adopting a radical and doctrinaire approach to using our awesome military might? How can we abandon diplomatic efforts when the turmoil in the world cries out for diplomacy?

Why can this President not seem to see that America's

true power lies not in its will to intimidate, but in its ability to inspire?

War appears inevitable. But, I continue to hope that the cloud will lift. Perhaps Saddam will yet turn tail and run. Perhaps reason will somehow still prevail. I along with millions of Americans will pray for the safety of our troops, for the innocent civilians in Iraq, and for the security of our homeland. May God continue to bless the United States of America in the troubled days ahead, and may we somehow recapture the vision which for the present eludes us.

ANAGRAM
....

George Walker Bush, President of the USA:
The bugger seeks of oil. He's a warped runt.

This email made the rounds during the build-up to the invasion of Iraq.

Warmonger Explains
War with Iraq to Peacenik

PEACENIK: Why did you say we are invading Iraq?

WARMONGER: We are invading Iraq because it is in violation of security council resolution 1441. A country cannot be allowed to violate security council resolutions.

PN: But I thought many of our allies, including Israel, were in violation of more security council resolutions than Iraq.

WM: It's not just about UN resolutions. The main point is that Iraq could have weapons of mass destruction, and the first sign of a smoking gun could well be a mushroom cloud over NY.

PN: Mushroom cloud? But I thought the weapons inspectors said Iraq had no nuclear weapons.

WM: Yes, but biological and chemical weapons are the issue.

PN: But I thought Iraq did not have any long range missiles for attacking us or our allies with such weapons.

WM: The risk is not Iraq directly attacking us, but rather terrorist networks that Iraq could sell the weapons to.

PN: But couldn't virtually any country sell chemical or biological materials? We sold quite a bit to Iraq in the eighties ourselves, didn't we?

WM: That's ancient history. Look, Saddam Hussein is an evil man that has an undeniable track record of repressing his own people since the early eighties. He gasses his enemies. Everyone agrees that he is a power-hungry lunatic murderer.

PN: We sold chemical and biological materials to a power-hungry lunatic murderer?

WM: The issue is not what we sold, but rather what Saddam did. He is the one that launched a pre-emptive first strike on Kuwait.

PN: A pre-emptive first strike does sound bad. But didn't our ambassador to Iraq, April Glaspie, know about and green-light the invasion of Kuwait?

WM: Let's deal with the present, shall we? As of today, Iraq could sell its biological and chemical weapons to Al Qaeda. Osama bin Laden himself released an audio tape calling on Iraqis to suicide attack us, proving a partnership between the two.

PN: Osama bin Laden? Wasn't the point of invading Afghanistan to kill him?

WM: Actually, it's not 100% certain that it's really Osama bin Laden on the tapes. But the lesson from the tape is the same: there could easily be a partnership between Al Qaeda and Saddam Hussein unless we act.

PN: Is this the same audio tape where Osama bin Laden labels Saddam a secular infidel?

WM: You're missing the point by just focusing on the tape. Powell presented a strong case against Iraq.

PN: He did?

WM: Yes, he showed satellite pictures of an Al Qaeda poison factory in Iraq.

PN: But didn't that turn out to be a harmless shack in the part of Iraq controlled by the Kurdish opposition?

WM: And a British intelligence report . . .

PN: Didn't that turn out to be copied from an out-of-date graduate student paper?

WM: And reports of mobile weapons labs . . .

PN: Weren't those just artistic renderings?

WM: And reports of Iraqis scuttling and hiding evidence from inspectors . . .

PN: Wasn't that evidence contradicted by the chief weapons inspector, Hans Blix?

WM: Yes, but there is plenty of other hard evidence that cannot be revealed because it would compromise our security.

PN: So there is no publicly available evidence of weapons of mass destruction in Iraq?

WM: The inspectors are not detectives, it's not their JOB to find evidence. You're missing the point.

PN: So what is the point?

WM: The main point is that we are invading Iraq because resolution 1441 threatened "severe consequences." If we do not act, the security council will become an irrelevant debating society.

PN: So the main point is to uphold the rulings of the security council?

WM: Absolutely . . . unless it rules against us.

PN: And what if it does rule against us?

WM: In that case, we must lead a coalition of the willing to invade Iraq.

PN: Coalition of the willing? Who's that?

WM: Britain, Turkey, Bulgaria, Spain, and Italy, for starters.

PN: I thought Turkey refused to help us unless we gave them tens of billions of dollars.

WM: Nevertheless, they may now be willing.

PN: I thought public opinion in all those countries was against war.

WM: Current public opinion is irrelevant. The majority expresses its will by electing leaders to make decisions.

PN: So it's the decisions of leaders elected by the majority that is important?

WM: Yes.

PN: But George B—

WM: I mean, we must support the decisions of our leaders, however they were elected, because they are acting in our best interest. This is about being a patriot. That's the bottom line.

PN: So if we do not support the decisions of the president, we are not patriotic?

WM: I never said that.

PN: So what are you saying? Why are we invading Iraq?

WM: As I said, because there is a chance that they have weapons of mass destruction that threaten us and our allies.

PN: But the inspectors have not been able to find any such weapons.

WM: Iraq is obviously hiding them.

PN: You know this? How?

WM: Because we know they had the weapons ten years ago, and they are still unaccounted for.

PN: The weapons we sold them, you mean?

WM: Precisely.

PN: But I thought those biological and chemical weapons would degrade to an unusable state over ten years.

WM: But there is a chance that some have not degraded.

PN: So as long as there is even a small chance that such weapons exist, we must invade?

WM: Exactly.

PN: But North Korea actually has large amounts of usable chemical, biological, AND nuclear weapons, AND long range missiles that can reach the west coast AND it has expelled nuclear weapons inspectors, AND threatened to turn America into a sea of fire.

WM: That's a diplomatic issue.

PN: So why are we invading Iraq instead of using diplomacy?

WM: Aren't you listening? We are invading Iraq because we cannot allow the inspections to drag on indefinitely. Iraq has been delaying, deceiving, and denying for over ten years, and inspections cost us tens of millions.

PN: But I thought war would cost us tens of billions.

WM: Yes, but this is not about money. This is about security.

PN: But wouldn't a pre-emptive war against Iraq ignite radical Muslim sentiments against us, and decrease our security?

WM: Possibly, but we must not allow the terrorists to change the way we live. Once we do that, the terrorists have already won.

PN: So what is the purpose of the Department of Homeland Security, color-coded terror alerts, and the Patriot Act? Don't these change the way we live?

WM: I thought you had questions about Iraq.

PN: I do. Why are we invading Iraq?

WM: For the last time, we are invading Iraq because the world has called on Saddam Hussein to disarm, and he has failed to do so. He must now face the consequences.

PN: So, likewise, if the world called on us to do something, such as find a peaceful solution, we would have an obligation to listen?

WM: By "world," I meant the United Nations.

PN: So, we have an obligation to listen to the United Nations?

WM: By "United Nations" I meant the Security Council.

PN: So, we have an obligation to listen to the Security Council?

WM: I meant the majority of the Security Council.

PN: So, we have an obligation to listen to the majority of the Security Council?

WM: Well . . . there could be an unreasonable veto.

PN: In which case?

WM: In which case, we have an obligation to ignore the veto.

PN: And if the majority of the Security Council does not support us at all?

WM: Then we have an obligation to ignore the Security Council.

PN: That makes no sense:

WM: If you love Iraq so much, you should move there. Or maybe France, with the all the other cheese-eating surrender monkeys. It's time to boycott their wine and cheese, no doubt about that.

PN: I give up.

Jonathan Schell's Cold War bestseller The Fate of the Earth *(1982) made the case for the elimination of nuclear weapons. More recently, he argued that Bush's policy of pre-emptive war would intensify the threat of nuclear proliferation.*

from The Case Against the War

from *The Nation* (3/3/03)

Jonathan Schell

THE LOST WAR

In his poem *Fall 1961*, written when the cold war was at its zenith, Robert Lowell wrote:

> All autumn, the chafe and jar
> of nuclear war;
> we have talked our extinction to death.

This autumn and winter, nuclear danger has returned, in a new form, accompanied by danger from the junior siblings in the mass destruction family, chemical and biological weapons. Now it is not a crisis between two superpowers but the planned war to overthrow the government of Iraq that, like a sentence of execution that has been passed but must go through its final appeals before being carried out, we have talked to death. (Has any war been so lengthily premeditated before it was launched?) Iraq, the United States insists, possesses some of these weapons. To take them away, the United States will overthrow the Iraqi government. No circumstance is more likely to provoke Iraq to use any forbidden weapons it has. In that event, the Bush Administration has repeatedly said, it will itself consider the use of nuclear weapons. Has there ever been a clearer or more present danger of the use of weapons of mass destruction?

While we were all talking and the danger was growing, strange to say, the war was being lost. For wars, let us recall, are not fought for their own sake but to achieve aims. Victory cannot be judged only by the outcome of battles. In the American Revolutionary War, for example, Edmund Burke, a leader of England's antiwar movement, said, "Our victories can only complete our ruin." Almost two centuries later, in Vietnam, the United States triumphed in almost every military engagement, yet lost the war. If the aim is lost, the war is lost, whatever happens on the battlefield. The novelty this time is that the defeat has preceded the inauguration of hostilities.

The aim of the Iraq war has never been only to disarm Iraq. George Bush set forth the full aim of his war policy in unmistakable terms on January 29, 2002, in his first State of the Union address. It was to stop the spread of weapons of mass destruction, not only in Iraq but everywhere in the world, through the use of military force. "We must," he said, "prevent the terrorists and regimes who seek chemical, biological or nuclear weapons from threatening the United States and the world." He underscored the scope of his ambition by singling out three countries—North Korea, Iran and Iraq—for special mention, calling them an "axis of evil." Then came the ultimatum: "The United States of America will not permit the world's most dangerous regimes to threaten us with the world's most destructive weapons." Other possible war aims—to defeat Al Qaeda, to spread democracy—came and went in Administration pronouncements, but this one has remained constant. Stopping the spread of weapons of mass destruction is the reason for war given alike to the Security Council, whose inspectors are now searching for such weapons in Iraq, and to the American people, who were advised in the recent State of the Union address to fear "a day of horror like none we have ever known."

The means whereby the United States would stop the prohibited acquisitions were first set forth last June 1 in the President's speech to the graduating class at West Point. The United States would use force, and use it preemptively. "If we wait for threats to fully materialize, we will have waited too long," he said. For "the only path to safety is the path of action. And this nation will act." This strategy, too, has remained constant.

The Bush policy of using force to stop the spread of weapons of mass destruction met its Waterloo last October, when Assistant Secretary of State for East Asian and Pacific Affairs James Kelly was informed by Vice Foreign Minister Kang Sok Ju of North Korea that his country has a perfect right to possess nuclear weapons. Shortly,

Secretary of State Colin Powell stated, "We have to assume that they might have one or two . . . that's what our intelligence community has been saying for some time." (Doubts, however, remain.) Next, North Korea went on to announce that it was terminating the Agreed Framework of 1994, under which it had shut down two reactors that produced plutonium. It ejected the UN inspectors who had been monitoring the agreement and then announced its withdrawal from the Nuclear Nonproliferation Treaty, under whose terms it was obligated to remain nuclear-weapon-free. Soon, America stated that North Korea might be moving fuel rods from existing reactors to its plutonium reprocessing plant, and that it possessed an untested missile capable of striking the western United States. "We will not permit . . ." had been Bush's words, but North Korea went ahead and apparently produced nuclear weapons anyway. The Administration now discovered that its policy of preemptively using overwhelming force had no application against a proliferator with a serious military capability, much less a nuclear power. North Korea's conventional capacity alone—it has an army of more than a million men and 11,000 artillery pieces capable of striking South Korea's capital, Seoul—imposed a very high cost; the addition of nuclear arms, in combination with missiles capable of striking not only South Korea but Japan, made it obviously prohibitive.

By any measure, totalitarian North Korea's possession of nuclear weapons is more dangerous than the mere possibility that Iraq is trying to develop them. The North Korean state, which is hard to distinguish from a cult, is also more repressive and disciplined than the Iraqi state, and has caused the death of more of its own people—through starvation. Yet in the weeks that followed the North Korean disclosure, the Administration, in a radical reversal of the President's earlier assessments, sought to argue that the opposite was true. Administration spokespersons soon declared that the North Korean situation was "not a crisis" and that its policy toward that country was to be one of "dialogue," leading to "a peaceful multilateral solution," including the possibility of renewed oil shipments. But if the acquisition by North Korea of nuclear arms was not a crisis, then there never had been any need to warn the world of the danger of nuclear proliferation, or to name an axis of evil, or to deliver an ultimatum to disarm it.

For the North Korean debacle represented not the failure of a good policy but exposure of the futility of one that was impracticable from the start. Nuclear proliferation, when considered as the global emergency that it is, has never been, is not now and never will be stoppable by military force; on the contrary, force can only exacerbate the problem. In announcing its policy, the United States appeared to have forgotten what proliferation is. It is not army divisions or tanks crossing borders; it is above all technical know-how passing from one mind to another. It cannot be stopped by B-2 bombers, or even Predator drones. The case of Iraq had indeed always been an anomaly in the wider picture of nonproliferation. In the 1991 Gulf War, the US-led coalition waged war to end Iraq's occupation of Kuwait. In the process it stumbled on Saddam Hussein's program for building weapons of mass destruction, and made use of the defeat to impose on him the new obligation to end the program. A war fought for one purpose led to peace terms serving another. It was a historical chain of events unlikely ever to be repeated, and offered no model for dealing with proliferation.

The lesson so far? Exactly the opposite of the intended one: If you want to avoid "regime change" by the United States, build a nuclear arsenal—but be sure to do it quietly and fast. As Mohamed ElBaradei, the director general of the International Atomic Energy Agency, has said, the United States seems to want to teach the world that "if you really want to defend yourself, develop nuclear weapons, because then you get negotiations, and not military action."

Although the third of the "axis" countries presents no immediate crisis, events there also illustrate the bankruptcy of the Bush policy. With the help of Russia, Iran is building nuclear reactors that are widely believed to double as a nuclear weapons program. American threats against Iraq have failed to dissuade Iran—or for that matter, its supplier, Russia—from proceeding. Just this week, Iran announced that it had begun to mine uranium on its own soil. Iran's path to acquiring nuclear arms, should it decide to go ahead, is clear. "Regime change" by American military action in that half-authoritarian, half-democratic country is a formula for disaster. Whatever the response of the Iraqi people might be to an American invasion, there is little question that in Iran hard-liners and democrats alike would mount bitter, protracted resistance. Nor is there evidence that democratization in Iraq, even in the unlikely event that it should succeed, would be a sure path to denuclearization. The world's first nuclear power, after all, was a democracy, and of nine nuclear powers now in the world, six—the United States, England,

France, India, Israel and Russia—are also democracies. Iran, within striking range of Israel, lives in an increasingly nuclearized neighborhood. In these circumstances, would the Iranian people be any more likely to rebel against nuclearization than the Indian people did—or more, for that matter, than the American people have done? And if a democratic Iran obtained the bomb, would pre-emption or regime change then be an option for the United States?

The collapse of the overall Bush policy has one more element that may be even more significant than the appearance of North Korea's arsenal or Iran's apparently unstoppable discreet march to obtaining the bomb. It has turned out that the supplier of essential information and technology for North Korea's uranium program was America's faithful ally in the war on terrorism, Pakistan, which received missile technology from Korea in return. The "father" of Pakistan's bomb, Ayub Qadeer Khan, has visited North Korea thirteen times. This is the same Pakistan whose nuclear scientist Sultan Bashiruddin Mahood paid a visit to Osama bin Laden in Afghanistan a few months before September 11, and whose nuclear establishment even today is riddled with Islamic fundamentalists. The BBC has reported that the Al Qaeda network succeeded at one time in building a "dirty bomb" (which may account for Osama bin Laden's claim that he possesses nuclear weapons), and Pakistan is the likeliest source for the materials involved, although Russia is also a candidate. Pakistan, in short, has proved itself to be the world's most dangerous proliferator, having recently acquired nuclear weapons itself and passed on nuclear technology to a state and, possibly, to a terrorist group.

Indeed, an objective ranking of nuclear proliferators in

order of menace would place Pakistan (a possessor of the bomb that also purveys the technology to others) first on the list, North Korea second (it peddles missiles but not, so far, bomb technology), Iran (a country of growing political and military power with an active nuclear program) third, and Iraq (a country of shrinking military power that probably has no nuclear program and is currently under international sanctions and an unprecedented inspection regime of indefinite duration) fourth. (Russia, possessor of 150 tons of poorly guarded plutonium, also belongs somewhere on this list.) The Bush Administration ranks them, of course, in exactly the reverse order, placing Iraq, which it plans to attack, first, and Pakistan, which it befriends and coddles, nowhere on the list. It will not be possible, however, to right this pyramid. The reason it is upside down is that it was unworkable right side up. Iraq is being attacked not because it is the worst proliferator but because it is the weakest.

The *reductio ad absurdum* of the failed American war policy was illustrated by a recent column in the *Washington Post* by the superhawk Charles Krauthammer. Krauthammer wants nothing to do with soft measures; yet he, too, can see that the cost of using force against North Korea would be prohibitive: "Militarily, we are not even in position to bluff." He rightly understands, too, that in the climate created by pending war in Iraq, "dialogue" is scarcely likely to succeed. He has therefore come up with a new idea. He identifies China as the solution. China must twist the arm of its Communist ally North Korea. "If China and South Korea were to cut off North Korea, it could not survive," he observes. But to make China do so, the United States must twist China's arm. How? By encouraging Japan to build nuclear weapons. For "if our nightmare is a nuclear North Korea, China's is a nuclear Japan." It irks Krauthammer that the United States alone has to face up to the North Korean threat. Why shouldn't China shoulder some of the burden? He wants to "share the nightmares." Indeed. He wants to stop nuclear proliferation with more nuclear proliferation. Here the nuclear age comes full circle. The only nation ever to use the bomb is to push the nation on which it dropped it to build the bomb and threaten others.

As a recommendation for policy, Krauthammer's suggestion is Strangelovian, but if it were considered as a prediction it would be sound. Nuclear armament by North Korea really will tempt neighboring nations—not only Japan but South Korea and Taiwan—to acquire nuclear weapons. (Japan has an abundant supply of plutonium and all the other technology necessary, and both South Korea and Taiwan have had nuclear programs but were persuaded by the United States to drop them.) In a little-noticed comment, Japan's foreign minister has already stated that the nuclearization of North Korea would justify a pre-emptive strike against it by Japan. Thus has the Bush plan to stop proliferation already become a powerful force promoting it. The policy of preemptive war has led to preemptive defeat.

I Hate Republicans READER They Said It . . .

"If we let our vision of the world go forth and don't try to piece together clever diplomacy, but wage total war . . . our children will sing great songs about us."
—Richard Perle, former chairman of the Defense Policy Board and cofounder of the Project for the New American Century

AND MORE . . .

FROM 888 REASONS TO HATE REPUBLICANS
BARBARA LAGOWSKI and RICK MUMMA–393

with a quote from Ronald Reagan;
excerpt from a novel by Marilyn T. Quayle and Nancy T. Northcott;
a quiz from Paul Slansky;
and anagrams

**"My name is Ronald Reagan.
What's yours?"**
—Reagan to his son Michael at Michael's
high-school graduation

Here are a few more random reasons to hate Republicans.

from 888 *Reasons to Hate Republicans*
(1996)

Barbara Lagowski and Rick Mumma

- Spiro Agnew, "a flat-out knee-crawling thug with the morals of a weasel on speed"—Hunter Thompson
- They prefer the Second Amendment to the Fifth.
- Antisodomy laws
- Assault weapons
- They would give more autonomy to the states, including the likes of Mississippi, Alabama, and Utah.
- "Republicans are . . . bloodsuckers with offices in Wall Street, princes of privilege, plunderers."—Harry S. Truman giving 'em hell in 1948
- Boards of Directors
- Fondness for bootstrap and grindstone metaphors
- They're boring.

- Bread lines
- Pat Buchanan
- William F. Buckley
- They would protect book burning and witch burning before flag burning.
- "The business of government is to keep government out of business—that is, unless business needs government aid."—Will Rogers
- "Capitalist pornography" (any book by or about Donald Trump, H. Ross Perot, Warren Buffett, Bill Gates, et al.)
- They have "careers" rather than lives.
- CEOs
- CFOs
- COOs
- They believe that when Christ comes back he'll be a social conservative with a trickle-down strategy for salvation.
- The myth of a classless America perpetuated by members of private clubs living off dividends.
- They coach Little League teams to win at all costs.
- They tend to confuse the accident of fortunate birth with virtue or hard work.
- Their credit cards are never rejected in full view of everybody else in the Wal-Mart checkout line.
- Reagan "Democrats"
- Disciplinarians
- They care more about their dogs than they do the homeless.
- Dress codes
- Dressing for dinner
- Dressing for success

- Flagrant flag wavers every Fourth of July who would have been temperamentally Tories on July 4, 1776.
- *Forbes:* Capitalist Tool
- *Fortune*
- The great 401k conspiracy to turn otherwise normal people into Republicans by tying all their retirement funds to the fate of the stockmarket
- Gated communities
- Go-getters, self-starters, and all the other eager beavers who make life hell for the rest of us
- Golf
- "Good" wars
- Hawks
- Homophobia
- Humorlessness
- They're rich enough to worry about inheritance taxes kicking in after the first one million.
- Pathological interest in interest rate fluctuations
- Investment bankers
- They're almost as proud of tearing down the Iron Curtain as they are building a ten-foot-high steel wall between California and Mexico.
- The Junior League
- Kennebunkport
- They know their tax brackets.
- Lean and mean workforces cut to the bone for the immediate gratification of fat and lazy stockholders
- Rush Limbaugh
- They live in suburbs where they never have to confront their racism.
- They look, without apparent irony, for business advice from Genghis Khan and Attila the Hun.

- LOVE IT OR LEAVE IT bumper stickers
- They became the majority party by pandering to the majority race.
- If you mention "the Market" to them, they think of the New York Stock Exchange, not the Piggly Wiggly.
- Military-style haircuts
- Military schools
- *Money*
- The National Rifle Association
- Negative campaigning
- "Nobody talks more of free enterprise and competition and of the best man winning than the man who inherited his father's store or farm."—C. Wright Mills
- Peggy Noonan, for crafting the greeting-card sentiments that made Reagan and Bush sound almost human
- Ollie North's gap-toothed smile
- Cutting nutrition programs for the poor
- In your heart, you know they're nuts.
- The 1 percent of American families who control 40 percent of American wealth
- They invented passive aggression.
- They consistently include electric chairs, firing squads, gas chambers, hanging, lethal injection, and the Right to Life as planks in their party platforms.
- They prefer property rights to civil rights.
- They insist upon imposing the Protestant Work Ethic on those who aren't.
- They proudly display photos of their dogs.
- They believe that the only public housing worthy of federal funding is the kind that comes equipped with electrified fences and guard towers.
- They define the pursuit of happiness as the pursuit of dollars.

- Random locker searches
- Redistribution of wealth from the middle class to the truly wealthy
- Right-to-Life as a euphemism for reproductive slavery
- Right-to-work as a euphemism for union busting
- The right to unfettered consumption
- They see selfishness as a virtue.
- They consider women, minorities, children, the poor, and the elderly "special interests": white men of business (who make up the other 10 percent of the population) are not.
- Sport utility vehicles (whose primary utility lies in keeping the American gasoline refineries operating at full capacity)
- Clarence Thomas
- They laugh *at* the Three Stooges, not *with* them.
- They think that wearing a Jerry Garcia tie to their job at the bank makes them different from their fathers.
- They trust big business more than big government.
- Type-A personalities
- Their unhealthy interest in their employees' urine
- The only values they're really concerned about are property values.
- Because, as Frank Zappa said, "Republicans stand for raw, unbridled evil and greed and ignorance smothered in balloons and ribbons."

"[Not] until now has there ever been a time in which so many of the prophecies are coming together. There have been times in the past when people thought the end of the world was coming, and so forth, but never anything like this."

—Ronald Reagan on Armageddon, 1983

ANAGRAM

PRESIDENT GEORGE BUSH:
There's God! Superbeing!
Bugger the depression!
Oh! Desert purge begins!

ANAGRAM

G. Dubya:
Bad guy.

Quiz

Paul Slansky

One of Bush's two nicknames for his political strategist, Karl Rove, is Boy Genius. What's the other one?

(a) Karl Marx
(b) The Rove Man
(c) Turd Blossom
(d) Roveewade

Answer: (c)

Excerpt

"She heard the door close behind her, but her eyes were held by the gaunt figure before her, her husband, Jose. Jose really was standing before her . . . They pulled apart slightly, each needing to see the other's face, to reassure himself. Jose, Jose, Ines's mind sang. It really was he . . ."

—From *Embrace the Serpent*, a novel by Marilyn T. Quayle and Nancy T. Northcott

Republican Senators (left to right) Trent Lott, Larry Craig, John Ashcroft and Jim Jeffords.[*]

[*] Jeffords later came to his senses and left the GOP. Rock on.

An I Hate Republicans *Timeline:*

1869–2003

Nate Hardcastle

September 24
Black Friday: Republican president Ulysses S. Grant's associates James Fisk and Jay Gould attempt to corner the gold market. Financial panic ensues; thousands of people are ruined.

November 2
Warren G. Harding is elected, ushering in the most corrupt administration in US history.

| 1869 | 1895 | 1920 | 1921 | 1946 |

May 15
Prescott Sheldon Bush is born in Columbus, Ohio. He will go on to make a fortune, be investigated for financial ties to Nazi Germany, and have a son and grandson who each become president.

July 6
George W. Bush is born under the sign of Cancer in the wealthy New York suburb of New Canaan, Connecticut.

The Teapot Dome Scandal begins: Edward L. Doheny gives a $100,000 bribe to Secretary of the Interior Albert B. Fall in exchange for exclusive rights to Wyoming's Teapot Dome oil fields. Fall eventually receives bribes worth more than $400,000 (about $4.5 million in today's dollars).

AN *I HATE REPUBLICANS* TIMELINE

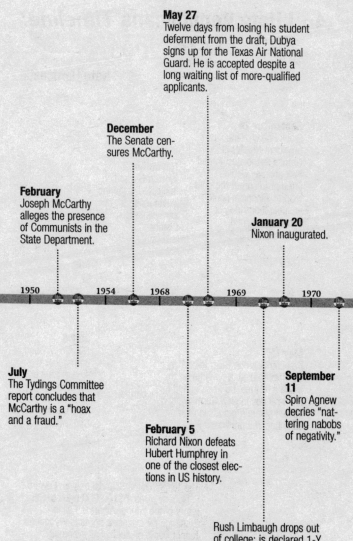

May 27
Twelve days from losing his student deferment from the draft, Dubya signs up for the Texas Air National Guard. He is accepted despite a long waiting list of more-qualified applicants.

December
The Senate censures McCarthy.

February
Joseph McCarthy alleges the presence of Communists in the State Department.

January 20
Nixon inaugurated.

1950   1954   1968   1969   1970

July
The Tydings Committee report concludes that McCarthy is a "hoax and a fraud."

September 11
Spiro Agnew decries "nattering nabobs of negativity."

February 5
Richard Nixon defeats Hubert Humphrey in one of the closest elections in US history.

Rush Limbaugh drops out of college; is declared 1-Y by the draft board because of a "pilonidal cyst."

AN *I HATE REPUBLICANS* TIMELINE

August–October
The *Washington Post* reports on links between the Watergate burglary and the Nixon reelection campaign.

October 20
The Saturday Night Massacre: Nixon fires special prosecutor Archibald Cox and abolishes the office of the special prosecutor.

June 13
The *New York Times* begins publishing the Pentagon Papers, exposing the secret history of the Vietnam War.

May 18
Senate Watergate Committee begins nationally televised hearings.

June 17, 2:30 A.M.
Five men are arrested trying to bug the Democratic National Committee headquarters in the Watergate hotel and office complex. One man claims links to the CIA.

November 7
Nixon is reelected in a landslide over Democratic candidate George McGovern.

1971   1972   1973

September 3
White House "plumbers" burglarize the office of former defense analyst Daniel Ellsburg's psychiatrist. They steal files on Ellsburg, the man who leaked the Pentagon Papers.

January 30
Former Nixon aides G. Gordon Liddy and James W. McCord, Jr., are convicted of conspiracy, burglary and wiretapping.

August
George W. Bush suspended from flight duty for missing a mandatory physical.

October 10
Vice-President Spiro Agnew resigns. Nixon chooses Gerald Ford to replace him.

September
George W. Bush transfers to an Alabama Guard unit. He never shows up for duty.

November 17
Nixon first says "I am not a crook."

AN *I HATE REPUBLICANS* TIMELINE

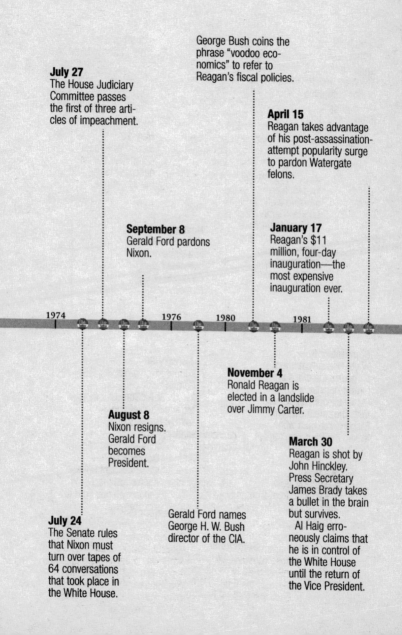

July 27
The House Judiciary Committee passes the first of three articles of impeachment.

George Bush coins the phrase "voodoo economics" to refer to Reagan's fiscal policies.

April 15
Reagan takes advantage of his post-assassination-attempt popularity surge to pardon Watergate felons.

September 8
Gerald Ford pardons Nixon.

January 17
Reagan's $11 million, four-day inauguration—the most expensive inauguration ever.

1974   1976   1980   1981

November 4
Ronald Reagan is elected in a landslide over Jimmy Carter.

August 8
Nixon resigns. Gerald Ford becomes President.

March 30
Reagan is shot by John Hinckley. Press Secretary James Brady takes a bullet in the brain but survives.
   Al Haig erroneously claims that he is in control of the White House until the return of the Vice President.

July 24
The Senate rules that Nixon must turn over tapes of 64 conversations that took place in the White House.

Gerald Ford names George H. W. Bush director of the CIA.

August 19
The Navy shoots down two Libyan jets. Attorney General Ed Meese decides not to wake Reagan.

April 14
Reagan denies that the administration is trying to overthrow the Sandanistas in Nicaragua: "That would be violating the law."

March 27
Nancy Reagan attends Washington's annual Gridiron Dinner dressed as a bag lady.

October 11
Nancy Reagan coins the phrase "just say no."

January 19
Ronald Reagan, whose tax returns show him giving 1.4% to charity, claims to believe in tithing.

July 1
Secretary of the Interior James Watt unveils his plan to open a billion acres of coastline to drilling during the next five years.

1982   1983

September 4
The Reagan administration, as part of a push to cut the size and quality of school lunches, declares that ketchup will be considered a vegetable.
  Nancy Reagan announces the acquisition of new White House china for $209,508.

June 7
Reagan falls asleep during a meeting with the Pope.

June 29
Reagan cites desegregation as a cause for the decline in public education.

November 25
Thanksgiving: Reagan Press Secretary Larry Speakes announces a plan to tax unemployment benefits in order to "make unemployment less attractive."

December 6
From Israeli newspaper *Maariv*: Reagan claimed to Israeli Prime Minister Yitzhak Shamir that during World War II he served in an army unit filming the horrors of Nazi concentration camps. Reagan in fact spent World War II in Hollywood making training films.

August
Reagan breaks air-traffic controllers strike.

February 9
George Bush claims he never used the phrase "voodoo economics." NBC broadcasts the tape of Bush doing so.

AN *I HATE REPUBLICANS* TIMELINE

August 13
White House deputy chief of staff Michael Deaver admits that Reagan sometimes falls asleep during Cabinet meetings.

February 16
Reagan repeats the story that he filmed death camps during World War II, this time to Rabbi Marvin Hier.

August 3
The percentage of Americans living in poverty hits 15.2%, the highest level in 18 years.

June 17
Chief Justice Warren Burger retires. Reagan replaces him with the reactionary William Rehnquist and promotes to the Supreme Court ultra-conservative Antonin Scalia—who later abandons his professed belief in judicial restraint to hand George W. Bush the 2000 presidential election.

May 20
Ed Meese names his pornography commission. While the commission proves completely ineffective at combating smut, it does succeed at compiling a hilariously comprehensive list of dirty book titles.

August 20
Jerry Falwell calls Bishop Desmond Tutu a phony.

1984   1985   1986

August 11
Reagan jokes during a sound check: "My fellow Americans, I'm pleased to tell you today that I've signed legislation that will outlaw Russia forever. We begin bombing in five minutes."

September 9
Nancy Reagan, participating in her very first rock video, sings a chorus of the anti-drug song "Stop the Madness."

March 13
Ed Meese admits having accepted a $15,000 interest-free loan from a man who later received a government job—an item he hadn't disclosed in his financial statements. His explanation: "It never occurred to me that an interest-free loan was a thing of value."

March 1
Reagan calls the Nicaraguan contras "the moral equal of our founding fathers."

March 18
Conservative gadfly William F. Buckley suggests that everyone with AIDS be tattooed on the forearm and the buttocks.

July 22
Reagan, during a speech explaining his opposition to sanctions on South Africa, refers to the country as South America.

January 9
The White House releases a January 17, 1986, document, bearing Reagan's signature, which authorizes the sale of arms to Iran and prohibits the CIA from telling Congress.

August 18
George H.W. Bush says "Read my lips: no new taxes!"—a promise he later has to rescind to combat the massive deficits he inherits from Reagan.

November 25
Ed Meese explains to the press that some proceeds from the Iran arms deal went to the contras. National security adviser John Poindexter resigns and his aide Oliver North is fired.

May 15
Reagan contradicts his previous claims of ignorance of the Iran-Contra affair, saying he was "very definitely involved in the decisions about support to the freedom fighters. It was my idea to begin with."

1987   1988   1989

December 9
North and Poindexter plead the fifth amendment during hearings before the House Foreign Affairs Committee.

November 8
George H.W. Bush is elected president, defeating Massachusetts governor Michael Dukakis.

November 13
Reagan admits authorizing "a secret diplomatic initiative" that entailed shipping arms to Iran "to effect the safe return of all hostages."

February 9
Former national security adviser Robert McFarlane attempts suicide by taking 20 Valiums the day before he is scheduled to testify before the Tower Commision's Iran-Contra hearings.

April 21
George W. Bush puts down $500,000 as part of a deal to buy the Texas Rangers. The ownership team later blackmails the city of Arlington into paying for a new stadium and trades Sammy Sosa.

AN *I HATE REPUBLICANS* TIMELINE

The Bahrainian government awards George W. Bush's oil company, Harken Energy, exclusive offshore drilling rights—despite the fact that the firm had never drilled offshore or outside the U.S. before. In keeping with Bush's oil-exploration track record, Harken finds no oil.

November 8
The Contract on America begins: Republicans pick up 52 seats in the House of Representatives.

November 1
George H.W. Bush loses the presidential election to Bill Clinton.

January 16
Operation Desert Storm begins.

1989   1990   1991   1992   1994

December 17
George H.W. Bush orders an invasion of Panama. The action is quickly condemned by the United Nations.

June 15
Dan Quayle, visiting a Trenton, New Jersey, middle school for a photo-op, watches twelve-year old pupil William Figueroa write the word "potato" on the blackboard. The Vice President insists over the student's objections that the word ends with an "e." His career never recovers.

June
George W. Bush sells $850,000 worth of Harken stock. Weeks later the company announces a $23 million quarterly loss and the stock plummets.

December
George H.W. Bush during his last days in office pardons six Reagan officials for their roles in Iran-Contra.

AN *I HATE REPUBLICANS* TIMELINE

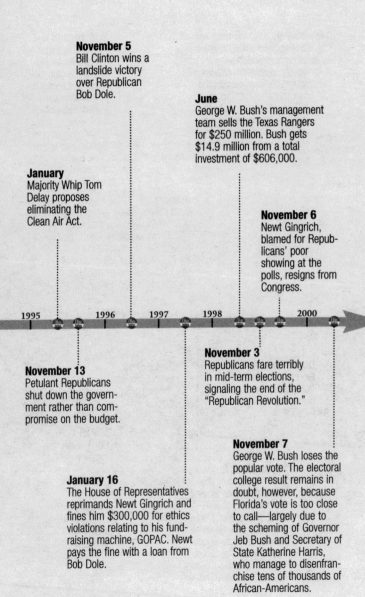

November 5
Bill Clinton wins a landslide victory over Republican Bob Dole.

June
George W. Bush's management team sells the Texas Rangers for $250 million. Bush gets $14.9 million from a total investment of $606,000.

January
Majority Whip Tom Delay proposes eliminating the Clean Air Act.

November 6
Newt Gingrich, blamed for Republicans' poor showing at the polls, resigns from Congress.

1995 1996 1997 1998 2000

November 13
Petulant Republicans shut down the government rather than compromise on the budget.

November 3
Republicans fare terribly in mid-term elections, signaling the end of the "Republican Revolution."

January 16
The House of Representatives reprimands Newt Gingrich and fines him $300,000 for ethics violations relating to his fundraising machine, GOPAC. Newt pays the fine with a loan from Bob Dole.

November 7
George W. Bush loses the popular vote. The electoral college result remains in doubt, however, because Florida's vote is too close to call—largely due to the scheming of Governor Jeb Bush and Secretary of State Katherine Harris, who manage to disenfranchise tens of thousands of African-Americans.

AN *I HATE REPUBLICANS* TIMELINE

December 9
The U.S. Supreme Court hands down its most political and ideological ruling in its history, ending the recount and handing Bush the presidency.

May 1
Vietnam-dodger George W. Bush, wearing a flight suit, lands in a fighter jet on the aircraft carrier *USS Abraham Lincoln* and declares that major combat operations in Iraq are over.

November 26
Katherine Harris certifies Bush's 537-vote victory in Florida. Al Gore's lawyers sue to contest the results.

January 20
George W. Bush is sworn in. He makes a number of promises he is soon to break.

January 28
Bush claims falsely in his State of the Union address that Iraq tried to buy uranium from Niger. Later revelations show the CIA and other administration officials knew months earlier this claim was untrue.

2000   2001   2002   2003

December 8
Florida's Supreme Court orders a manual ballot recount.

January 13
Bush faints after choking on a pretzel.

March 17
Bush orders the invasion of Iraq.

September 11
Terrorists destroy the World Trade Center and part of the Pentagon.
  Five hours later, Donald Rumsfeld tells his aides to develop plans to attack Iraq, despite the fact that there is no evidence Iraq was connected to the terrorist attacks.

August 6
Three U.S. soldiers are killed in Iraq, bringing the total number of American casualties to 256—118 since Bush declared that major combat operations in Iraq were over.

Acknowledgments

Many people made this anthology.

At Thunder's Mouth Press and Avalon Publishing Group:
Thanks to Will Balliett, Kristen Couse, Maria Fernandez,
Linda Kosarin, Dan O'Connor, Neil Ortenberg, Paul Pad-
dock, Susan Reich, David Riedy, Michelle Rosenfield,
Simon Sullivan, and Mike Walters for their support, dedi-
cation and hard work.

At The Writing Company:
I am especially grateful to Nate Hardcastle, who made a
huge contribution to this book. He did most of the
research, participated fully in editorial decisions at every
stage, wrote a selection (see page 226), created the Republican timeline that begins on page 401, chased down rights
and solved assorted problems. Taylor Smith and
Nathaniel May took up slack on other projects.

At the Portland Public Library in Portland, Maine:
The librarians helped collect books from around the
country.

Finally, I am grateful to the writers and artists whose work
appears in this book.

Permissions

Bibliography

Abraham, Rick. *The Dirty Truth: George W. Bush's Oil and Chemical Dependency.* Houston, Texas: Mainstream Publishers, 2000.

Begala, Paul. *Is Our Children Learning? The Case Against George W. Bush.* New York: Simon & Schuster, 2000.

Begala, Paul. *It's Still the Economy, Stupid.* New York: Simon & Schuster, 2002.

Bennett, Drake, and Heidi Pauken. "All the President's Lies." Originally published by *The American Prospect,* May 1, 2003.

Byrd, Senator Robert. "The Arrogance of Power." Speech to the U.S. Senate, March 19, 2003. http.byrd.senate.gov/byrd_speeches.

Byrd, Senator Robert. "We Stand Passively Mute." Speech to the U.S. Senate, February 12, 2003. http.byrd.senate.gov/byrd_speeches.

Carville, James. *We're Right, They're Wrong.* New York: Random House, 1996.

Chait, Jonathan. "Defense Secretary." Originally published by *The New Republic,* June 10, 2002.

Chait, Jonathan. "Get Lucky." Originally published by *The New Republic,* December 23, 2002.

Dershowitz, Alan M. *Supreme Injustice.* New York: Oxford University Press, 2001.

Floyd, Chris. "American Dominance." Originally published by *The Bergen Record,* February 23, 2003.

Franken, Al. *Rush Limbaugh Is a Big Fat Idiot and Other Observations.* New York: Delacorte Press, 1996.

Furgurson, Ernest B. *Hard Right: The Rise of Jesse Helms.* New York: W.W. Norton, 1986.

Gibson, Bridget. "Scandals and Lies." Originally published by Democratic Underground, www.democraticunderground.com, March 29, 2002.

Helvarg, David. "Unwise Use: Gale Norton's New Environmentalism." Originally published by *The Progressive,* June 2003.

Huffington, Arianna. *Pigs at the Trough.* New York: Crown Publishers, 2003.

Ivins, Molly, and Lou Dubose. *Shrub: The Short, Happy Political Life of George W. Bush.* New York: Random House, 2000.

Krugman, Paul. "Standard Operating Procedure." Originally published by *The New York Times,* June 3, 2003.

Kutler, Stanley I. "There Will Absolutely Be No Dissension.". Originally published by *The Chicago Tribune,* March 18, 2003.

Lagowski, Barbara, and Rick Mumma. *888 Reasons to Hate Republicans.* Secaucus, New Jersey: Carol Publishing Group, 1996.

Moore, Michael. *Stupid White Men . . . And Other Sorry Excuses for the State of the Nation!.* New York: Regan Books, 2001.

The Onion. "Bush: 'Our Long National Nightmare of Peace and Prosperity is Finally Over'" and "Bill of Rights Pared Down to a Manageable Six." www.theonion.com.

Palast, Greg. *The Best Democracy Money Can Buy.* New York: Plume, 2003.

Schell, Jonathan. "The Case Against the War." Originally published in *The Nation,* March 3, 2003.

Seely, Hart. "The Poetry of D. H. Rumsfeld." Originally published by Slate.com, April 2, 2003.

Shawn, Wallace. "Fragments from a Diary." Originally published in *The Nation,* March 21, 2003.

Slansky, Paul. *The Clothes Have No Emperor.* New York: Simon & Schuster, 1989.

Thompson, Hunter S. *Better Than Sex: Confessions of a Political Junkie.* New York: Ballantine Books, 1994.

CLINT WILLIS has edited more than 30 anthologies, on subjects ranging from meditation *(Why Meditate)* to mountaineering *(Epics on Everest)*. He is the editor (with Nathaniel May) of *We Are the People: Voices from the Other Side of American History*. Clint studied politics at Williams College and the Yale University Graduate School of Political Science. He lives with his family in Maine.